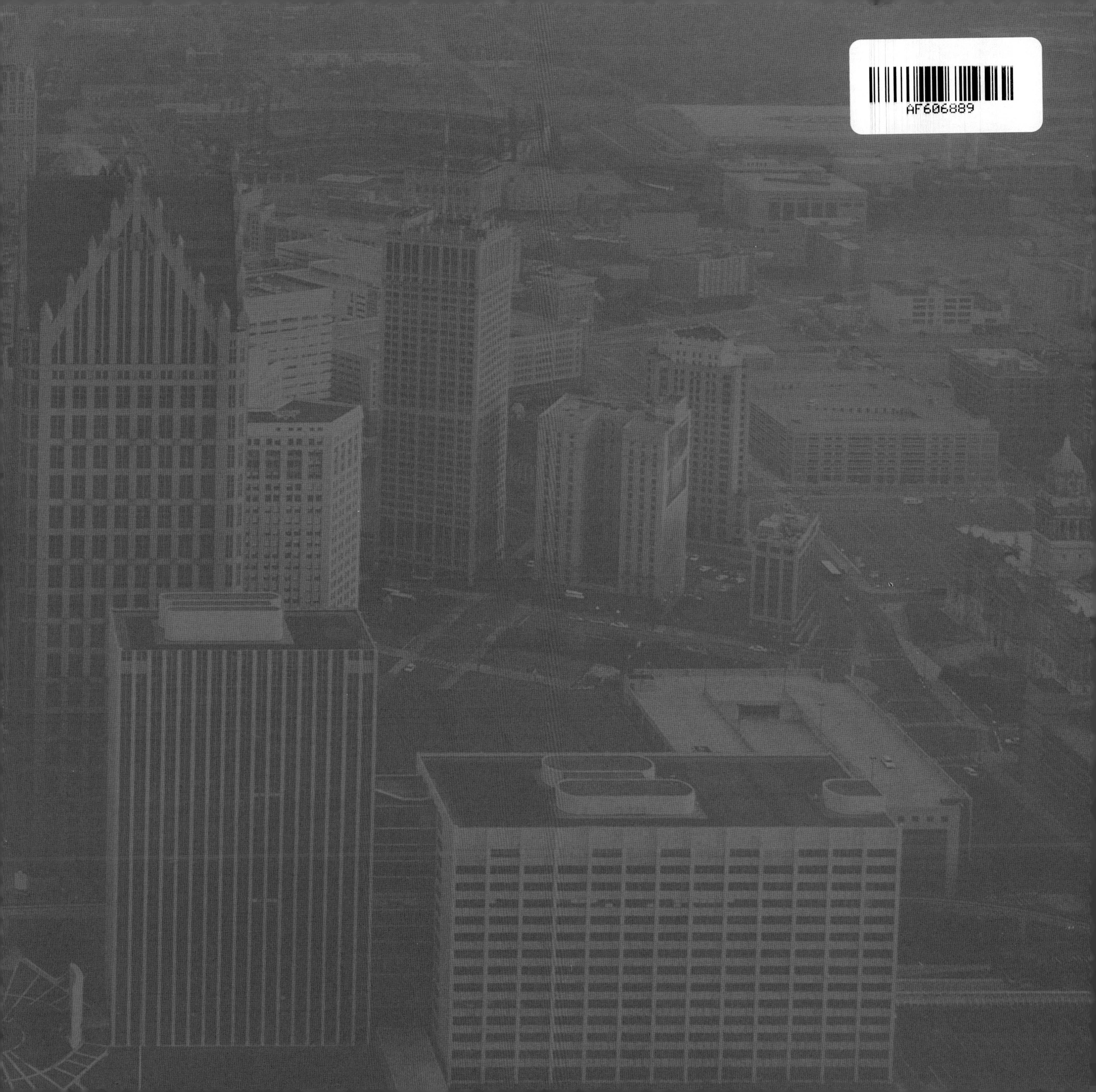

DETROIT STYLE

CAR DESIGN IN THE MOTOR CITY, 1950–2020

BENJAMIN W. COLMAN | DETROIT INSTITUTE OF ARTS

DISTRIBUTED BY YALE UNIVERSITY PRESS | NEW HAVEN AND LONDON

Detroit Style: Car Design in the Motor City, 1950–2020 is organized by the Detroit Institute of Arts.

Major funding is generously provided by the Ford Motor Company Fund and General Motors.

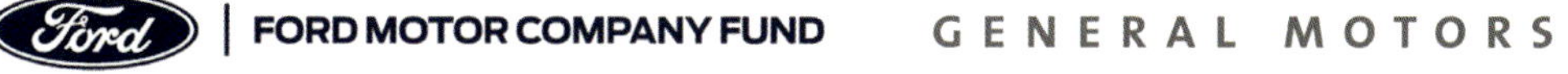

Additional funding is provided by the Marvin and Betty Danto Family Foundation, FCA US LLC, and The Suburban Collection, Jennifer & David Fischer and Darcy & David Fischer, Jr.

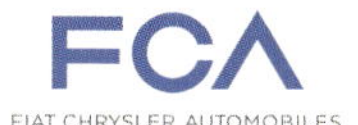

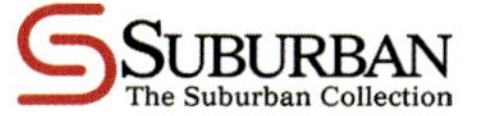

Additional support is provided by Barbara and William U. Parfet and TCF National Bank.

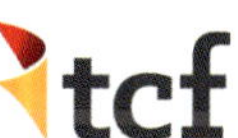

Major funding for the exhibition catalog is generously provided by the Margaret Dunning Foundation.

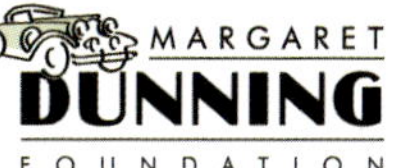

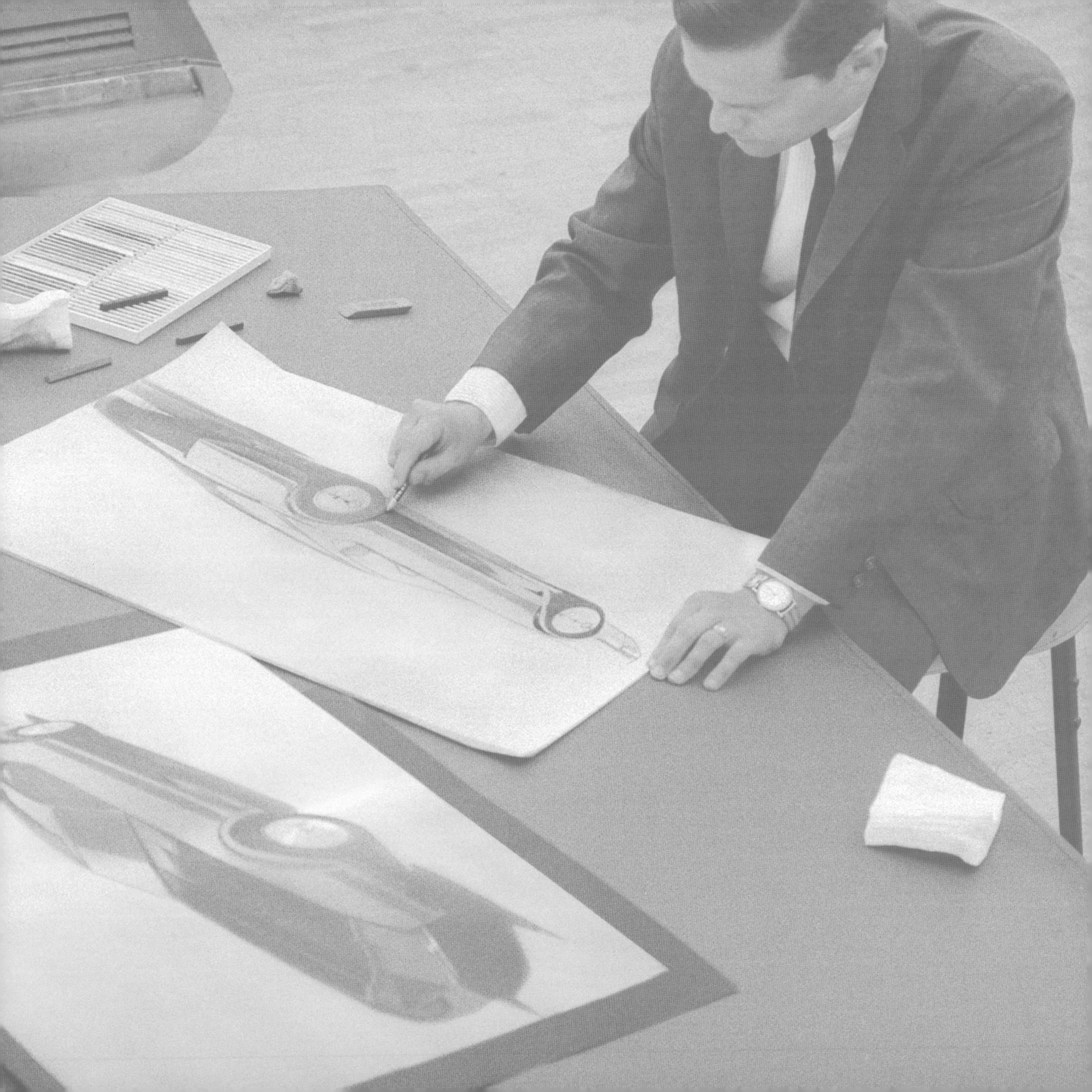

TABLE OF CONTENTS

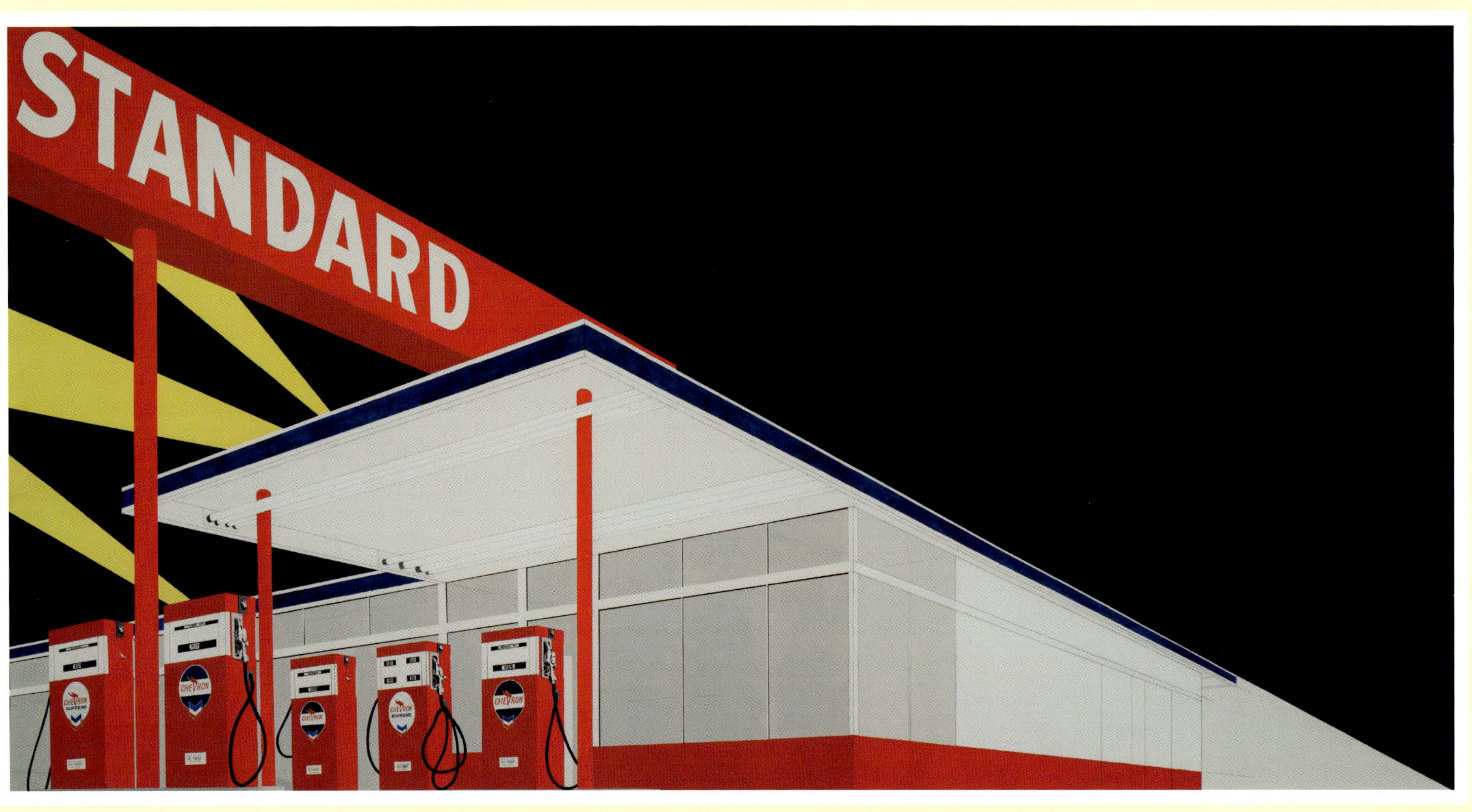

EDWARD JOSEPH RUSCHA

Standard Station, Amarillo, Texas, 1963, oil on canvas

The Detroit Institute of Arts (DIA) is inextricably linked to the American automobile. As the city grew and prospered in the twentieth century alongside the automotive industry, the museum expanded into a thriving institution celebrating the grand scope of human creativity. At its center were Diego Rivera's glorious *Detroit Industry Murals* (1932–33), which depict with monumental vision the workers powering Ford's River Rouge factory. With the exhibition *Detroit Style: Car Design in the Motor City, 1950–2020*, the DIA celebrates the remarkable artistry of the stylists and designers who define the look of American automobiles.

Standing in a city surrounded by the studios that shape American cars and across the street from the College for Creative Studies (CCS), where upcoming generations of designers study, the DIA is uniquely suited to celebrate the ingenuity of the complex process of designing a car and the art it produces. Although other art museums have displayed cars, *Detroit Style* is distinctive for its focus on the practice of car design and the unique perspective of the designer. Rather than treat the car as static sculpture, it honors the chorus of voices that work together to create its dynamic form and function. There is much to be learned from their experimental methods, built around trial and error.

Like painters and sculptors, car designers work with an awareness of form, surface, and beauty, taking risks and making ambitious proposals that ask us to reimagine what is possible. Their work takes place years before a car is introduced to the public and involves a careful balance of foresight and uncertainty as they try to predict what consumers will want. The discipline of car design also has unexpected parallels to the historic modes of art making displayed throughout the museum. The structure and collaborative work of thriving design studios, for example, are similar to those of Renaissance workshops, where artists labored on monumental frescoes or sculptures following the direction of the oil sketches or clay models created by a renowned master. Surrounded by galleries of the museum's world-class collections of art and design, the exhibition is a testament to the significant achievements of the artists who conceived these beautiful machines.

By celebrating the art of automobile design, we also honor the immense contribution the car has made to the arts in the city of Detroit. The Detroiters who built the automotive industry have always been some of the museum's most important supporters, and in 2014, Fiat Chrysler, the Ford Motor Company, and General Motors joined the thousands of donors who contributed to the Grand Bargain that established the DIA as an independent museum and saved its extraordinary collection. As we continue to serve our community by bringing it inspiring art, we are reminded of the immense creativity of the city that put the "world on wheels" and recognize that car design belongs in the museum galleries as one of the great accomplishments of humankind.

When we began to think about this project more than three years ago, we had conversations with our colleagues at CCS, members of the scientific community, and museum professionals around the country about how to make the exhibition accessible and engaging. It was also important to bring to the forefront the scholarly research of curators, collectors, and car designers. I am grateful to the legendary automotive designer Bill Porter for his expertise and passion, and to DIA curator Benjamin Colman, who stewarded this important project and helped make it a success. I am also deeply thankful to the DIA exhibition team and staff who made it a reality.

Salvador Salort-Pons, PhD
Director, President, and CEO
Detroit Institute of Arts

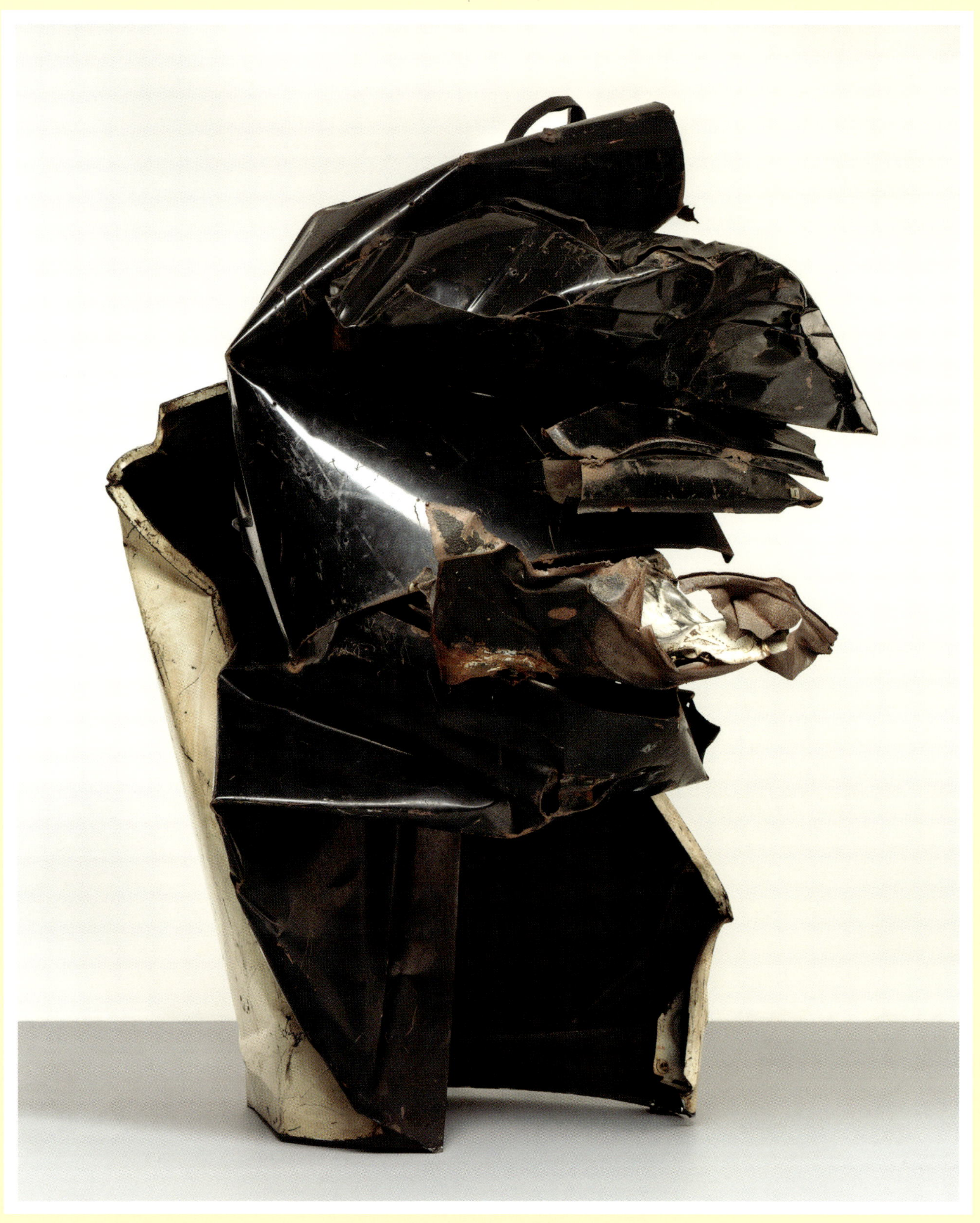

JOHN CHAMBERLAIN

Coo Wha Zee, 1962, painted steel

Detroit has long been a major hub for automotive design. As the city became the center of the American automobile industry in the early twentieth century, its design studios began to incubate new ideas and new styles. Working on paper, with clay models, and with wood and metal prototypes, the city's designers have driven American car culture and shaped the way we get around every day. This catalog and the concurrent exhibition explore the stories of twelve coupes and sedans, both experimental show cars created for display and landmark production models sold to the mass market, made by Detroit-based manufacturers between 1950 and 2020. They represent the work of many visionary designers and illustrate some of the important automotive style trends during this period. These cars, alongside working design sketches, American paintings and sculpture that examine cars and car culture, and the interviews with designers included in this volume, highlight the beauty, ingenuity, and importance of Detroit car design.

Detroit Style: Car Design in the Motor City, 1950–2020, presents an opportunity to assess with fresh eyes the aesthetic significance of car design in American culture. From the invention of the automobile in the late nineteenth century, the American public and art museums have been slow to recognize the automobile as an art form worthy of aesthetic attention. In the 1930s the French were known for their Concours d'Elegance, outdoor gatherings where prestigious custom automobiles were shown and judged along with women's fashions created by top couturiers. In 1951 the Museum of Modern Art in New York held a groundbreaking exhibition, *8 Automobiles*. In the foreword to the accompanying catalog, MoMA's then-curator of architecture, Arthur Drexler, proclaimed, "automobiles are hollow, rolling sculpture."[1] Other art museums have followed suit in recent decades, often exhibiting the most expensive custom luxury cars. In 1985 the Detroit Institute of Arts held a show composed solely of American production automobiles created between 1925 and 1950.

The current exhibition and this catalog pick up the story of Detroit car design where the previous show left off. By the mid-twentieth century, the domestic automobile industry was dominated by the so-called Big Three companies: General Motors, the Ford Motor Company, and Chrysler (now Fiat Chrysler). Other older, smaller, independent manufacturers such as Hudson, Nash, Packard, and Studebaker have made important contributions to the evolution of American design, but they perished in the ferocious competition after the car-starved post–World War II era came to an end. The automobiles in this exhibition highlight some of the different ways Detroit designers have navigated changing tastes, new technologies, and ever-changing consumer demands.

By 1950 the US automobile had evolved from a collection of separate elements into an overall envelope form where most, if not all, body parts (hood, fenders, passenger compartment, trunk, etc.) were fused into a relatively smooth, uniform body. The characteristic and very distinct American automotive style of the 1950s was ushered in by the General Motors Le Sabre show car, the first great concept car employing aircraft imagery. The prevalence of that imagery faded at the start of the 1960s and a totally new view of the automobile as a pure abstract expression of its own being took its place. This abstraction allowed for the creation of a decade of design masterpieces, swept clean of referential aircraft imagery by understated designs such as the 1966 Oldsmobile Toronado.

Imported cars, both European and Asian, began to arrive in numbers in the 1960s, heightening worldwide competition. The decade also gave rise to market segmentation. Small cars made in America finally came into prominence. Intermediate-size cars soon appeared with full-size car engines and became known as muscle cars. Some smaller cars morphed into sporty pony cars such as the eponymous Ford Mustang. The Mustang's outstanding success in the marketplace soon spawned a host of imitators. Thus the relatively large family of American pony cars such as the 1970 Plymouth Barracuda came into being.

The early 1970s saw an increase in the regulation of the automotive industry by the federal government. Among the most noticeable manifestations from the buyer's viewpoint were seat belts to restrain driver and passengers in the event of a collision and much larger and heavier bumpers. All of this took place against the background of world oil crises in 1973 and 1979. These events prompted a newly serious interest in automotive aerodynamics, an appropriate and cost-effective response to the need for increased vehicle fuel economy that informs designs for cars such as the 1983 Ford Probe IV and the 1987 Chrysler Lamborghini Portofino. The 1980s saw a continued concentration on automotive safety and efficiency throughout the industry. Wind tunnel testing and crash impact studies became routine elements of the design process and, as might be expected, have become more sophisticated with the passage of time.

During the 1990s the largest manufacturers flirted briefly with new body themes that featured more rounded shapes and amoebic, free-form window graphics. This style trend may have been fed by the application of aerodynamics during the design process. Automotive nostalgia, the thirst for bygone vehicle styles evident in the 1997 Chrysler Chronos, 2002 Ford GT Concept, and 2017 GT has been a long-standing undercurrent in both American and European automobile design between 1950 and 2020.

This exhibition is unique in its focus on designers and the design process. The car is both a tool for mobility and an icon filled with personal resonance. Successful designers deftly navigate the space between these two realms, creating cars that meet practical demands and drive the cultural aspirations of their day. Many of the cars in this exhibition are concept cars—experimental one-off custom designs intended for display. Detroit designers began creating concept cars in the 1930s. They are meant to introduce the motoring public and, incidentally, corporate management, to fresh ideas. Concept cars also test public acceptance of forthcoming styles prior to the company's commitment of the heavy financial investment required for mass production. As style statements, concept cars often have more flare and exaggeration than production cars because they are designed without many of the functional limitations imposed by mass production and marketing. Generally speaking, they more nearly represent the far-reaching imagination of the designer.

Philosophically speaking, car design is an expressive, interpretive, and often personal practice. Yet like other large, complicated, and collaborative art forms, such as architecture, the finished automobile is seldom the work of a single designer. Production automobile studios are normally devoted to a single brand, such as Chevrolet, Dodge, Lincoln, etc., all under the direction of a corporate vice president of design. Designers in these brand-specific studios contribute ideas that are examined, tested, and adjusted countless times by a number of specialists working as a team. The designers are the creative core of the team, communicating their ideas in sketch form to sculptors who shape full-scale clay models and engineers who ensure the machine's functionality. Initially, designers concentrate on the overall theme. Once it is developed, they focus on specific features—details that must then take their place in a harmonious whole. Production studios also do the work of face-lifting cars between major body changes. This usually consists of creating new details, such as grille textures and taillights, while major body forms are left unchanged. Although a single designer or a small group is sometimes associated with a specific car, the final product is always the work of many hands, approved by design executives for the corporation. It is, however, customary to credit the studio chief or lead designer with the design.

Detroit design has long been a distinctive component of the global automotive scene. During the time period covered by this exhibition, the American auto industry has weathered both major style changes and perilous financial times. American cars tended, at least throughout the majority of the twentieth century, to be larger and more forcefully sculpted than their international equivalents. On the streets around us we see vehicles of European and Asian origin that are built and sold here in the US, while vehicles designed in Detroit are built and sold both here and abroad. But in spite of the fact that automotive design is a truly global art form today, it is usually possible for the keen eye to identify those quintessentially American products originating from Detroit.

William L. Porter
Automobile Designer

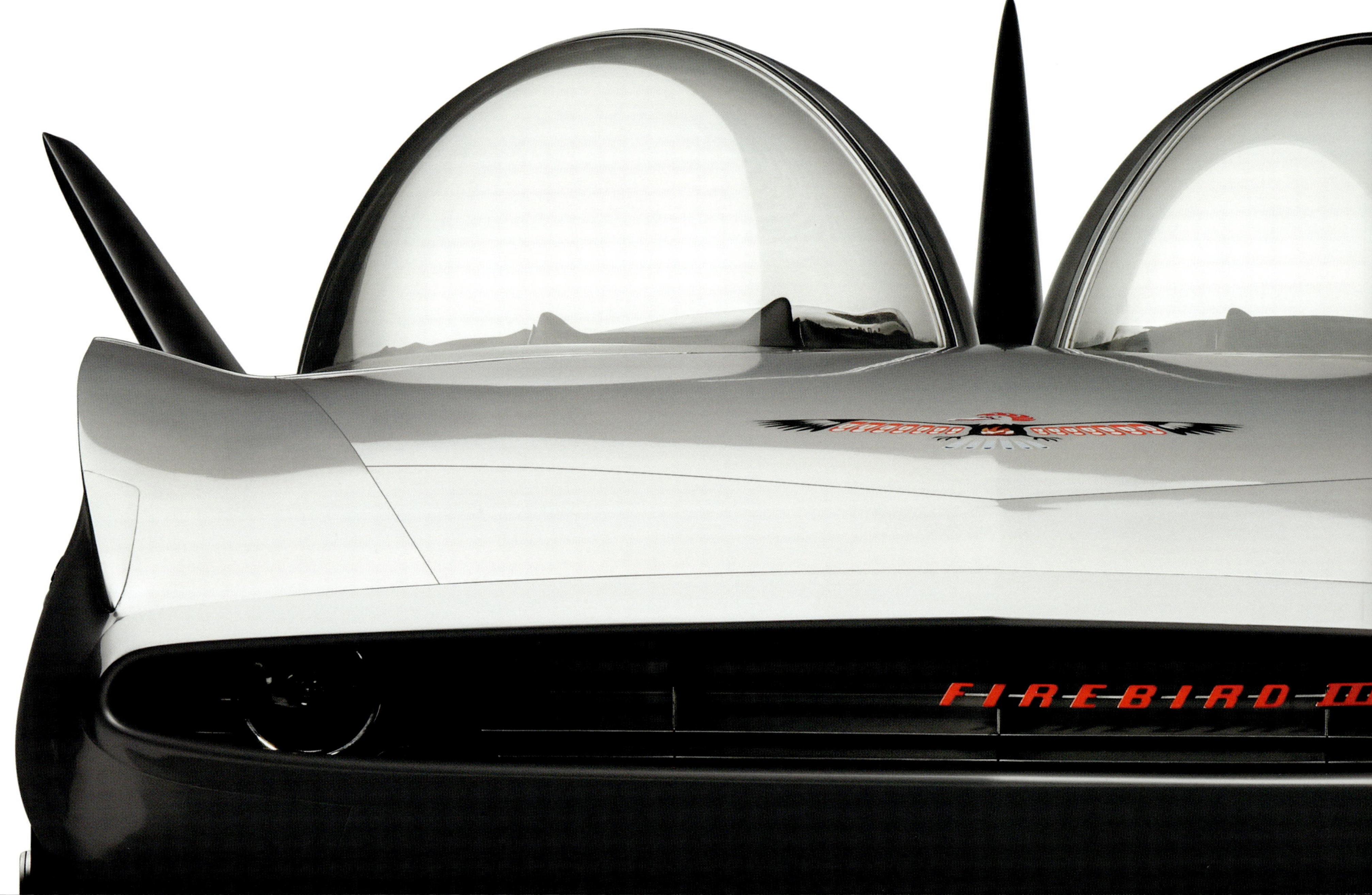
FIREBIRD II

DETROIT STYLE

CAR DESIGN IN THE MOTOR CITY, 1950–2020

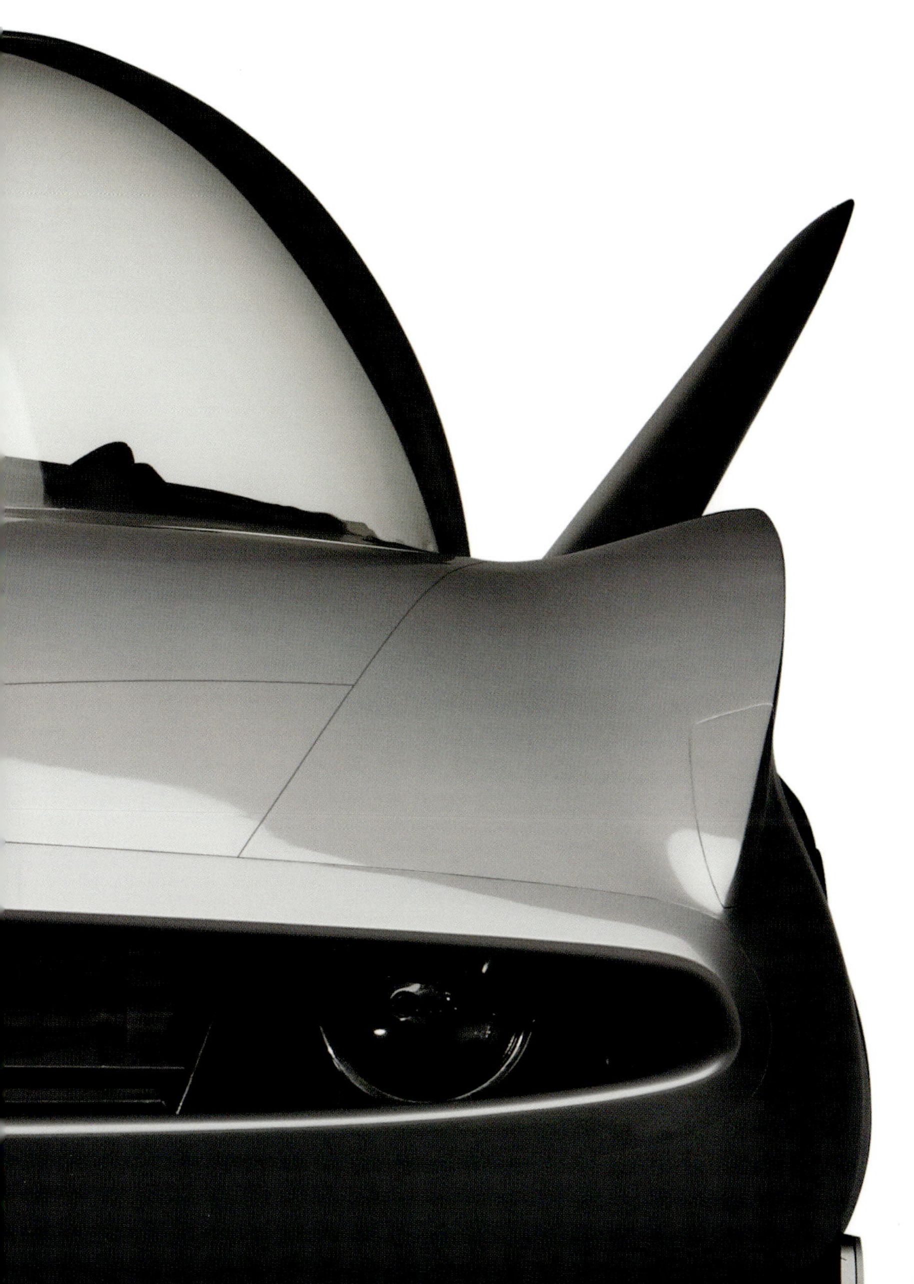

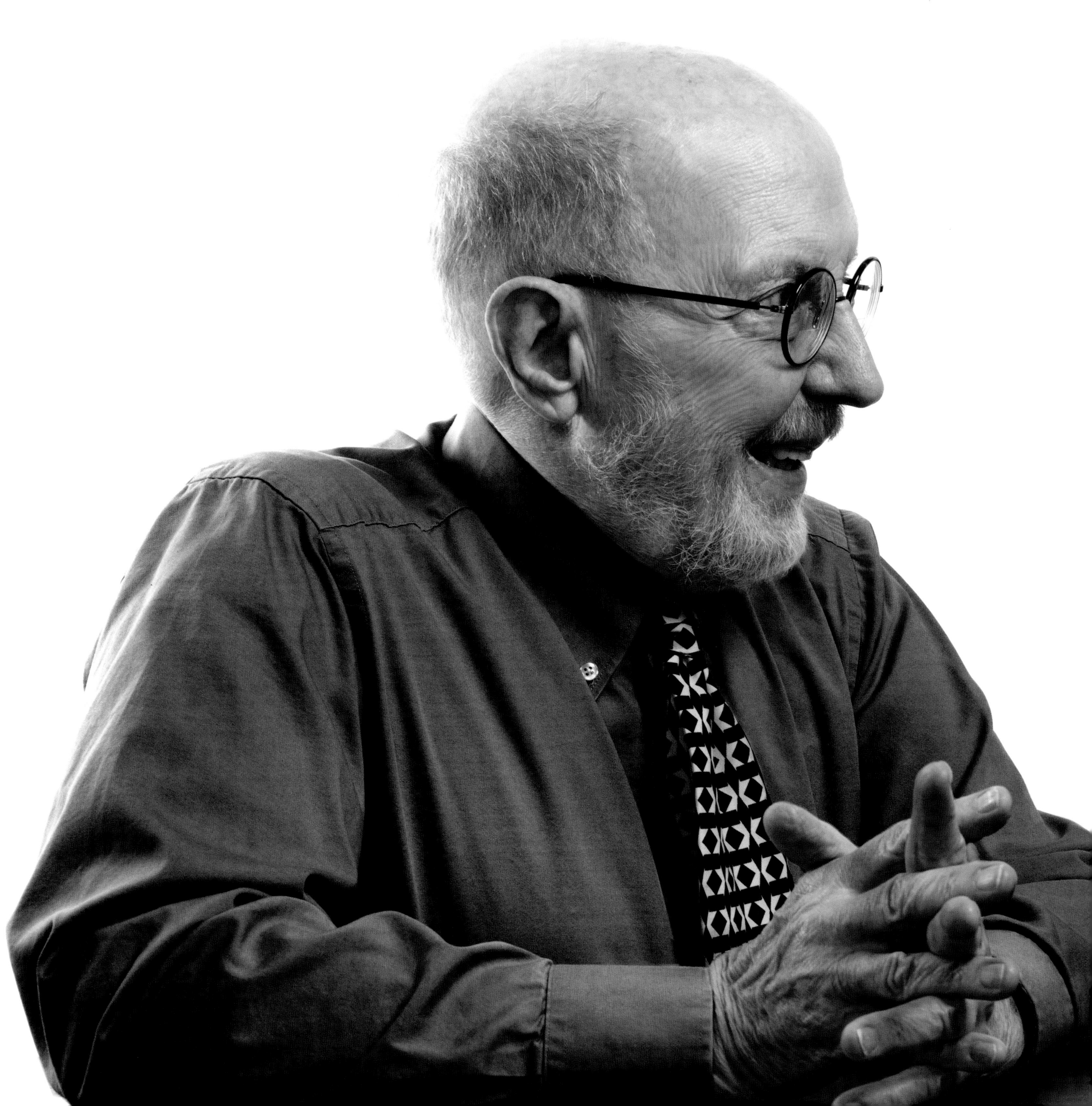

INTERVIEW WITH WILLIAM L. PORTER

William L. Porter began his career as a car designer at General Motors in 1958 and stayed at the company until he retired in 1996. He served as studio chief for Pontiac styling from 1963 to 1979 and studio chief for the Buick 1 exterior studio from 1979 to 1996.

Benjamin W. Colman: How did you become interested in car design?
William L. Porter: I had a bachelor's degree in fine art from the University of Louisville, where I concentrated in painting. But even as an undergraduate I had wanted to be an automobile designer. After I got out of school, the first and best job I could find was designing neon signs for a company called Neon Art. I worked there for a few months and learned lettering. I loved that. Then I was drafted. This was the end of the Korean War (1950–53).

BC: How did you find your way to Pratt Institute for graduate school?
WP: While I was in the army, I entered an automobile design contest in a magazine and won second prize. I designed a sports car with a station wagon back end. At the time there was nothing on the market like that, so it was perceived as original and fresh and workable. That pushed me toward trying to be a car designer. All the guys in the army thought it was a crazy idea, but I was encouraged by winning the contest.

My dad knew a man in Detroit who knew a man at General Motors, who was in the design section, called styling at that time. I interviewed with him at GM. My portfolio was from the neon sign company, so I had all kind of signs and lettering and a few drawings of cars, including the design that won second place in the contest.

They called in a guy named Homer LaGassey, and someone else, who came in and looked at my work. Homer recommended Pratt Institute in New York. The other guy recommended Art Center School in Pasadena [now Art Center College of Design], which provided the majority of designers to the industry at that time. Pratt was in New York, and my idea of modern art had more to do with New York than Los Angeles, so I went to New York.

BC: Was there a particular style or look to Pratt design at the time?
WP: Most of the professors of design were heavily influenced by the Bauhaus, which affected me, but I realized after talking to GM that if I adhered strictly to the Pratt look of sculptural shapes, I was not going to achieve the GM look. At that time the American automobile industry was celebrating rockets and bombs and aircraft shapes, which were absolutely detested by those interested in the Bauhaus look.

I participated in the GM summer program in 1957. I wanted to find out how I could dig in and eventually move their vocabulary of shapes in a direction I thought was more appropriate, away from bombs and fins. I was hired back as a permanent employee after I graduated. My career went quite well.

BC: At what point did you begin to have the chance to put your personal stamp on cars?
WP: After the introductory studio, where young designers started, I was assigned to work in an advanced area for a man named Bernie Smith, who had a broad understanding of design. Gradually things turned away from bombs and fins. When Harley Earl retired, Bill Mitchell, I think, was ready to dump them. They'd had their run in the 1950s.

BC: Can you describe the redesign process for the Pontiac GTO?
WP: I was promoted and became the chief designer at one of the little advanced studios. While I was there I did some experimental cars, one of which became the Pontiac Tempest for 1966 or 1967. The Tempest was the basis for the GTO. In 1963 and 1964 we were working on a new body for the 1968 GTO. I came up with this idea with line shapes and cutouts and bulges around the wheels.

I was trying to find a simple body shell, essentially a cylinder, and slice out the window shapes and so on. The shell in cross section was roughly an oval. I wanted a sense of power in the wheels, almost like an electric force that was pulsing, bulging out those sides, not a bomb shape or a fin. This was an organic bulge, like the magnetic field in the earth. Instead of being a defined form of muscle, it would be more of a force field stretching the rest of the form toward it.

BC: Later in your career, when you came to Buick, one of the luxury lines at GM, how did you adapt your design sensibility to that brand?

WP: I went into Buick 1, the studio designing all the big cars and some of the intermediates. I was assigned to work on the Park Avenue, which was a big car, and the Riviera, a special luxury car. The Buick Park Avenue was built on the new C-body platform. That was a big job. I didn't have a lot of time to adjust or develop a design philosophy. I was trying to develop a formal vocabulary, insofar as you could with all the shared parts for the different cars using the C-body, that was identifiably Buick.

I went back to a car in the garage, the 1946 car. In the 1930s and 1940s Buicks were evolving into kind of a—we called it muscular grace. Buick was going to be bulky, like a football player in a tuxedo. Formal, but with a muscularity under it.

I was trying to recapture the power, grace, and flair of the '40s.

BC: When did you have the idea to introduce ellipsoidal lines into your designs for Buick?

WP: It was all part of trying to capture that grace and power. We felt like that needed to be Buick. Oldsmobile could be something else, a little more academic. Cadillac could be edgier.

To get at this idea of muscular grace, we booked the auditorium for a couple of weeks. We put up light tents, big circles, and we put the Buicks in there with objects we thought epitomized their character. We had a cello, for example, which has a muscularity but is still very graceful.

BC: So you wanted to connect the design you were creating for Buick with classic examples of design?

WP: We were trying to define Buick. All of the middle- and upper-middle-class cars were in trouble because most of them had become homogenized. How can you get somebody to pay $10,000 to $20,000 more for a car that is not distinctive?

I had loved Buicks as a boy. When I was in high school, a friend's dad was the Buick district sales manager. At the end of the war, his dad drove the first Buick I'd ever seen in the streets. He got the green super sedan, which just wiped me out. It was breathtaking.

BC: So Buick was a fitting place to end your career in design?

WP: There are cars I really wish—to this day, when I see them coming down the street, I want to turn into an alley so I don't have to look at them.

One of the things that's so hard about designing a car is there's just so damn much to it. It's like designing a building. You've got so much freedom, but there's so much you need to take into consideration. How long the doors need to be. How much curve you can put into a panel, if they need to stamp it two times. You have to know all of that, and yet it has to be buried so deep you forget it. If you want it to be angular. If you want it to have the beauty of a rattlesnake's mouth, with those fangs, or the beauty of a seal in the water. The question is, What kind of beauty do you want? And what kind of beauty can you get in a particular package?

You're dealt a particular hand—someone puts the cab in the middle of the car, that's one kind of hand. They slide it back, that is a different hand. It all becomes the hand you're dealt.

This April 11, 2019, interview has been edited and condensed.

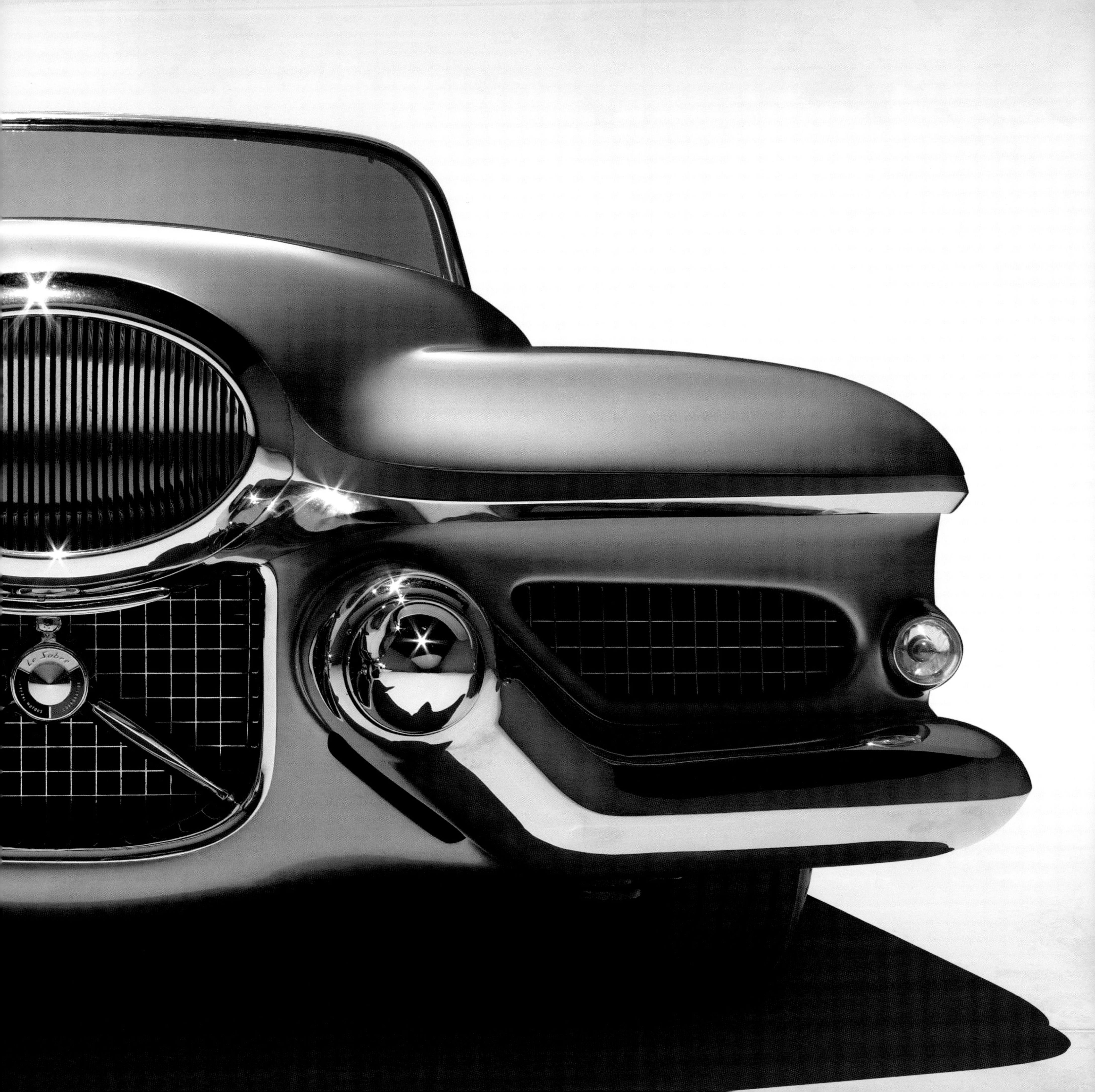
Le Sabre

1951

GENERAL MOTORS

LE SABRE

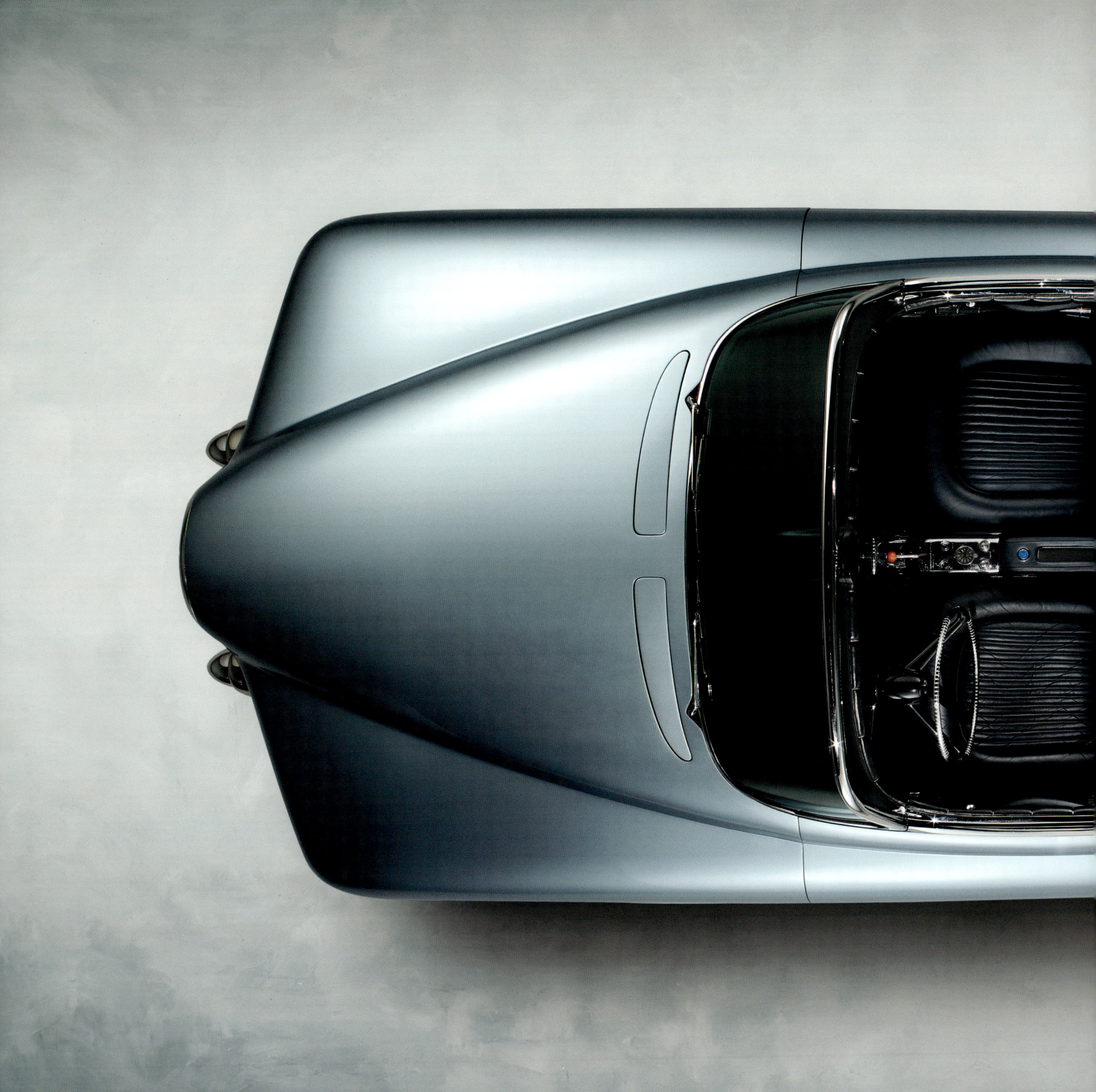

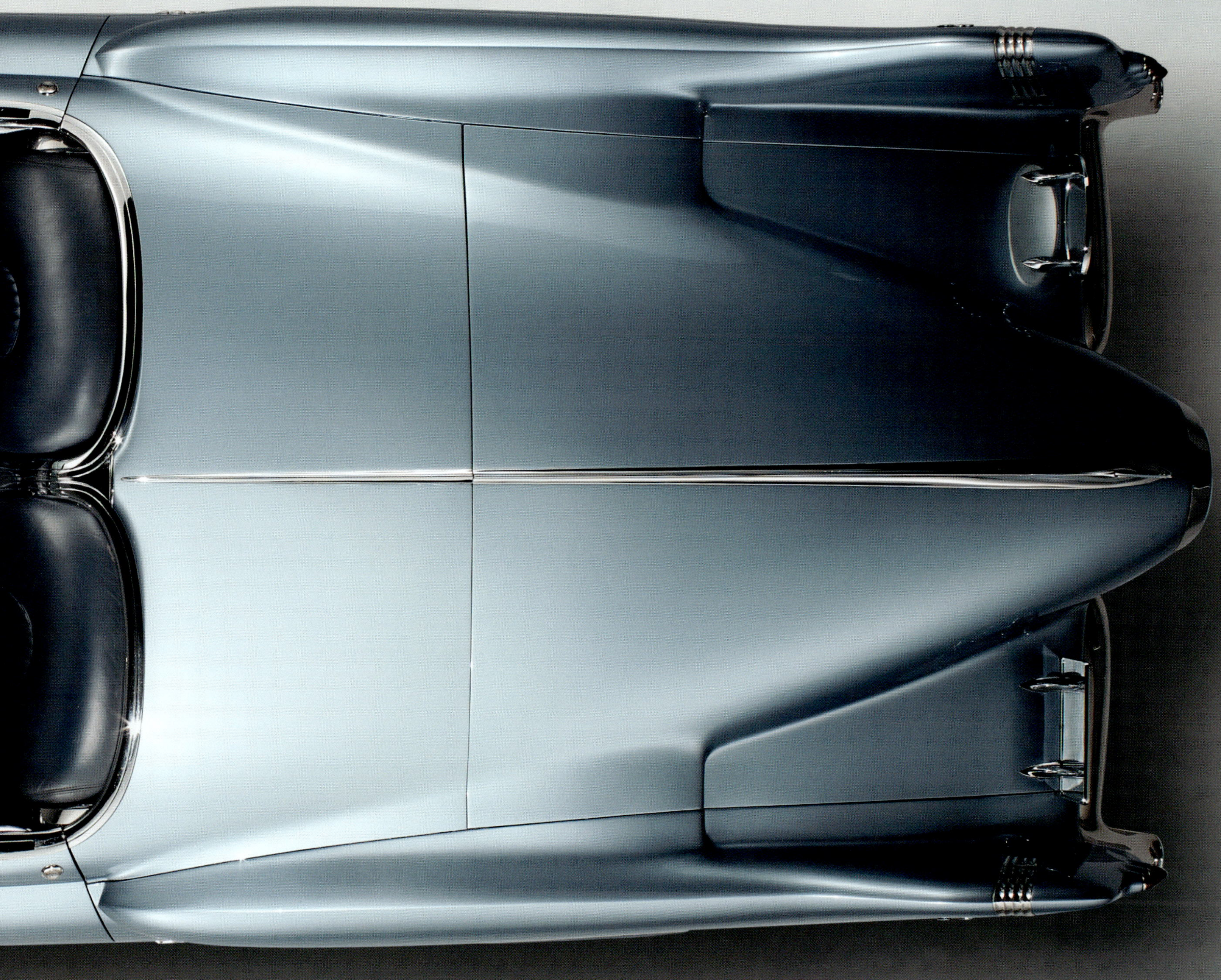

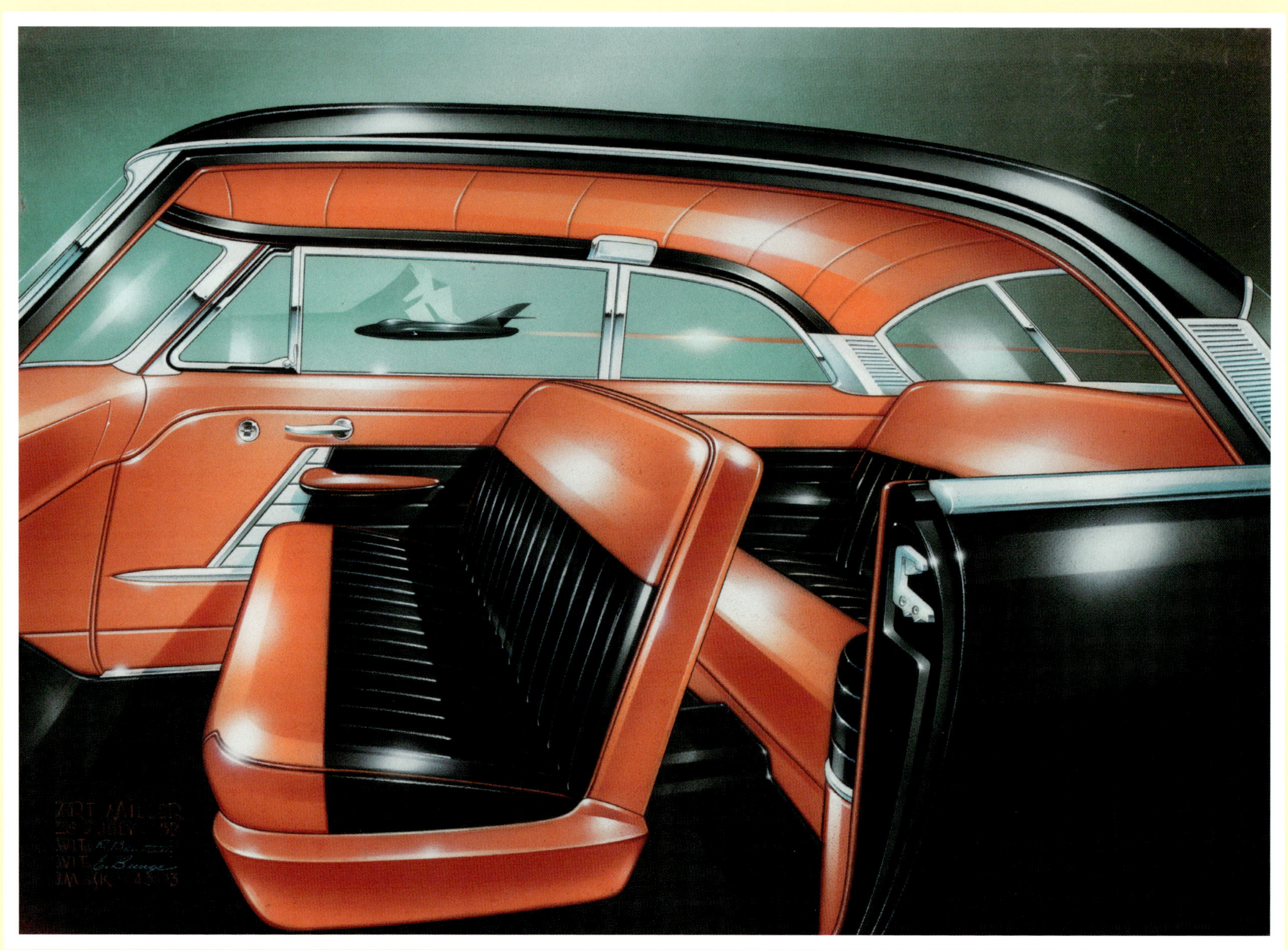

ART MILLER

Rendering of Automobile Interior, 1952, airbrush and pastel on paper

The General Motors Le Sabre show car set the tone for American car design of the 1950s. With forms evoking fighter planes, the sleek and low-slung convertible reflected a feeling of celebratory optimism in American popular culture in the wake of World War II. Many of its functional elements—the wing-shaped bumper with pointed bomb shapes, applied propeller grille, extended nose, projecting tail, and finlike fenders—recalled the planes that carried the Allied forces to victory.

The car also marked the beginning of a remarkable period for the theatrical display of experimental cars at auto shows and expositions. In the following years, American car stylists created ambitious and progressive designs for prototypes that suggested to the public what they might see on the road in years to come.

The Le Sabre was shepherded from concept to production by designer Harley Earl (1893–1969), who joined GM in 1926, when the mass market for American cars was beginning to reflect a desire for vehicles that were both functional and stylish. First hired by GM as a consultant for Cadillac, Earl brought to the company a design sensibility that harmonized the interior and exterior of a car. He also pioneered the practice of sculpting a full-size clay model of a car in the design studio, which allowed stylists to experiment with and refine subtle variations in form and surface. Clay models soon became the standard across the industry, replacing the wooden models that had been used for decades.[1] Over the course of his career with GM, Earl transformed the new art and color section into the powerful styling division, which oversaw the design of cars across the company's brands.[2] From his position at styling, Earl redefined both the practice of car design and the role of the car stylist within the industry.

The Le Sabre was meant to follow in the tracks of Earl's first successful concept car for GM, the 1938 Buick Y-job. While, in Earl's words, the Y-job had "served a useful purpose affecting many cars now in the hands of customers," its modern lines and style had fallen out of fashion by the mid-1940s.[3] Hoping for another similarly influential design, he assembled a team to create the Le Sabre. With the support of Harlow Curtice, general manager for Buick, in the winter of 1946–47 Earl began working in earnest on car XP-8, which would become the Le Sabre. The engineering challenges for the XP-8 were assigned to Buick engineer Charles Chayne. Buick designer Edward E. Glowacke (1921–62) contributed to the exterior styling.[4]

An eager public was offered glimpses of the car and its anticipated technology, still in clay model form, in a January 1951 article in *Life* magazine that proclaimed, "'Sabre' Is the Car of the 1960s."[5] Experiments with materials such as cast magnesium for the hood and doors and an aluminum honeycomb floor meant the Le Sabre weighed less than comparable cars. A radically shortened engine allowed for the low profile of the hood. The tail fin–shaped rear fenders had a practical function, holding rubber fuel storage bladders—one for gasoline, another for methanol. The oval-shaped front grille spun to reveal front headlamps at the push of a button. Built-in hydraulic jacks lifted the car when a tire needed to be changed. A water sensor between the seats automatically extended the top of the car at any sign of rain. The bent glass of its wraparound windshield, which gave the driver an expanded field of vision, would become ubiquitous in the years that followed.[6]

Perhaps because of the years Earl spent working for his father's custom car company in Los Angeles, where many of their clients were involved in the movie industry, he understood the potential for popular media and spectacle to drive consumer interest. The Le Sabre made its public debut to a crowd of roughly 100,000 at Watkins Glen, New York. From there it traveled to Toronto to the Canadian National Exhibition and to Paris for the Salon de l'Automobile. As he had with the Y-job, Earl drove the Le Sabre as his personal car when it was not on display, and many recall seeing it on the streets of Detroit and suburban Grosse Pointe.[7]

In a 1955 promotional brochure about car design titled *Styling: The Look of Things,* Earl described the task of the growing practice of industrial designers as "making these useful things beautiful, not in the sense of applying superficial ornamentation, but in developing a form of beauty exactly suited to the purpose."[8] For show cars he balanced that modernist sensibility with a keen understanding of how best to generate excitement. As he once said, "people like something new and exciting in an automobile as well as in a Broadway show—they like visual entertainment and that's what we stylists give them."[9] ❖

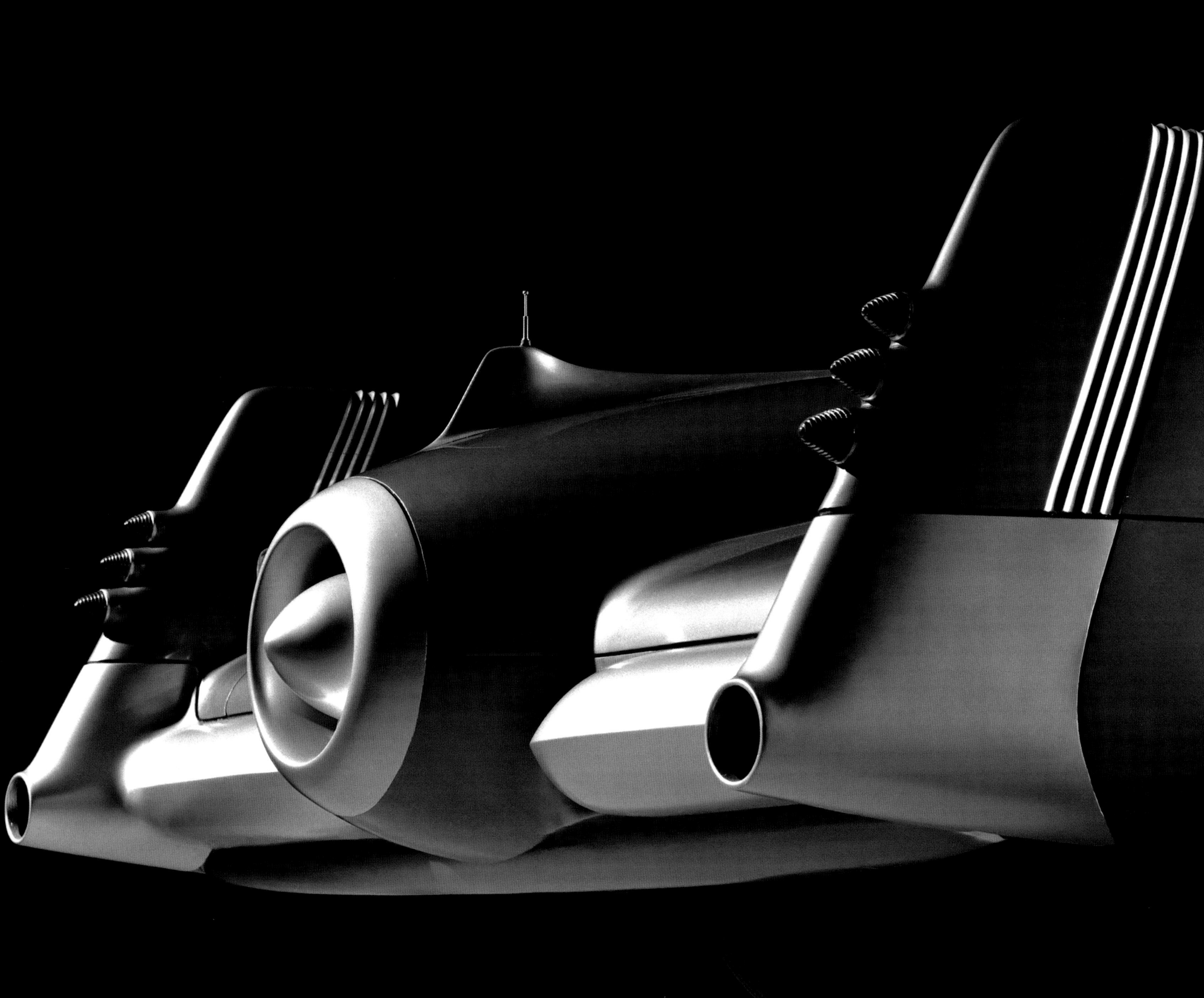

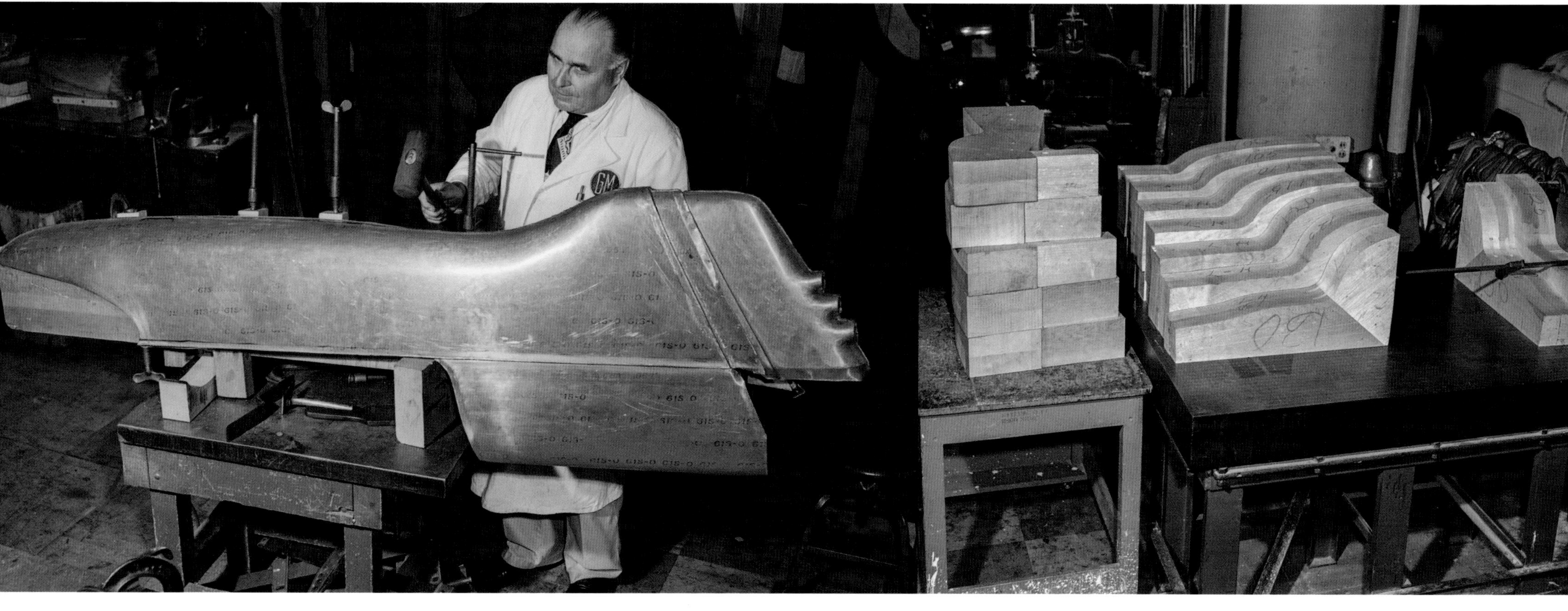

General Motors, Le Sabre, 1951. *p. 18:* Front view (detail); *pp. 20–21:* Top view; *opposite:* Rear view of clay model showing fender and exhaust, circa 1949; *above left:* Shaping rear fin, 1950; *above right:* Wooden forms for fins, 1950.

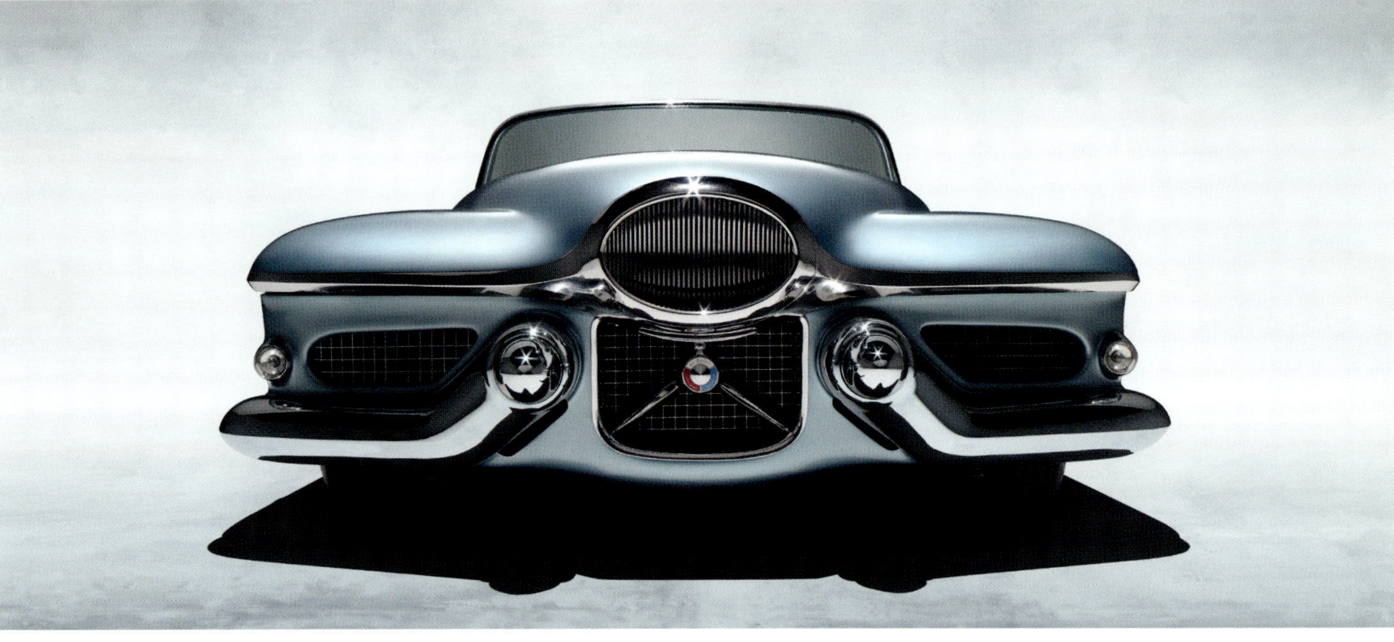

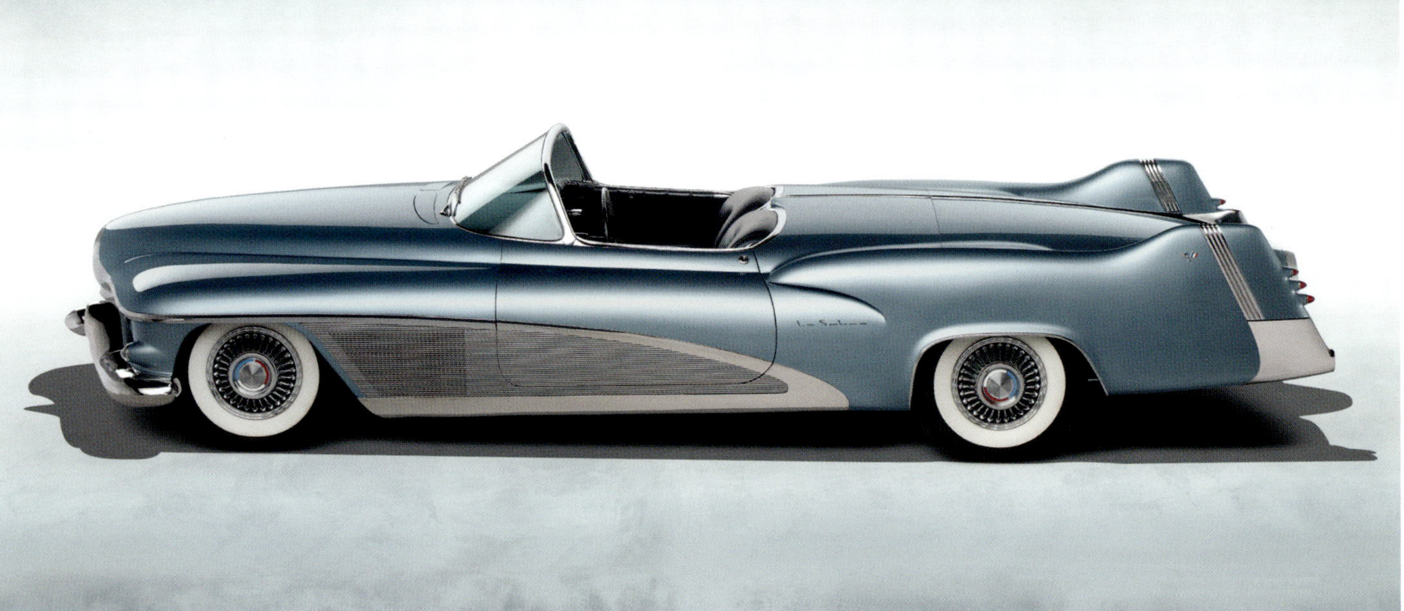

General Motors, Le Sabre, 1951. *above:* Front view showing airplane-inspired propeller details; *below:* Left side view showing wraparound windshield and fin profile; *opposite:* Front view showing pointed and projecting form referencing airplane design.

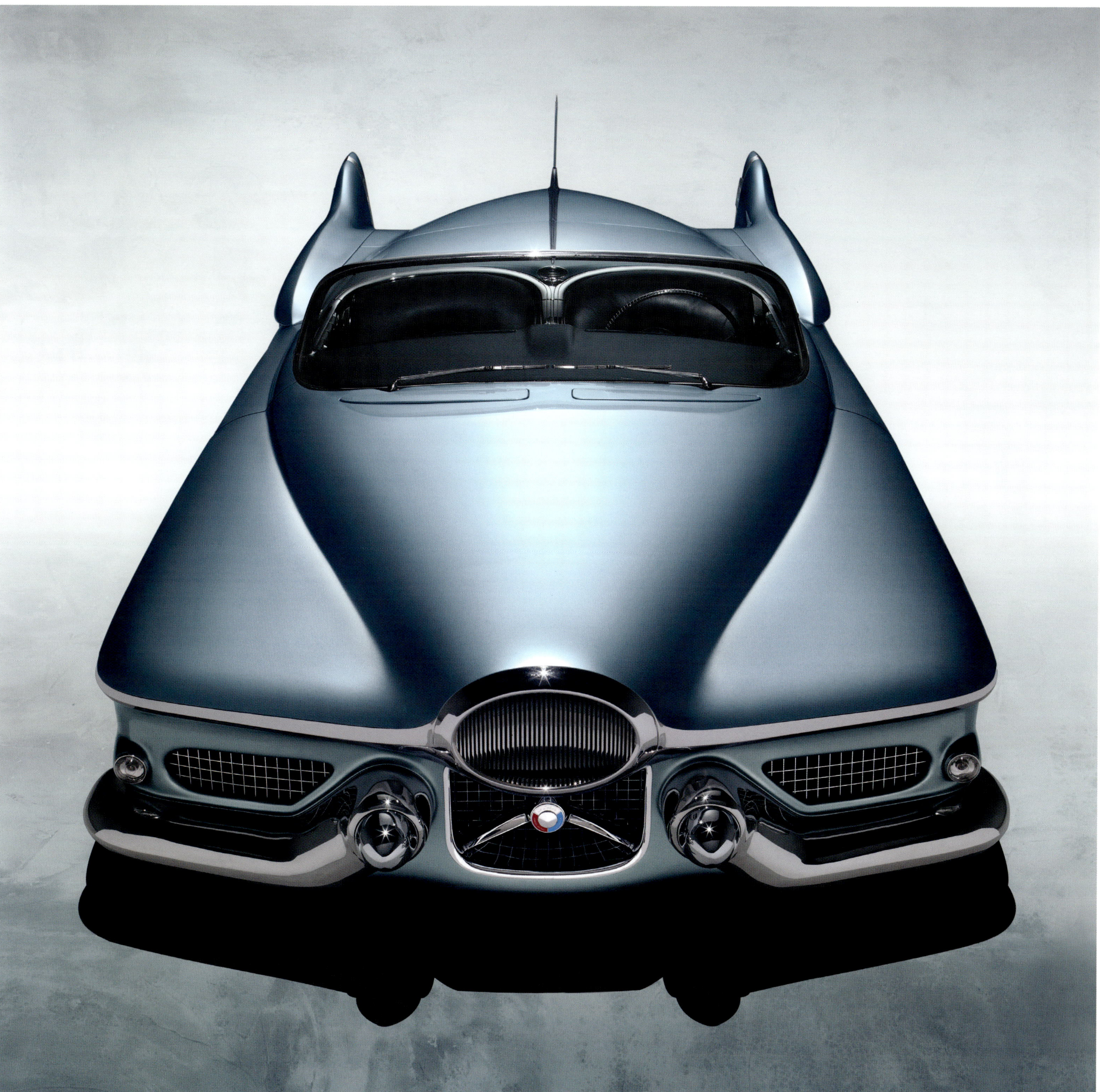

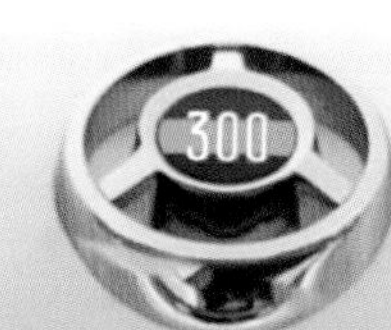
300

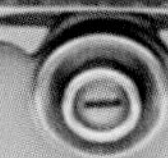

1957 CHRYSLER 300C

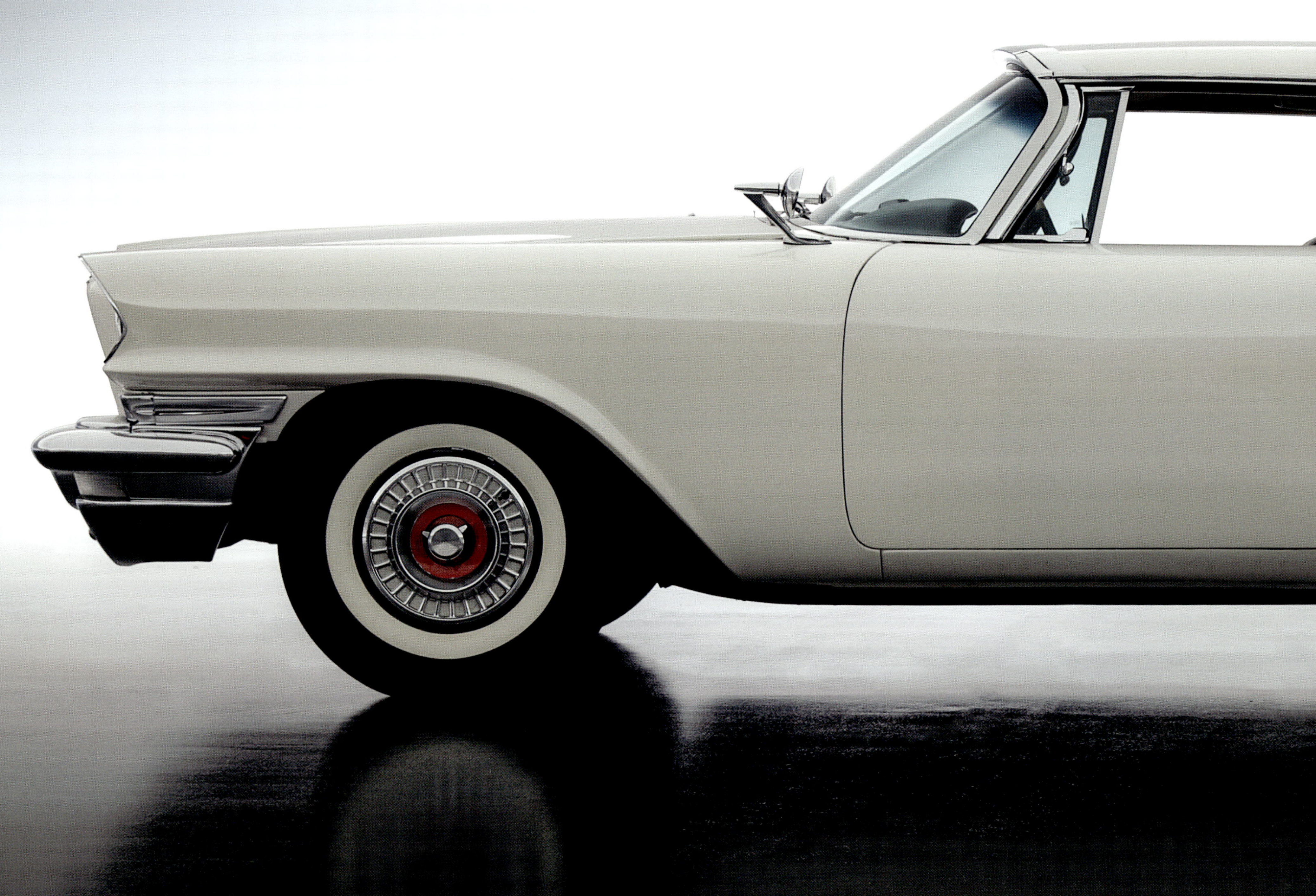

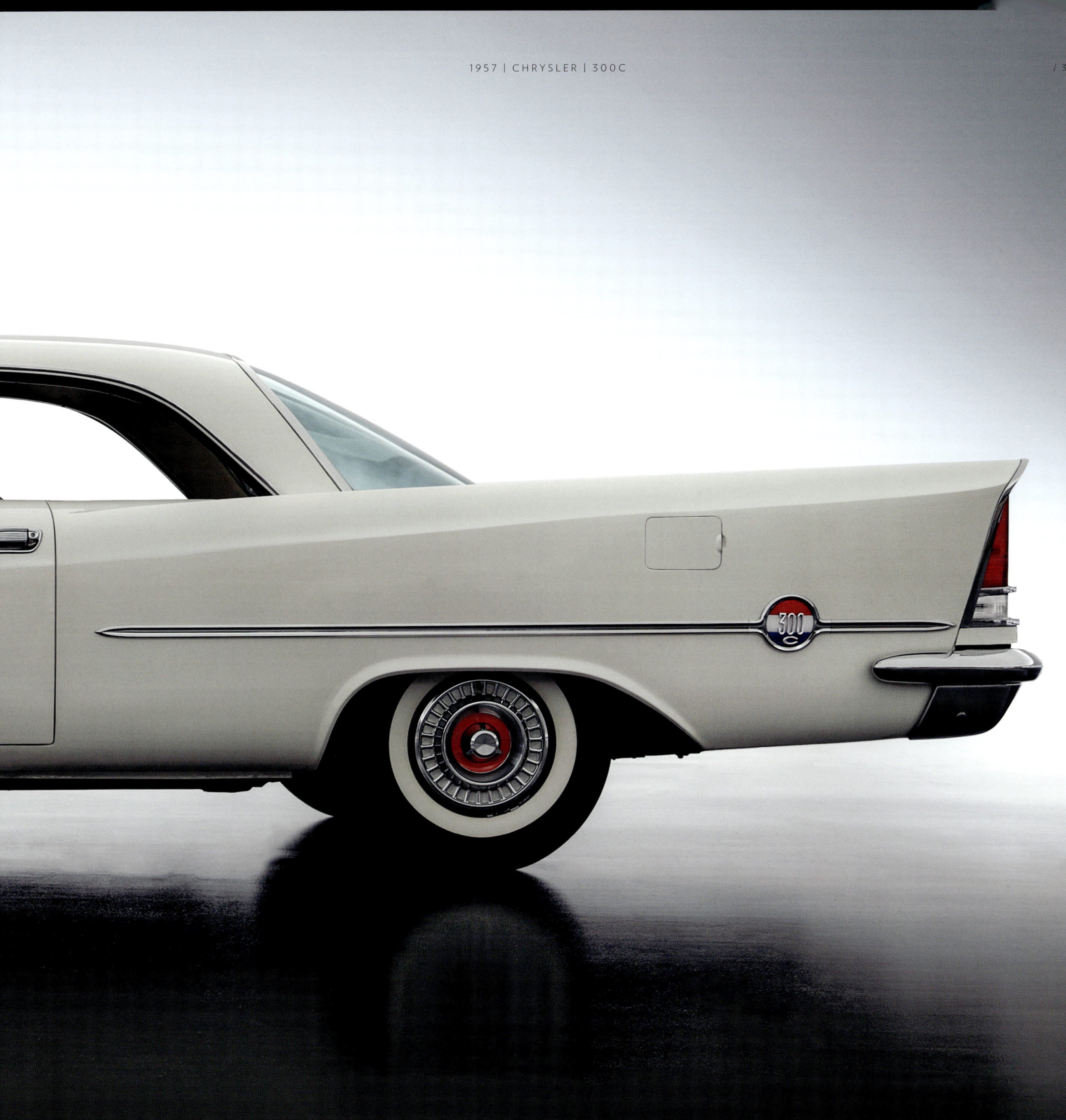
300
C

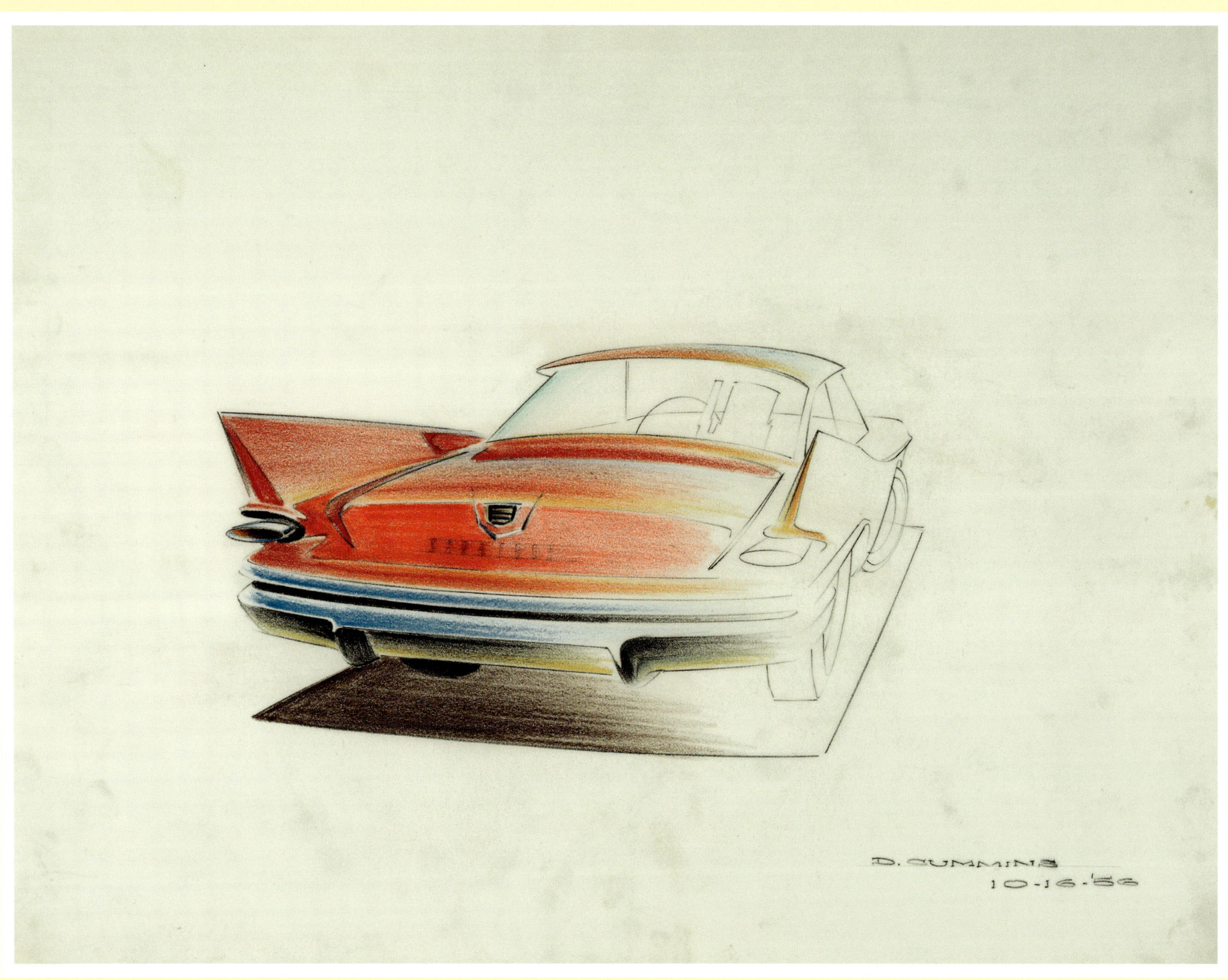

DAVE CUMMINS

Design Drawing for 1960 Chrysler, 1956, Prismacolor on vellum

The pointed fins, smooth sides, and swept-back wraparound windshield of Chrysler's 1957 300C brought the aeronautic motifs of the high-concept show cars of the 1950s to the production line. The 1957 model year car was the third in a successful campaign by designer Virgil Exner (1909–73) to create a "Forward Look" across Chrysler's brands. That campaign tapped into a zeitgeist hungry for powerful engines and streamlined forms interpreted for the new highways and suburbs of the postwar American landscape.

Virgil Exner was well positioned to offer Chrysler a new vision when he became director of styling within the engineering division in 1953. Trained as an artist at the University of Notre Dame, he began working as a stylist in Harley Earl's art and color department at General Motors in the 1920s. He left GM to work with the pioneering industrial designer Raymond Loewy (1893–1986), focusing on automotive work for Studebaker. After joining Chrysler in 1949, Exner quickly rose through the ranks alongside executives like the young president L. L. "Tex" Colbert, who understood that the company's old-fashioned designs—marketed with the slogan "Bigger on the inside, smaller on the outside"—would no longer work. Exner expanded the styling department to include designers such as William Brownlie and Donald Kopka.[1]

Design and styling were important business in the 1950s in Detroit. As the Big Three car companies—Chrysler, Ford, and General Motors—vied for market share along with smaller companies such as Packard, American Motors, and Studebaker, the imprimatur of a well-regarded stylist offered assurance that the enormous expense of development and factory retooling required to produce a new car would pay off. Prior to the 1950s, Chrysler and its associated brands had a reputation for conservative styling. Beginning in 1951, Exner began to define a new vocabulary for the company. The introduction of the Forward Look in 1955 marked a turning point.[2] Describing the formal influences of his Forward Look, Exner said, "in the modern jet fighter plane the nose is tapered and the bulk seems concentrated toward the rear, crowned by the upsweep of the tail. Big racing boats take the same general form."[3] The clean lines of the 1957 300C emphasize the massing and geometry he saw speeding across the water and through the air. Sales and profits increased dramatically from 1954 to 1955, lifting the company's share of the market from 11 percent in 1954 to 18 percent in 1955.[4]

While Chrysler's 1955 offerings repositioned the company in relation to its competitors, it became a victim of its own success. The C-300 model introduced in 1955 was a curvy two-door coupe with a chrome-covered, split-grille front end and unassuming rear fender fins. Based on the increase in sales in 1955, the company offered only modest face-lifts to its lineup for 1956 models like the 300B. Sales dropped 36 percent—consumers clearly wanted something new. In 1957 Chrysler introduced the strikingly redesigned 300C, which offered dramatic, angular rear fins, a simplified front end with a single grille, and reduced chrome to emphasize the broad, flat sides. Once consumers were primed to expect new thinking and progressive styling from Chrysler, they would not readily accept something too familiar. When Exner maintained his tall fins for 1959, one journalist blithely dismissed the offerings from "the prematurely white-haired Virgil Exner" as "another set of racily finned models."[5]

Although the fins on 1950s American cars are often recalled as exuberant flights of styling, Exner argued that this feature served a practical function. In a 1958 paper delivered to the Society of Automotive Engineers, he described wind tunnel testing undertaken at the University of Detroit using a five hundred–pound model of the 1957 Chrysler. He argued that while the modified teardrop shape of the car's body and hood effectively reduced wind resistance, a wedge-shaped silhouette with rear fins stabilized the car against crosswinds.[6]

Exner's Forward Look was both a design and an astute marketing success that captured the attention of a public eager for something new. When Chrysler released a string of television commercials for its Plymouth-brand 1957 model year cars, their slogan proudly boasted, "Suddenly ... it's 1960."[7] The bold design of his 1957 cars helped to strengthen Chrysler's reputation as a bellwether of car styling to come—a position that had often been held by Harley Earl at General Motors during the 1950s. The role of the stylist, and the public perception that certain studios would lead the pack, had lucrative implications for these massive corporations.[8] ❖

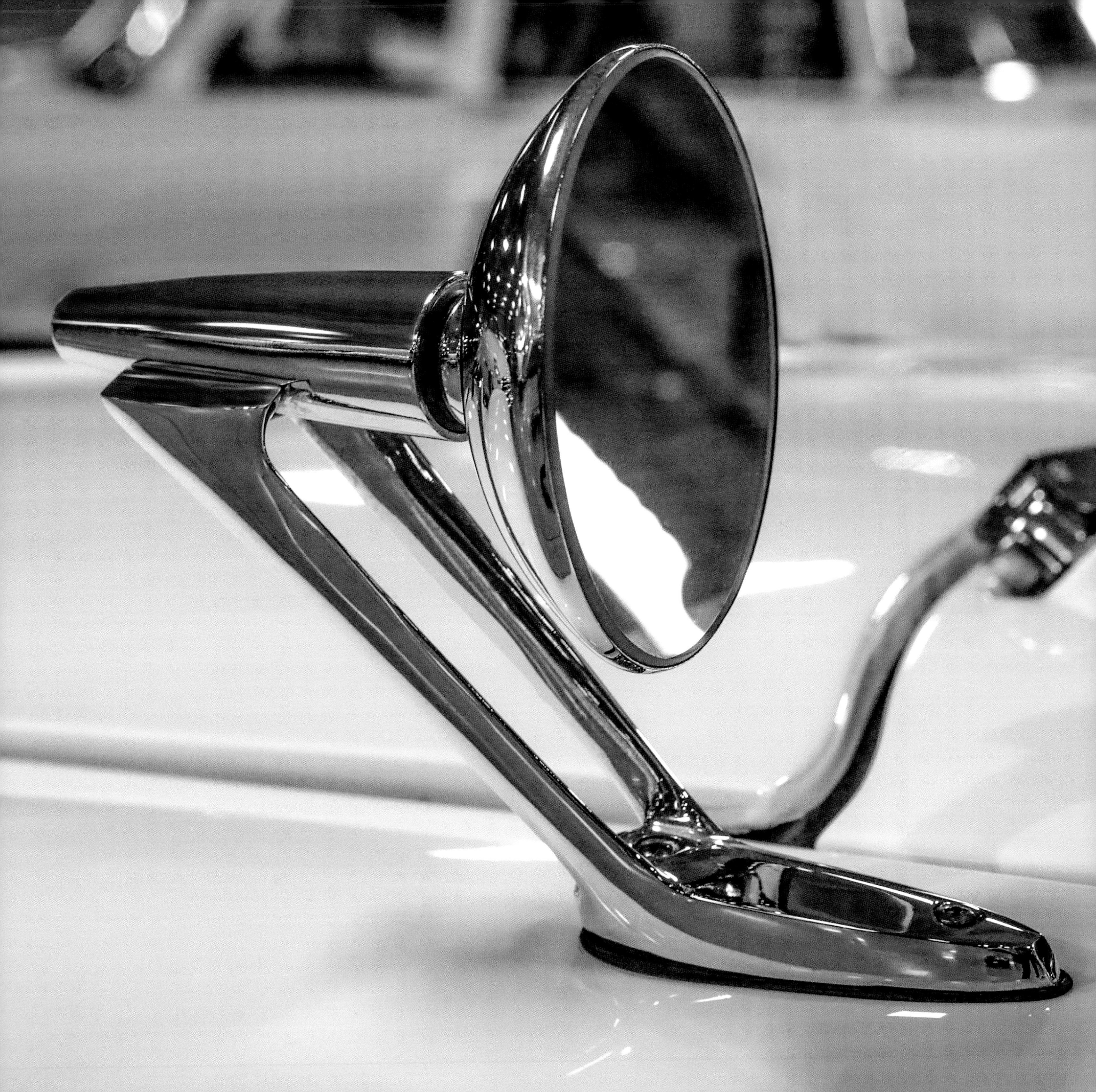

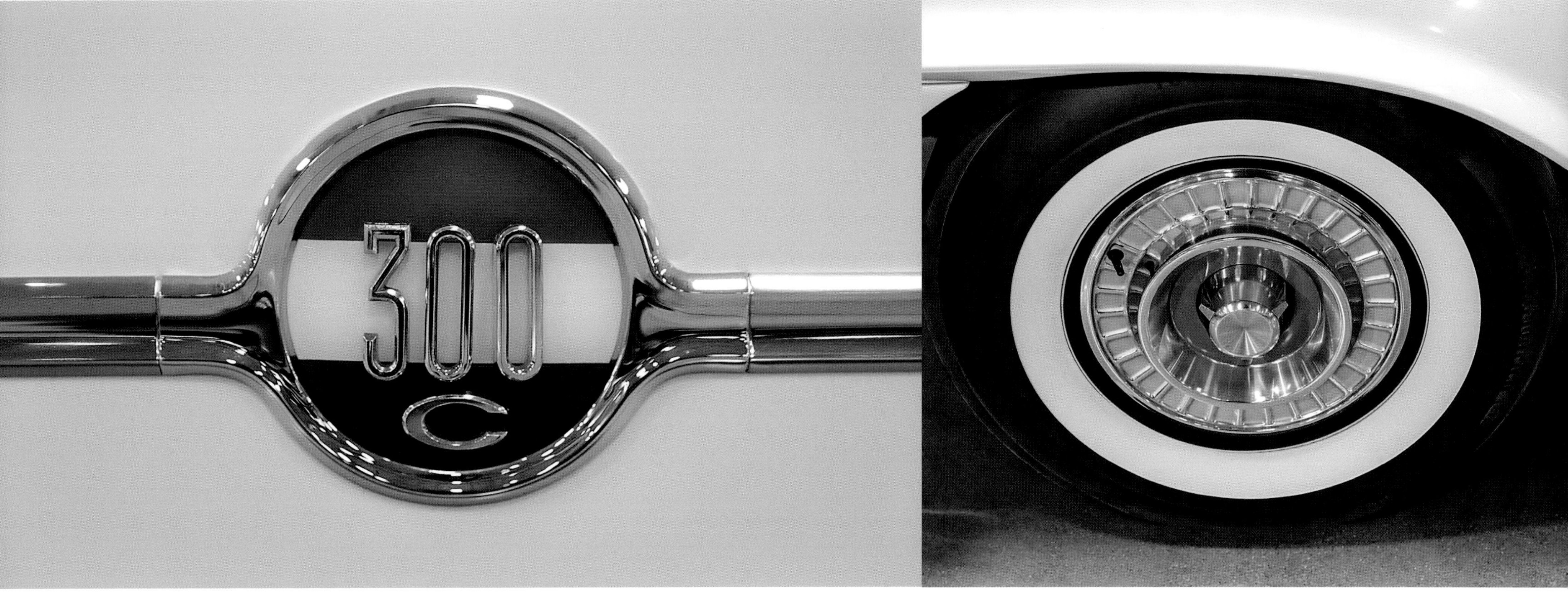

Chrysler Corporation, 300C, 1957. *p. 28:* Rear view (detail); *pp. 30–31:* Left side view; *opposite:* Angular chrome detailing on side view mirror; *above left:* Model insignia; *above right:* Hubcap.

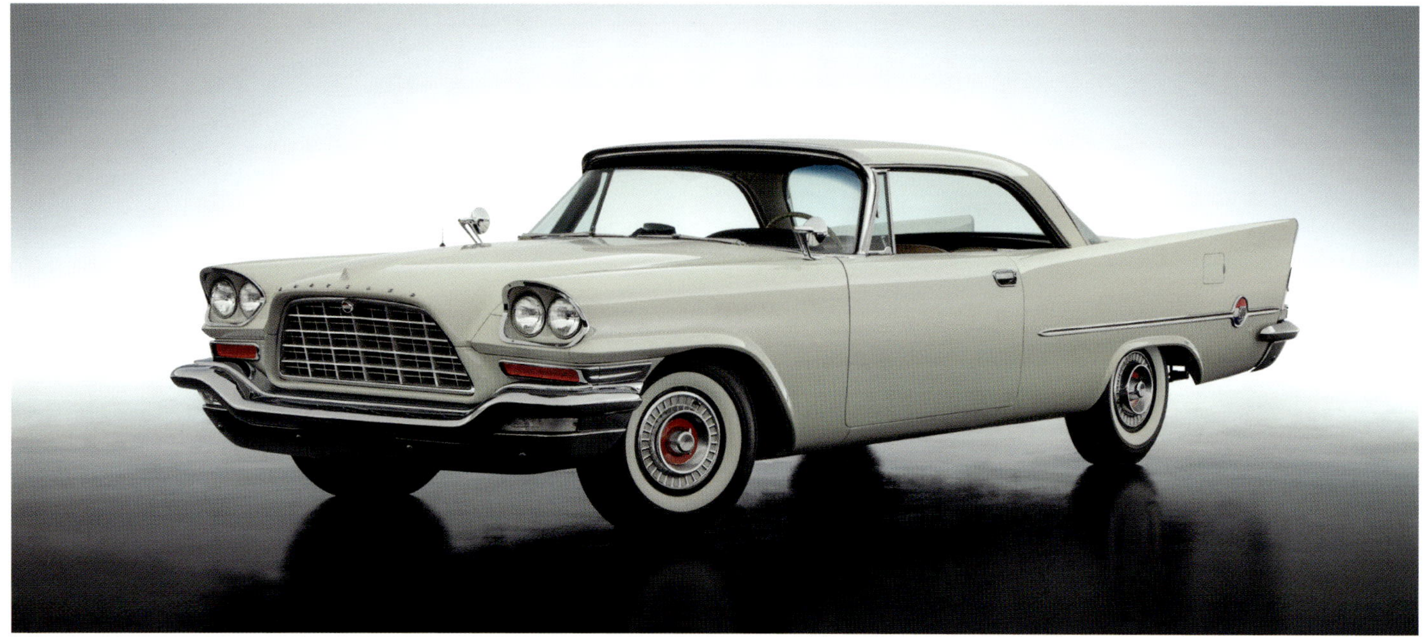

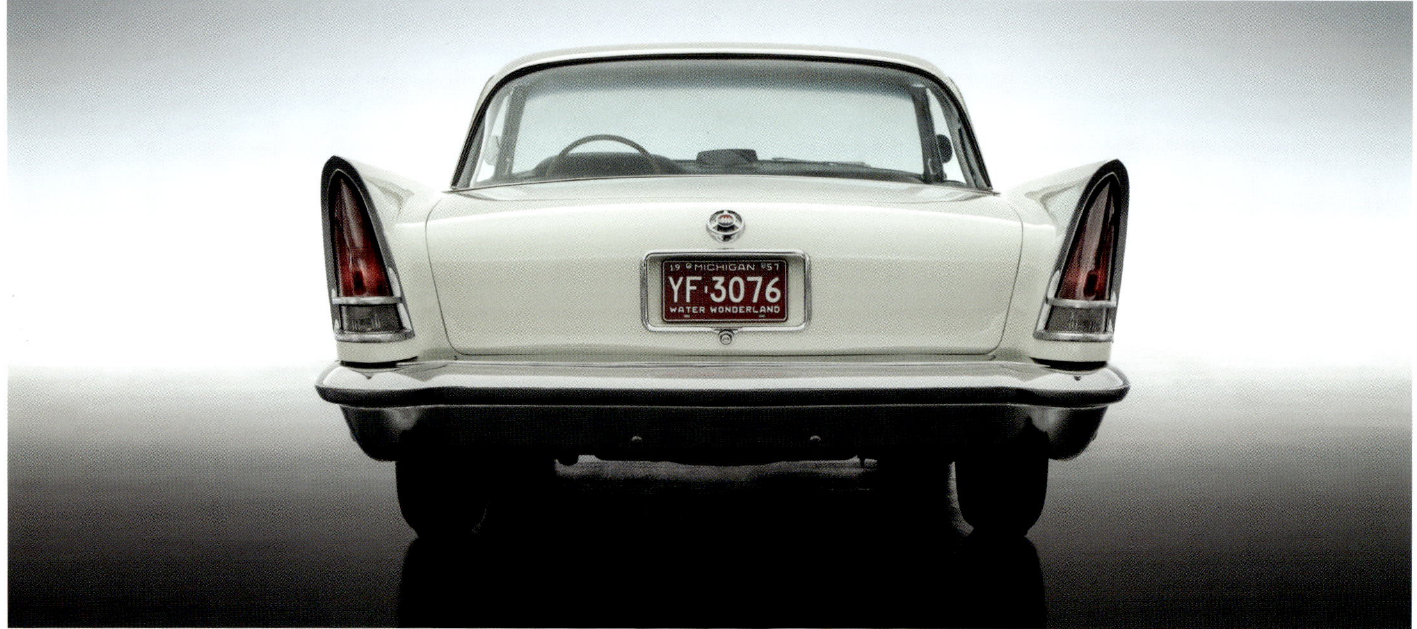

Chrysler Corporation, 300C, 1957. *above:* Front three-quarter view showing angular profile; *below:* Rear-end view showing taillights built into peaked fins; *opposite:* Front view showing trapezoidal grille.

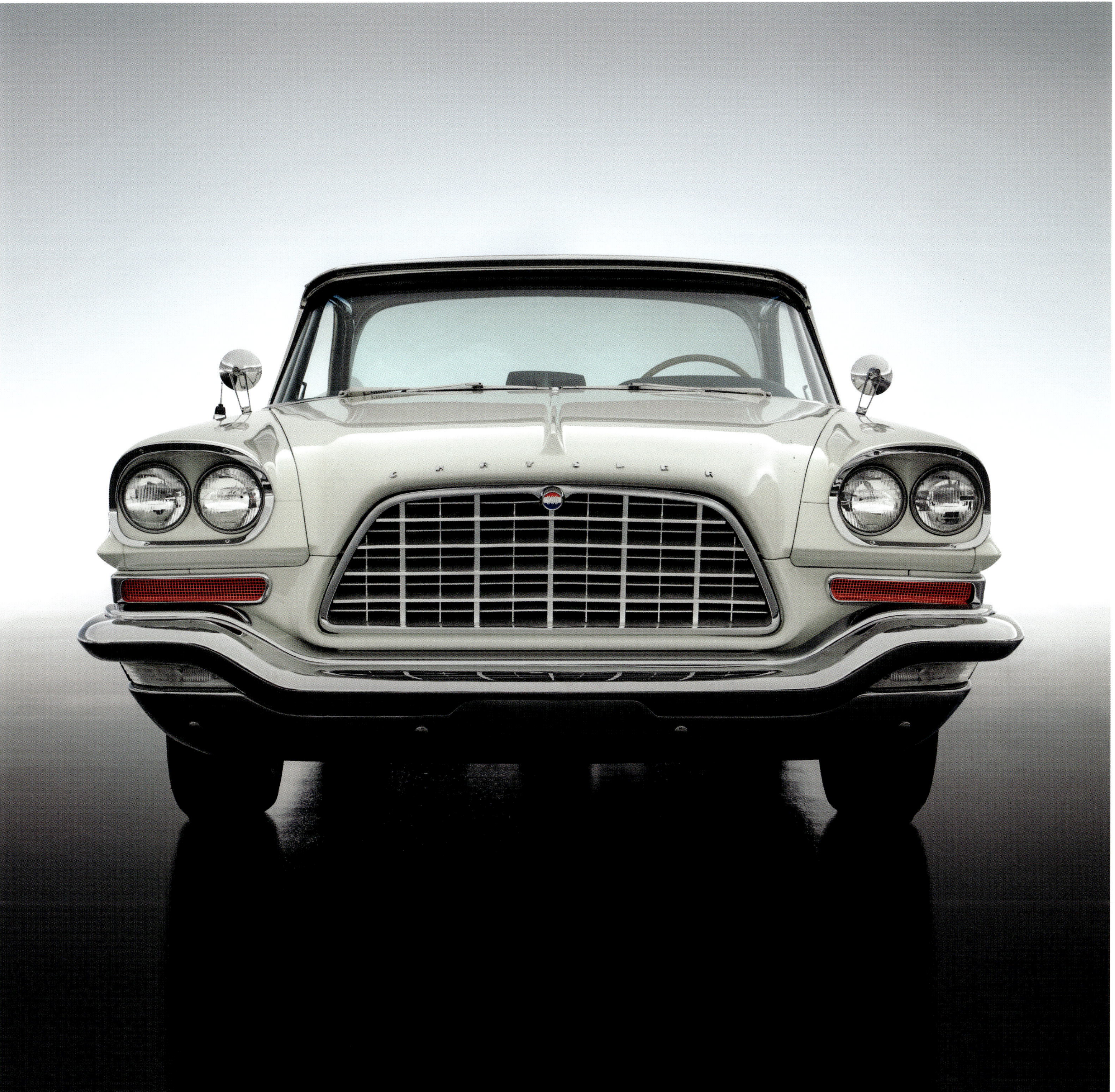
CHRYSLER

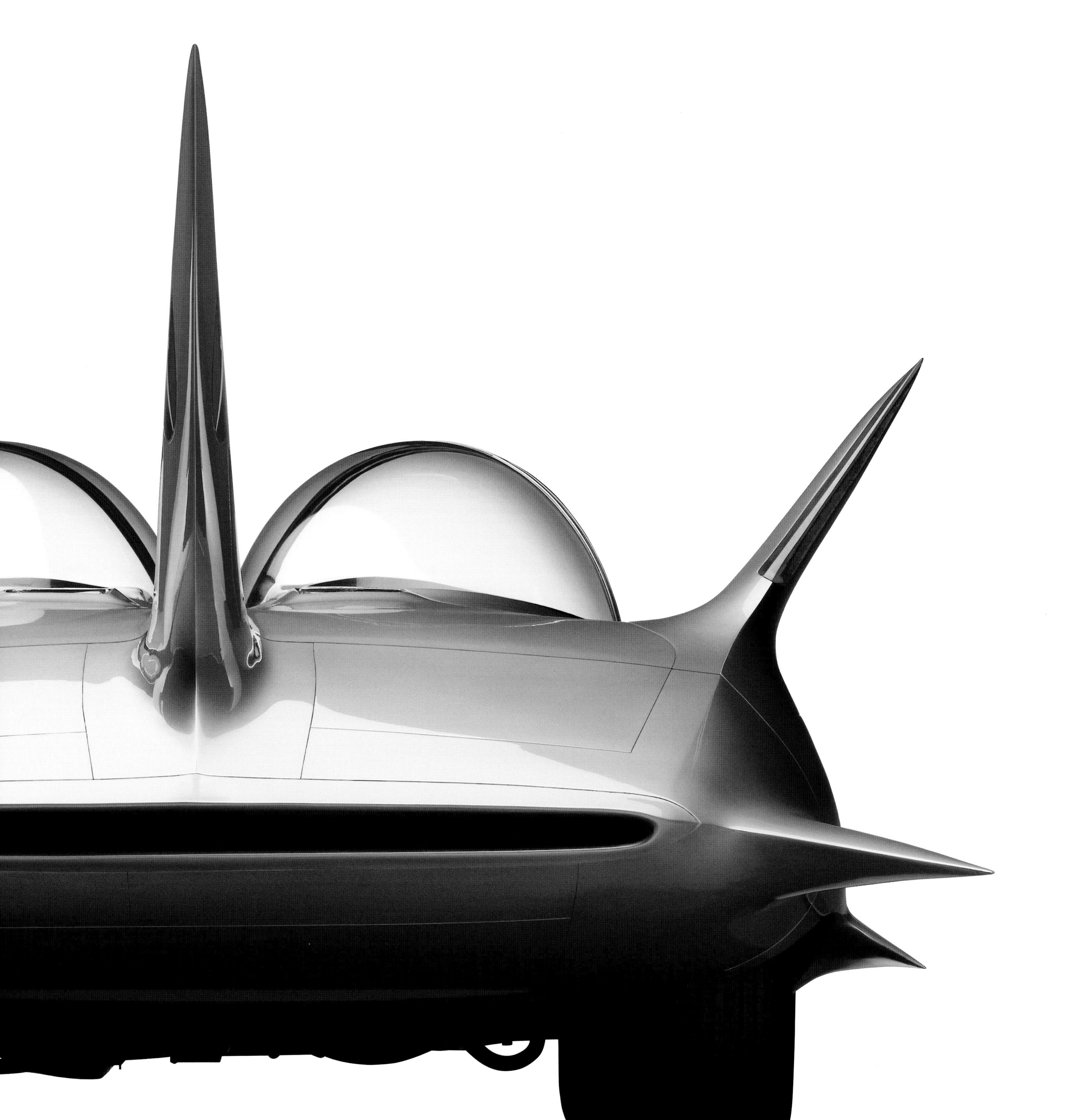

1958

GENERAL MOTORS

FIREBIRD III

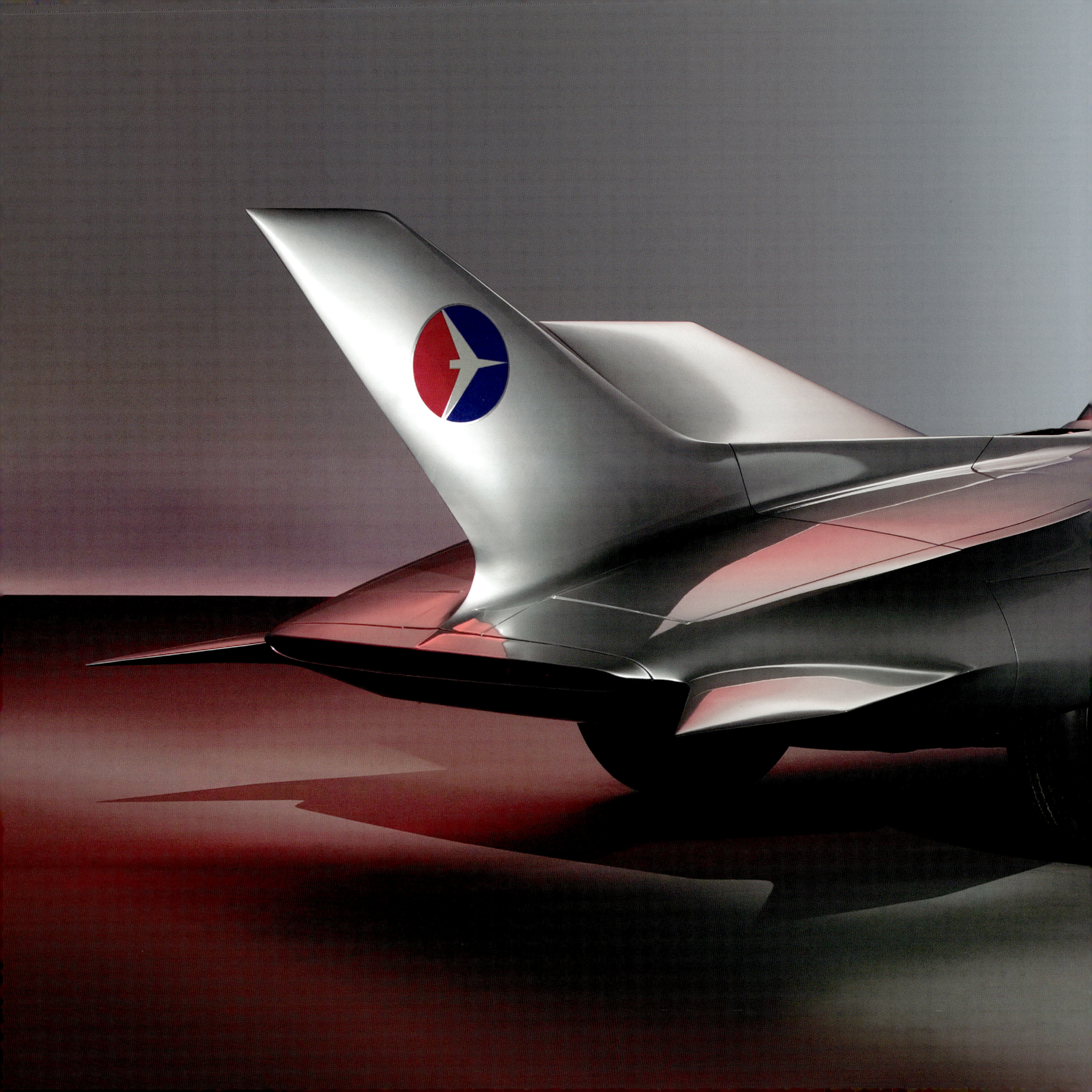

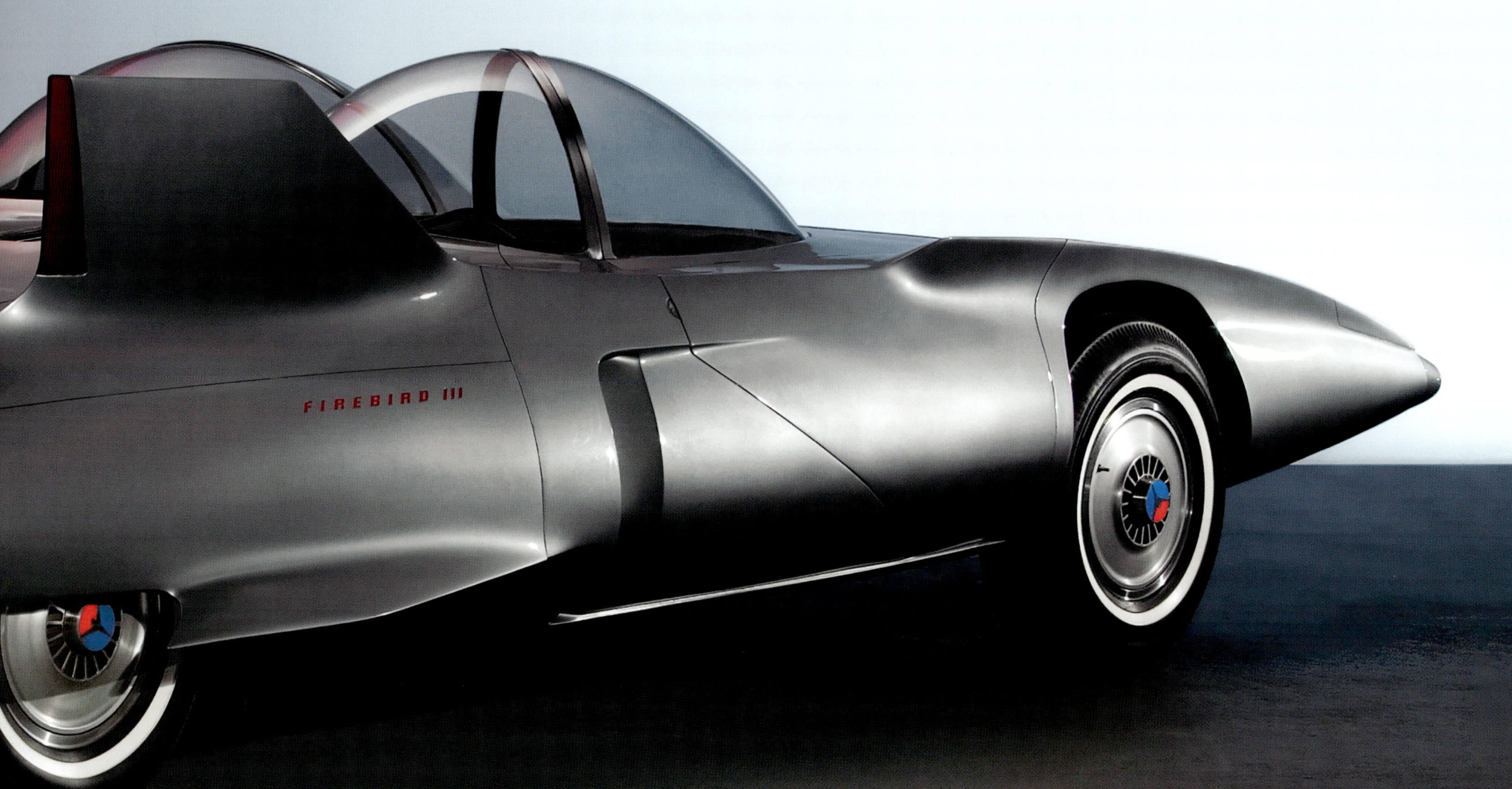
FIREBIRD III

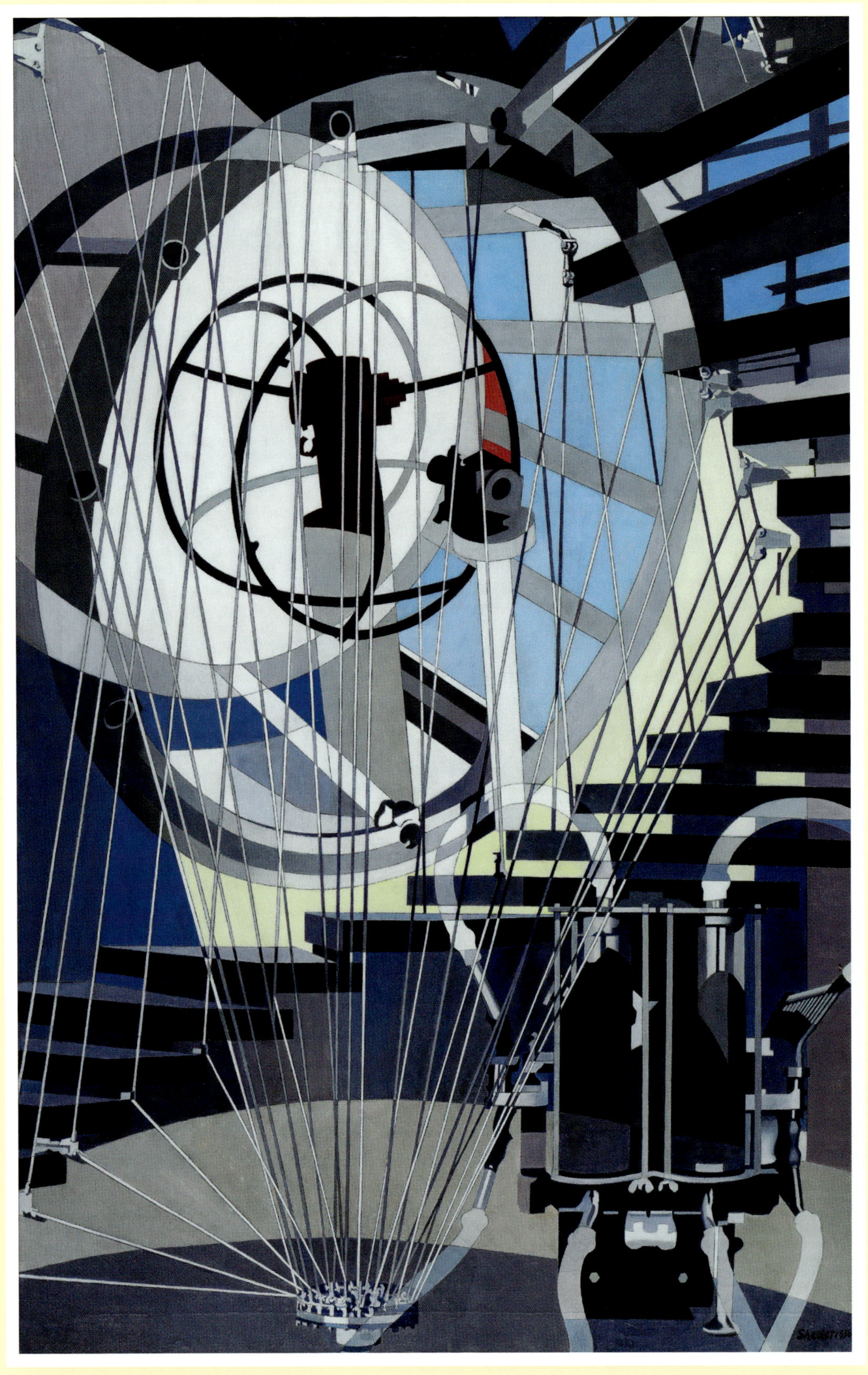

CHARLES SHEELER

General Motors Research, 1955, oil on canvas

General Motors' futuristic Firebird III was designed to shock the public with visions of space-age technology brought to earth. It debuted against the backdrop of the space race between the United States and the USSR, when the ability to approach new frontiers became a matter of patriotic pride and rival victories like the successful Soviet launch of the satellite Sputnik I in 1957 were cause for anxiety. With its streamlined body, towering fins, and protruding bubbles for the cabin, this 1958 show car powerfully evoked a supersonic jet or a spaceship from a science fiction movie.

The third Firebird built on the success of two earlier models. A promotional brochure for the 1959 Motorama where it debuted described the evolving goals for the program: Firebird I was built "for high performance," Firebird II was an experiment in "futuristic family car design," and Firebird III "refines the outstanding features of both."[1] The Firebird I was created in 1953. Harley Earl, GM's vice president for styling, is credited with developing its plastic body. A single-seat car with a teardrop-shaped bubble over the driver, it was the first American car powered by a gas turbine. The Firebird II, created in 1956, was a turbine-powered car with an expanded four-person cab. Among many ambitious features, it had automated navigation when driven on roads embedded with an electric system that could communicate with the car.

When Earl explained his concept to the team working on the third Firebird project, then called XP-73, he asked them to design "what you would expect the astronauts to drive to the launch pad on their way to the moon."[2] The designers sought to create a show car that would dazzle crowds and act as a functional laboratory for testing the usability and feasibility of features for consumer models. It was styled and engineered in GM's new technical center in suburban Warren, Michigan, a sprawling, modern campus designed for the company in the latest midcentury style by Finnish American architect and designer Eero Saarinen (1910–61) and completed in 1956. The company commissioned the American modernist painter Charles Sheeler (1883–1965) to create a new work for the research division building. The resulting 1955 painting is a celebration of the technological sublime that emerged as Americans looked to scientists and engineers to offer better understandings of the world around them (opposite).

Fittingly, the Firebird III was a collaboration between two divisions of General Motors. The styling division, under Earl's leadership, took the lead on the exterior and interior design—as a show car, the Firebird III needed to look as futuristic as the technology whirring under its hood. The research division was tasked with developing the chassis, engines, and running gear, including a number of novel features such as a joystick monocontroller used to steer, accelerate, and brake the car. In addition to the turbine engine that drove the car, the sophisticated electronics required a small secondary engine to power auxiliary functions.[3] To allow the sculptural body surface to maintain its integrity and power, it is relatively devoid of the applied chrome ornaments or color variation that were otherwise common in consumer models of the era.[4]

With his showman's sensibility for generating spectacle, Earl described the crowds that would gather in New York City at the ballroom of the Waldorf Astoria hotel for the car's debut. The designer Norman James (born 1932), taking the directive to heart, included in his initial concept sketches features like projecting fins to guide the crowds around the car.[5] As with the debut of the Le Sabre, Firebird III drew widespread popular attention for its dramatic styling and innovative technological features. The promotional literature for the 1959 Motorama display advised visitors, "Don't be deceived by this Firebird III—it may look like a dream car, but it is a practical workshop for testing advancements that could very well improve your General Motors car of the next few years."

While the Firebird III was not for sale, its motifs were immediately diffused to the mass market, and consumers could look for related style features when they purchased a new car. As the car prepared to make its debut, the fins on production models rose higher than ever. *Popular Science* asked in October 1958: "Who said fins would disappear? GM has seen the Chrysler Corp. in kings and queens and raised the ante in aces and deuces."[6] The 1959 Cadillac, for example, had towering tail fins that measured 46 inches high off the ground. Although that fell short of the Firebird's 57.3-inch tail fins, it was taller than those of its peers introduced that model year.[7] ❖

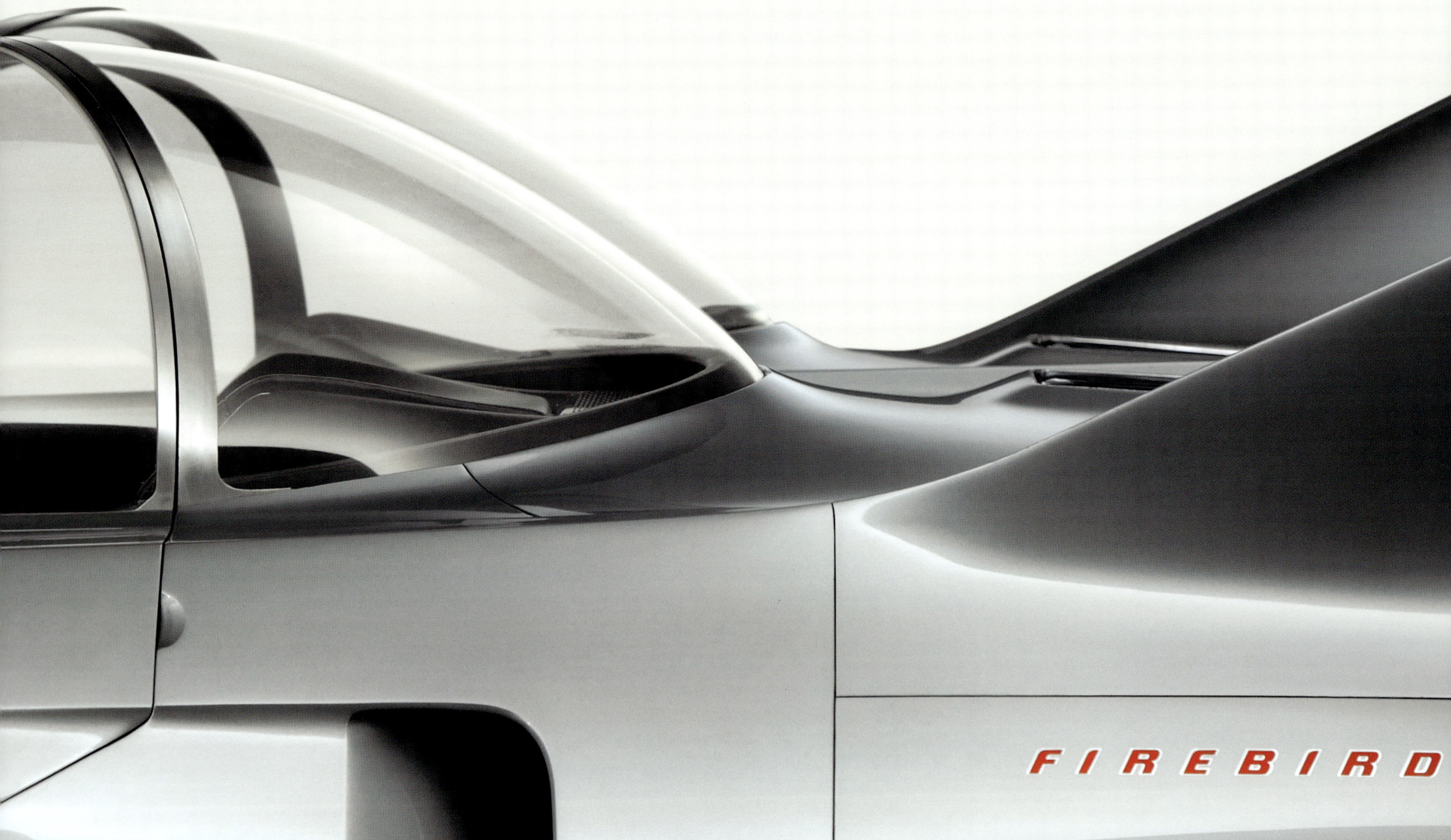
FIREBIRD

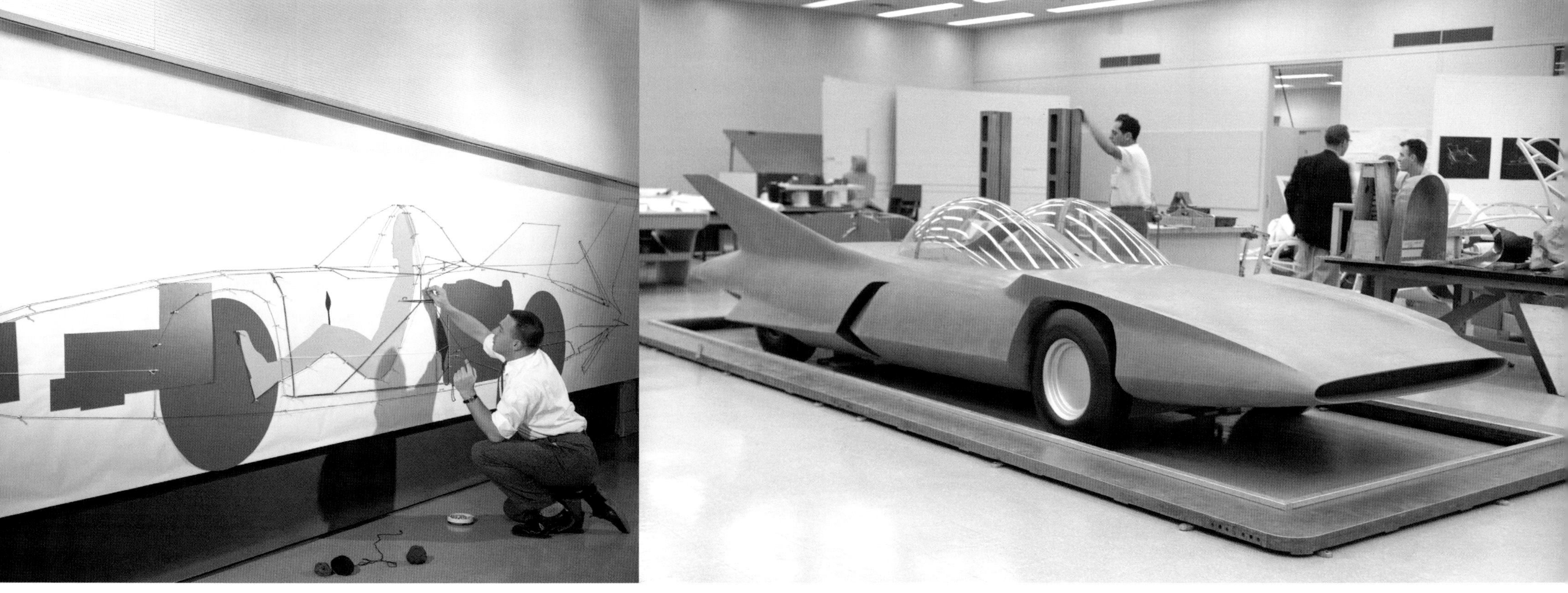

General Motors, Firebird III, 1958. *p. 38:* Rear view (detail); *pp. 40–41:* Rear three-quarter view; *opposite:* Left side view showing fin modeling and cabin bubble; *above left:* Creating yarn drawings, 1957; *above right:* Clay model in the design studio, 1957.

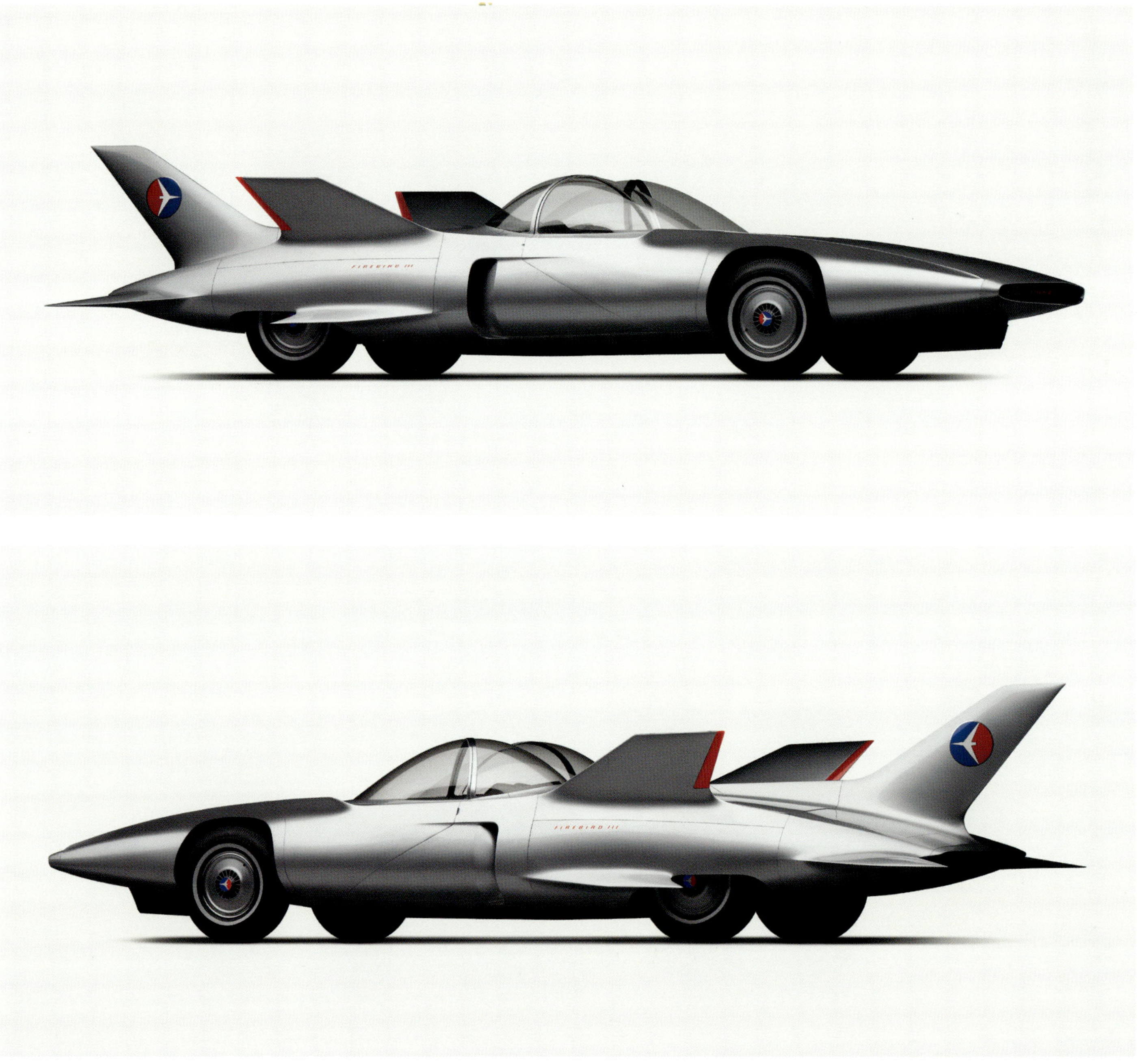

General Motors, Firebird III, 1958. *above:* Right profile view showing fins in relation to cabin; *below:* Left profile view; *opposite:* Front end view showing oval grille and dual bubble covers for cabin.

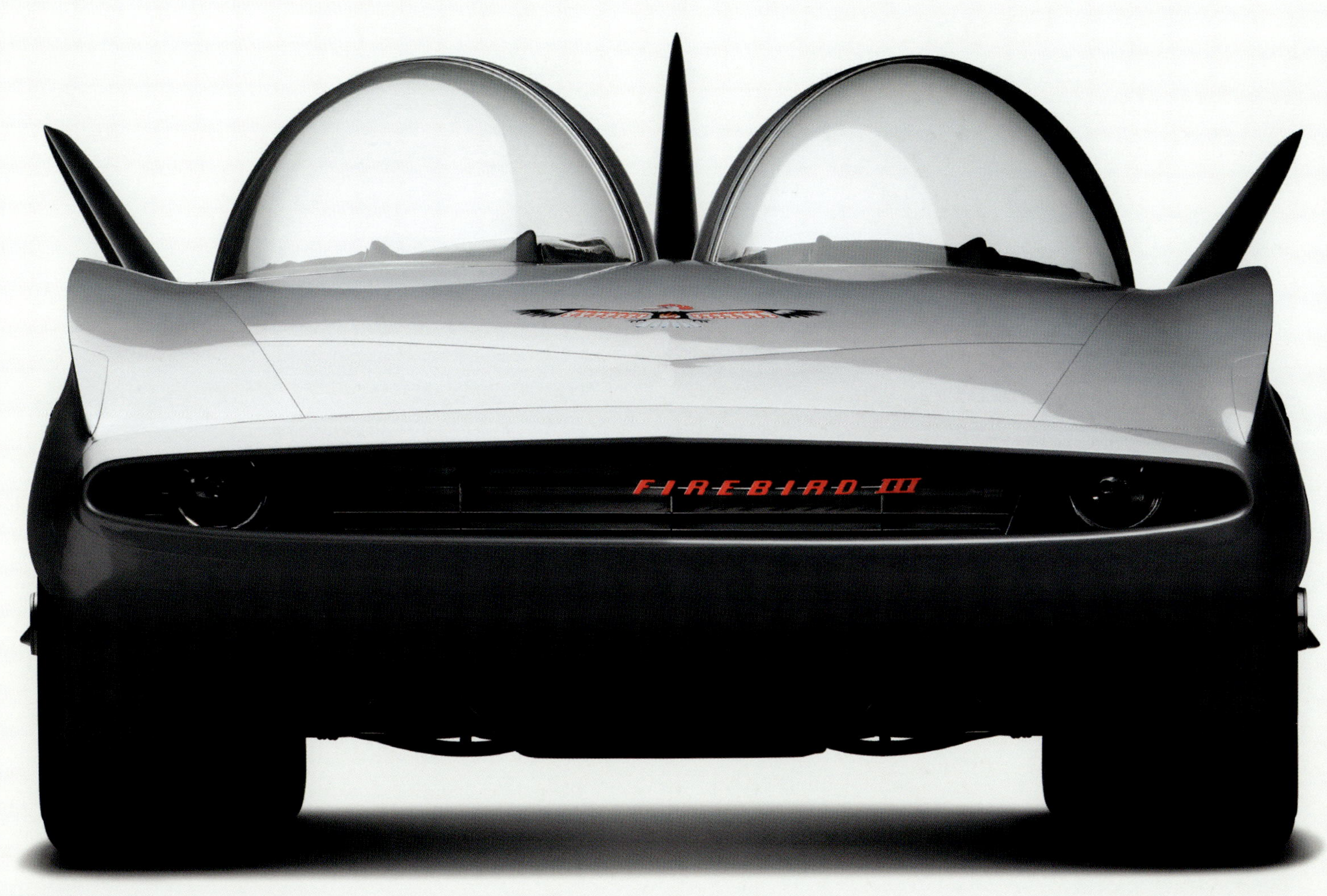
FIREBIRD III

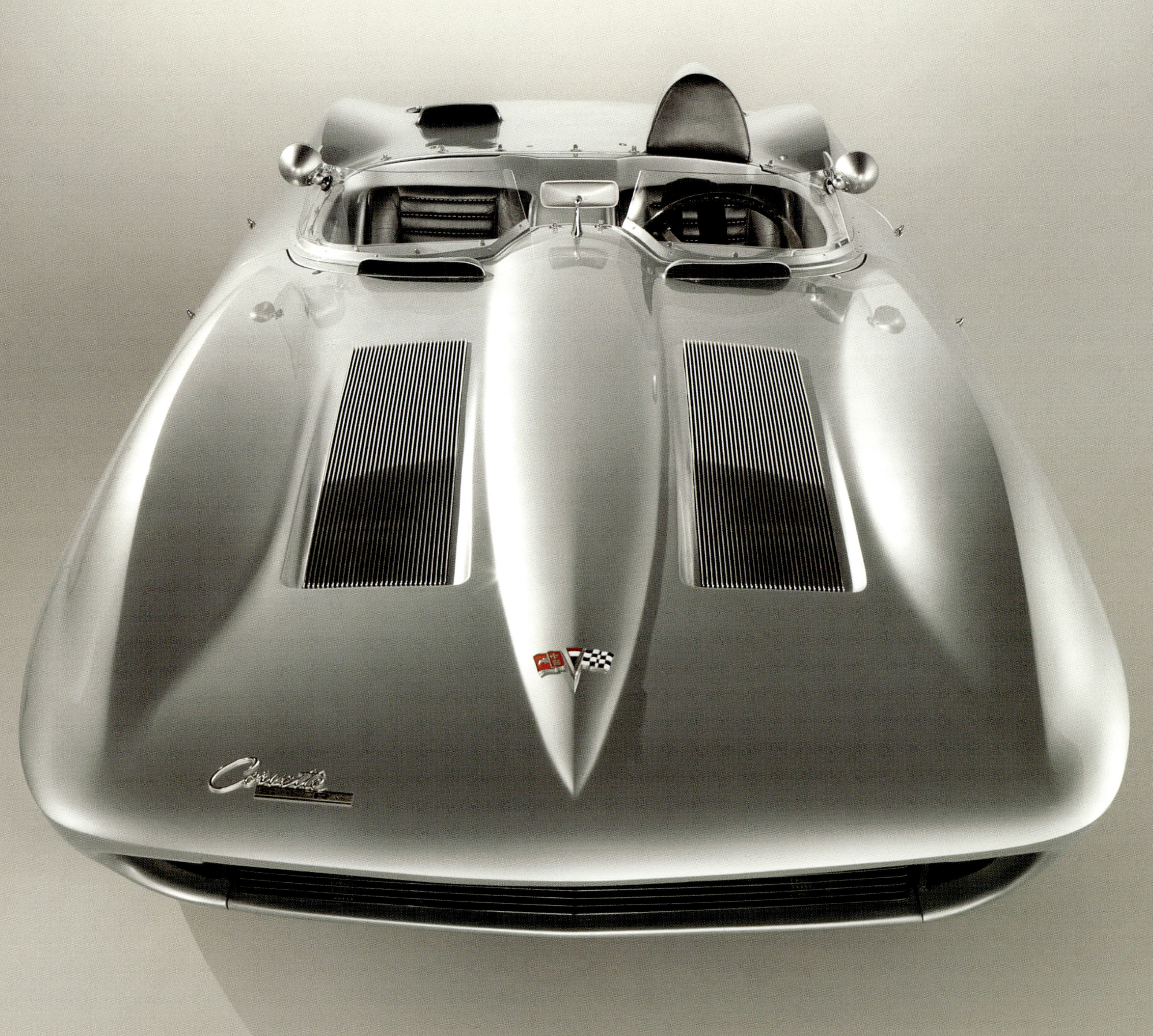

1959 GENERAL MOTORS CORVETTE STINGRAY RACER

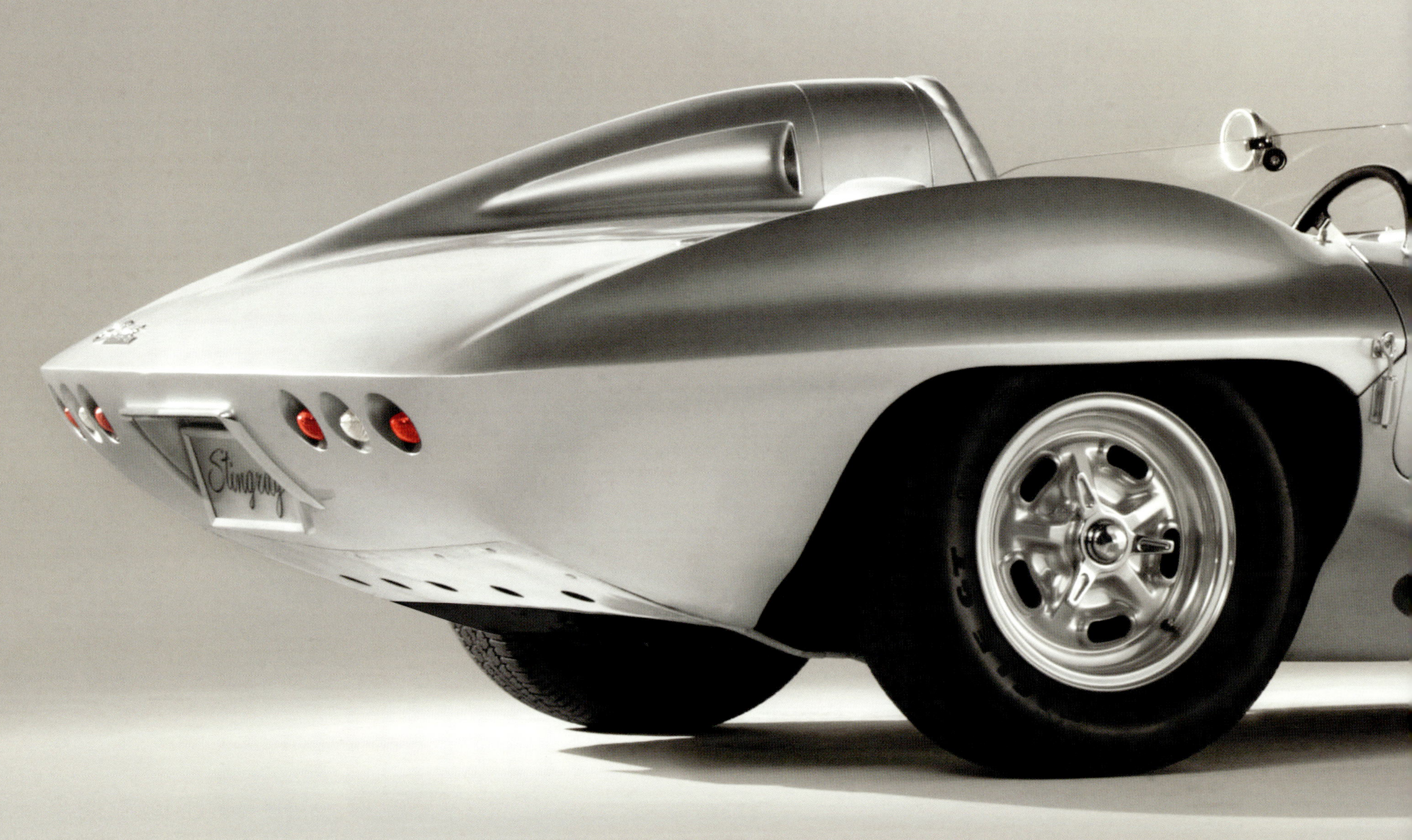
Stingray

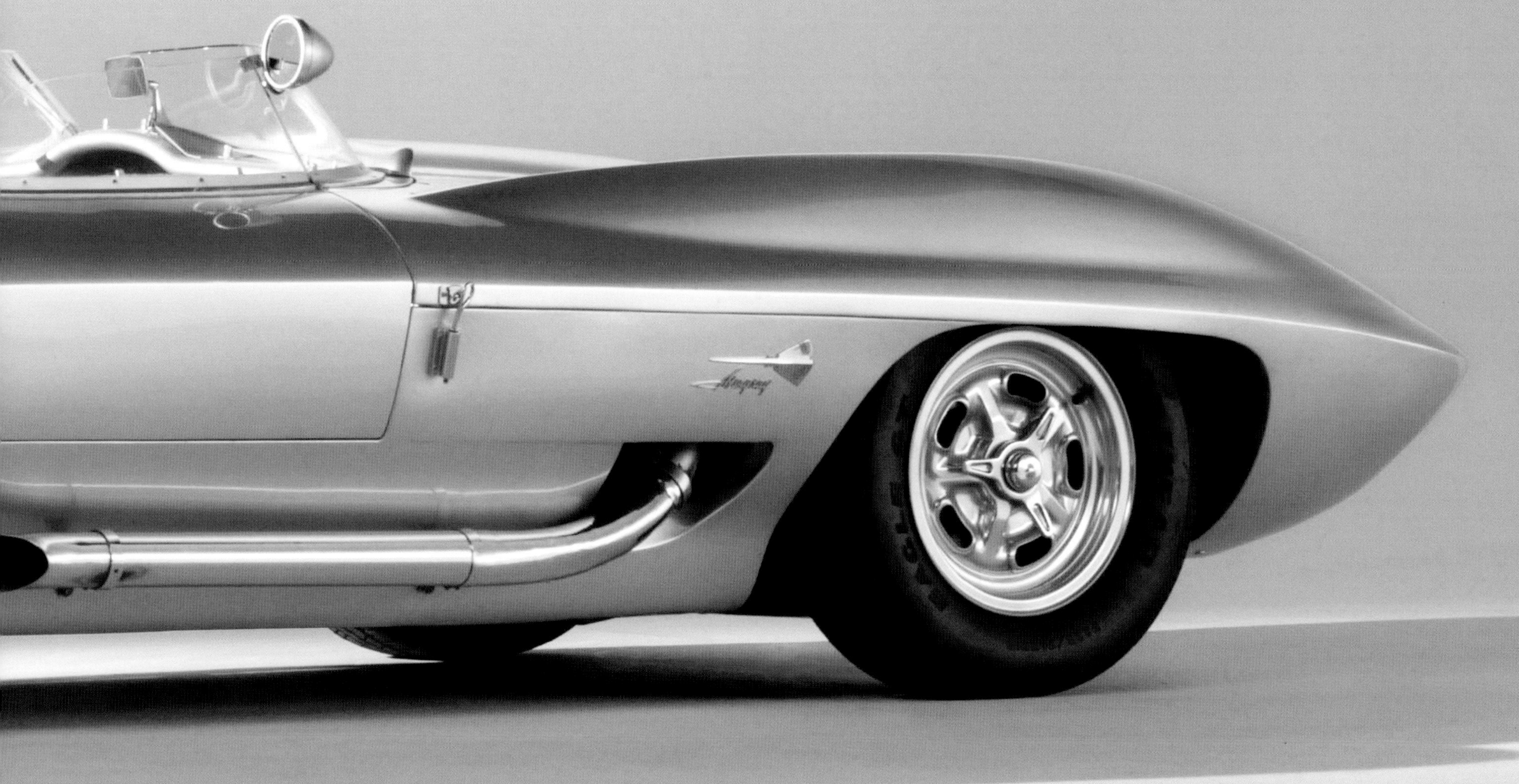

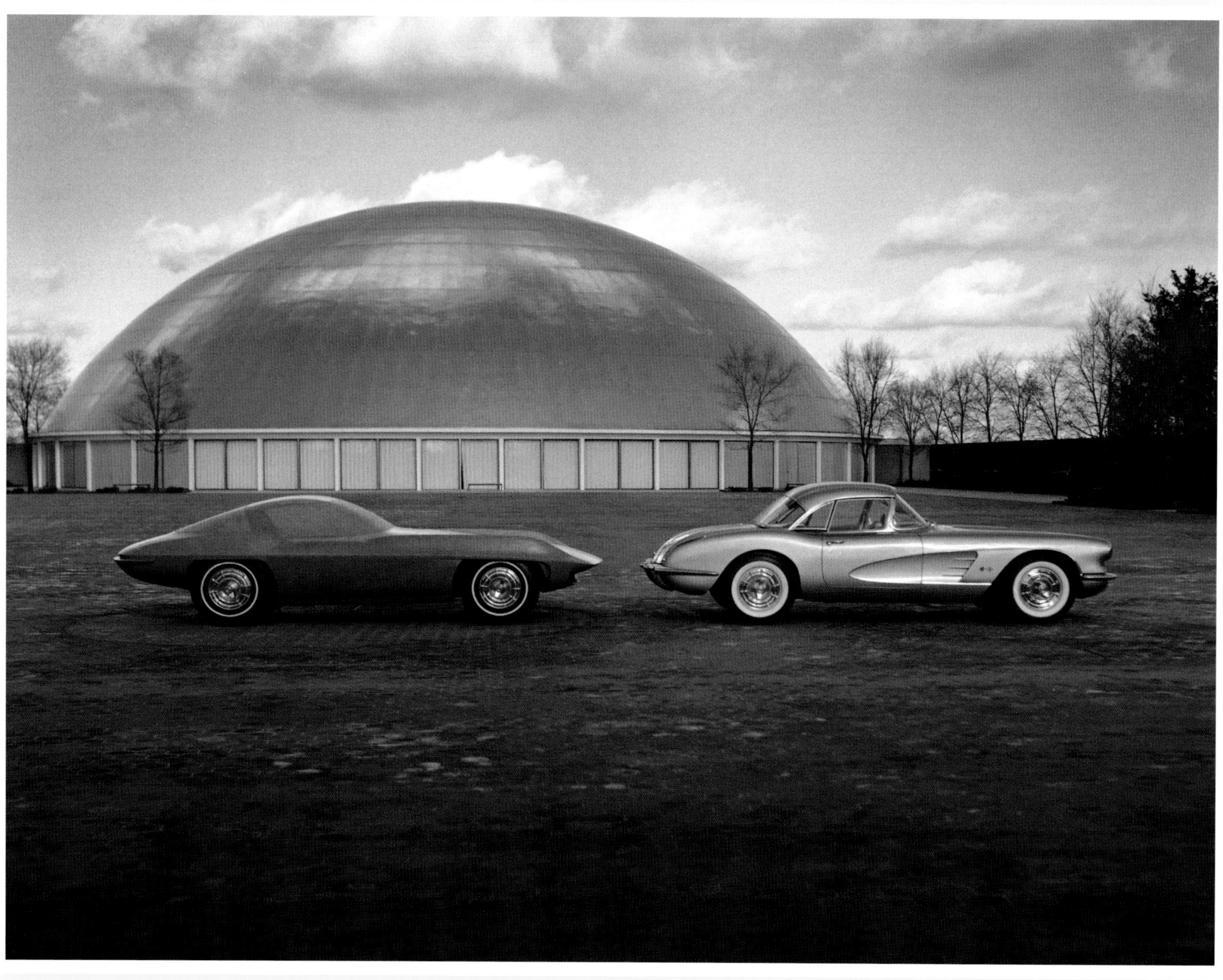

Clay model for XP-87 alongside 1958 Corvette, 1957.

The custom 1959 Corvette Stingray Racer looks nothing like the production model Corvettes sold to the public that year. Completed in a secret studio at General Motors for stylist William Mitchell (1912–88), it reflects his enthusiasm for the look and speed of race car driving and the youthful attitude that accompanied that dangerous endeavor. The car was produced against the wishes of GM corporate leadership during a period when the Detroit auto industry had officially severed ties with car racing. Despite, or perhaps because of, its position outside the officially sanctioned design program of its day, the custom 1959 Corvette Stingray helped inspire the shape of iconic Corvettes introduced in the 1960s.

Mitchell joined GM's art and color department as a young designer in 1935 after studying at the Carnegie Institute in Pittsburgh, and the Art Students League in New York City. He rose through the ranks of the Cadillac studio before leaving GM between 1949 and 1953 to take a position with Harley Earl's independent product design firm Harley Earl Inc. He returned to GM in 1953 with the new title of assistant director of styling. When Earl retired in 1958, Mitchell was promoted to the position of vice president for styling. Despite his thorough training in Earl's studios, as Mitchell began putting his mark on new GM designs, the differences between their sensibilities were immediately clear.[1]

When Chevrolet first introduced the lightweight fiberglass Corvette in 1953, the two-door, two-seat, and often convertible-roof car was marketed to youthful drivers or as a second car alongside a family sedan. Its low profile, small size, and novel materials stood in marked contrast to the large sedans dominating the market and helped to tempt American consumers to the market for a sports car. The Corvette soon sparked challengers from other Detroit companies, like Ford's Thunderbird or Studebaker's Golden Hawk.[2]

While Earl had begun efforts to redesign the Corvette, as he approached retirement, his taste was increasingly out of touch with the demands of young consumers no longer thrilled by chrome and fins. During the fall of 1957, in his role as assistant director of styling, Mitchell brought photographs of recent European sports cars to Research Studio B at General Motors, then headed by Robert Veryzer. The young designers associated with the studio included the racing enthusiast Peter Brock, Larry Shinoda, Chuck Pohlman, Tony Lapine, and Gene Garfinkle.[3] Mitchell challenged that studio to rethink the Corvette with the European images in mind, saying, "I want this form to be a complete breakaway from what we've seen around here in the past."[4] This nascent project began with the unassuming name XP-87.

A December 1957 photograph shows a clay model for the proposed XP-87 alongside the 1958 production Corvette (opposite). The latter has many features associated with Earl's era at GM, including an inset swipe, applied chrome stripes on the sides, and bomblike headlamps. In sharp contrast, the model XP-87 is a low-slung, angular, hard-edged racer. In place of the rounded fenders of the '57 Corvette, it has taut, muscular fenders sculpted around the wheel wells. Instead of a chrome grille split by the bumper line, it has a pointed front end concealing a modest air intake. The dramatically angled front and rear windshields merge cleanly into the roof to create an aerodynamic teardrop shape that could cut across the road or racetrack. The dramatic contrast reflects both the birth of a new era in car design, one that would react to the youthful sensibilities and rebellious spirit of the coming 1960s, and the introduction of a new personality shaping design and styling at General Motors.

Mitchell's youthful alternative to Earl's design sensibility was not without controversy. As the dangers of racing attracted increased scrutiny in the wake of a number of widely publicized deadly crashes, the Automobile Manufacturers Association instituted a ban in 1957. Within the design division at GM, this immediately halted any projects too closely associated with racing.[5] As the XP-87 progressed from sketch, to one-fifth-scale clay model, to full-size clay model, the team retreated deep into the design building at the Warren, Michigan, campus, away from the prying eyes of executives committed to the ban on racing. Their work took place in the secret Studio X, hidden behind a false wall in a room used to store tools. The XP-87 was no longer a model for potential production; it was developed as a personal car for Mitchell himself to race.

When it debuted to the public in the spring of 1959, it was not marked as a GM car, or as a Corvette. Officially, it was known only as the Stingray. Despite a lackluster racing performance due to aerodynamic inefficiency, the car attracted immediate attention for its striking design.[6] Although created as a unique prototype, the 1959 Stingray Racer influenced the styling of the second-generation Corvettes introduced as the Sting Ray for the 1963 model year. The low-slung body, pointed front end, and fender forms of that production model were all informed by this forward-thinking experiment. ❖

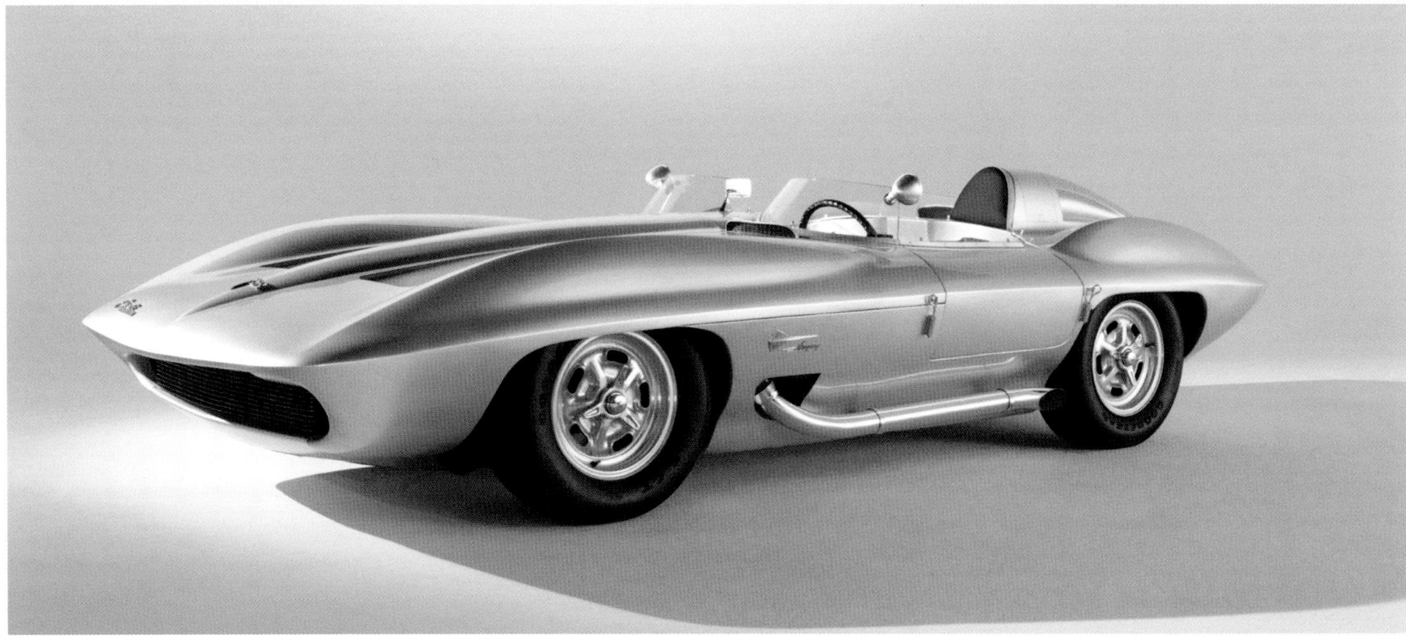

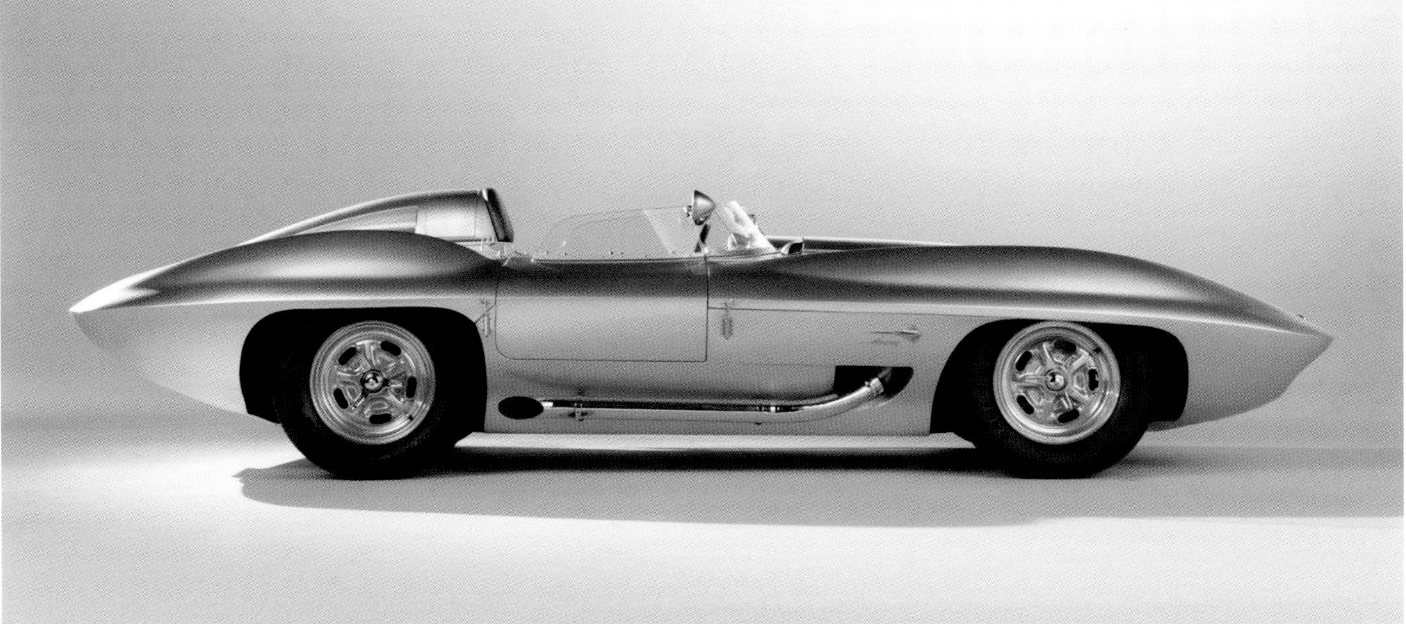

General Motors, Corvette Stingray Racer, 1959. *p. 48:* Front view; *pp. 50–51:* Rear three-quarter view; *above:* Front three-quarter view showing curved fender form; *below:* Right profile view showing side pipe exhaust; *opposite:* Rear three-quarter view showing interior.

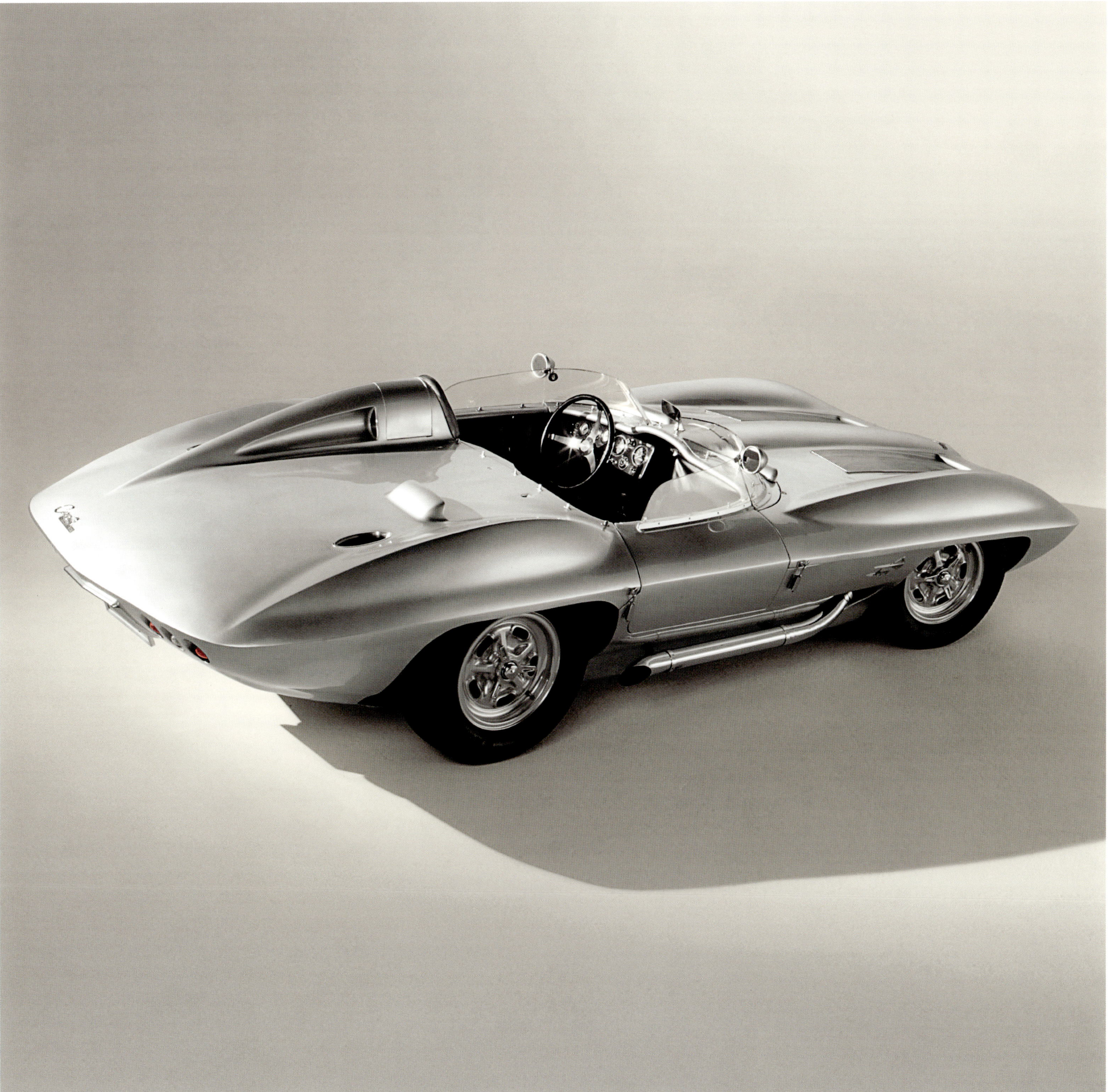

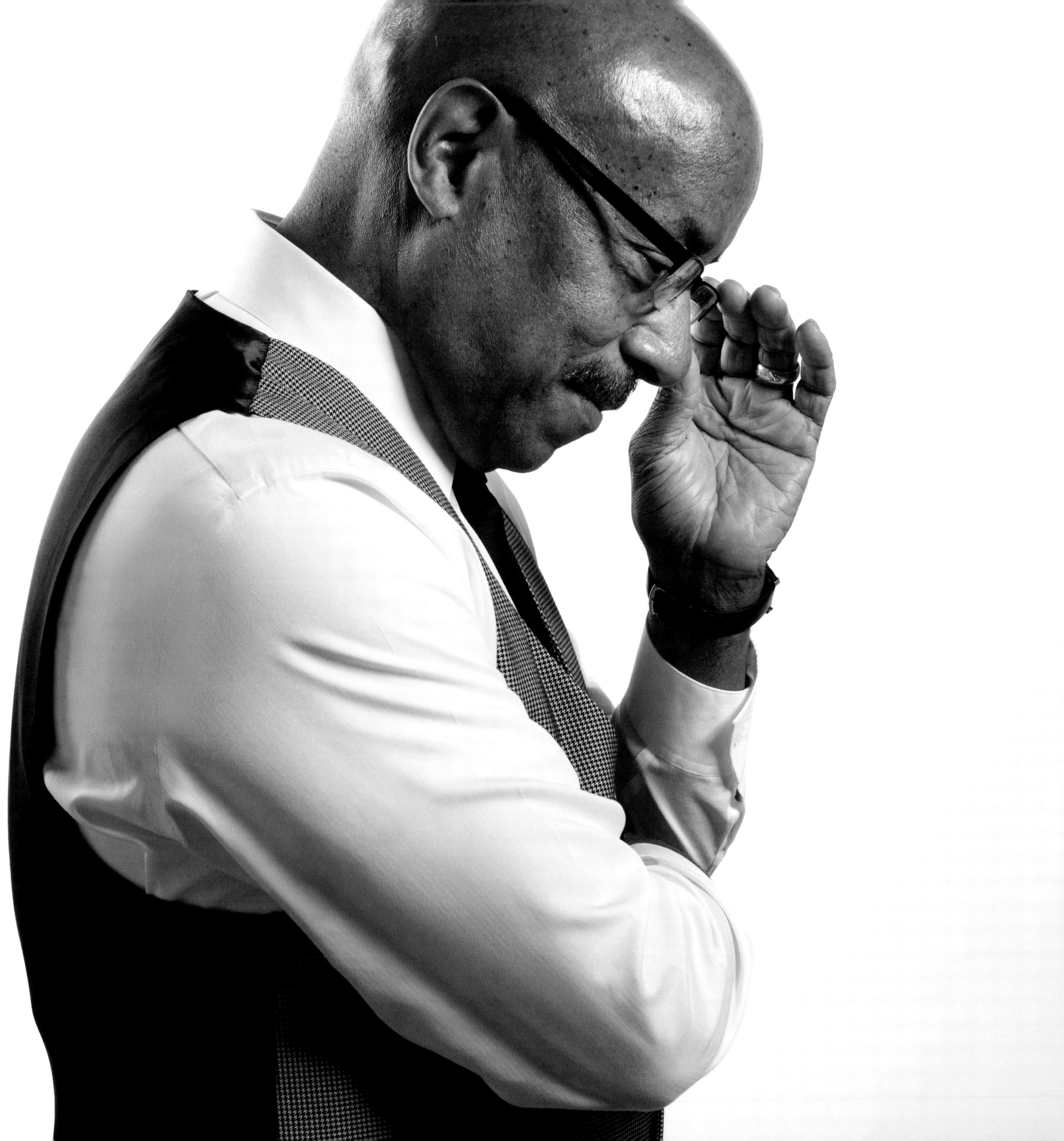

INTERVIEW WITH EDWARD T. WELBURN

Edward T. Welburn began his career at General Motors as an associate designer in 1972. He became vice president of GM Design North America in 2003 and vice president of GM Global Design in 2005. He held the latter position until he retired in 2016.

Benjamin W. Colman: How did you know you wanted to become a car designer?

Edward T. Welburn: When other toddlers were drawing stick figures of horses and people, I was drawing cars. By age eight I had decided I wanted to be a car designer, and at age eleven I wrote my first letter to General Motors asking for information about careers in design. They sent me career information, and I followed their lead.

BC: It is remarkable you knew at such a young age what you wanted to do.

EW: I didn't know if it was engineering or art. I didn't know which path. Did I need to study math or design or art? They helped me in that regard. They gave me a list of schools so I would have an idea of what was out there.

BC: Were there particular cars that you were drawn to at that young age?

EW: Definitely Corvettes. My uncles drove Cadillacs, and that was exciting to me, but I'll never forget the very first Corvette I saw. I was probably about six years old and it just struck me. It was the design of the car, not the performance or the engineering, that had the impact on me.

BC: Where did you attend design school?

EW: I went to Howard University in Washington, DC. I was in the school of fine arts. Back then—I entered Howard in 1968—there weren't many schools that had a concentration or a major in transportation design. At Howard the instructors knew what my mission was, because I was very focused, and they did everything they could to tailor the curriculum to help me reach that goal through design, sculpture, and painting.

BC: So this was a classic art school curriculum?

EW: Yes, and I majored in design and sculpture. I felt that the best automobiles were very sculptural, and I really believe the course in sculpture went a long way to helping me develop as a designer.

BC: What happened after your BFA?

EW: Following my junior year I was accepted into a summer internship program at GM. I had stayed in touch with the company since my first letter, and they suggested I enter into the summer internship program at the end of my junior year. After that they told me to finish my senior year and they would hire me as a designer.

BC: Who were the key designers at GM when you were a summer intern?

EW: Bill Mitchell was the head of design at the time. He was one of my heroes, and it was mainly the vehicles done under his leadership I was drawn to. They were some spectacular cars.

BC: How would you describe your own sensibility during those years? Did you have particular cars or design vocabularies that you were most excited about?

EW: I have always been interested in performance cars, but it seemed as though my greatest success was in luxury vehicles, cars like the Buick Riviera or Park Avenue. Those were the very first cars to which I made a significant contribution.

BC: Did your training in sculpture, and the kind of formal thinking you brought from art school, inform that?

EW: Absolutely. Having spent a significant amount of time in sculpture, painting, and life drawing had an influence in a number of ways. And the fact that I was in a university environment at Howard is quite a bit different than most art schools. A university experience helped me quite a bit.

BC: Other designers I have spoken to described the 1970s as a challenging period to work as a car designer. Was that your experience?

EW: It was a very creative period at the beginning. It was difficult for many designers who had been around for some time because at the time the government was dictating elements of the design that no one had ever dictated in the past. It was regulating bumpers—not only specifying that the cars needed to have bumpers, but at what height they needed to be located and how large they needed to be. Designers never had those controls before. For some designers it was very difficult. For me it was all new and it wasn't as much of a challenge.

BC: In the '70s was the design process still done largely on paper and in clay, beginning with a small sketch and building up to a full-size drawing and clay model?
EW: Exactly. It would begin with countless sketches, and you would funnel the ideas from many down to a few. The very basics of the process have not changed—funneling down from many ideas to a single design. The technologies have changed radically, but the fundamental process is the same.

BC: You began your career at GM during what is considered a legendary period of design at the company. How did you engage with that legacy of design and design innovation?
EW: I think I've always been looking forward and I've always wanted the team to look forward, but at the same time you need to understand the history of design. One of the things that was very important to me was to lead the restoration of many of GM's historic concept vehicles. These are the crown jewels of the company. Some were in good shape and some were in disrepair, tucked away in warehouses. During the period that I led design, we restored seventeen of them.

BC: It seems like an interesting balance to celebrate the legacies of past GM design executives like Harley Earl and Bill Mitchell, and also to look forward. How did you approach the challenge of staying relevant?
EW: That is the challenge. You want to build on the history. It's all about brands and building strong identities for the brands. In markets as competitive as ours today, the brand has to stand for something. It's an advantage to have a great history to build upon, but you've got to do it in a fresh, contemporary way. I think the most important thing I could do as the leader of design was to create an environment where creative people felt free to come forward with their ideas. They felt free to explore, make mistakes, and try things.

BC: How do you think the role of design has changed in the industry?
EW: If you look at the history of the auto industry, there's a pendulum swinging back and forth. There are periods when engineering dominates and design plays a support role. Then it swings the other way and design dominates and engineering is deep in the shadows. It swings back and forth. I think over the past ten years, it has been pretty much centered. That's when you get some of your best work.

The 1960s were a spectacular period in design. You had great collaboration with engineering. You just can't get wonderful proportions without that collaboration. One of the best examples is the Corvette—engineers, designers, marketing, racing, all worked together. When I was named vice president of design, the first thing I did was instruct the team to send Bill Mitchell's 1959 Stingray Racer to our shop to be restored. Every Corvette since then has been inspired by that vehicle. Ultimately the customer benefits.

BC: What drew you to the Stingray Racer?
EW: I thought it was one of the most influential designs in the history of the company. Not only had it inspired every Corvette, but other Chevrolets were influenced by that design. If you look at the fenders on that Stingray Racer, and you look at the fenders on Chevrolet Impalas in the '60s and other Chevrolets in that period, the root of it was the '59 Stingray Racer.

BC: Where do you see design heading in the near future?
EW: We could talk for quite a while about that. The first thing that comes to mind is a great debate I've had with a friend, Bob Lutz. He feels as though the autonomous vehicles of the future will just be pods and we will no longer have great designs. I disagree with that. I think it's an opportunity for very expressive design and probably a wider variety of designs than we have today. I'm very excited about it.

This April 9, 2019, interview has been edited and condensed.

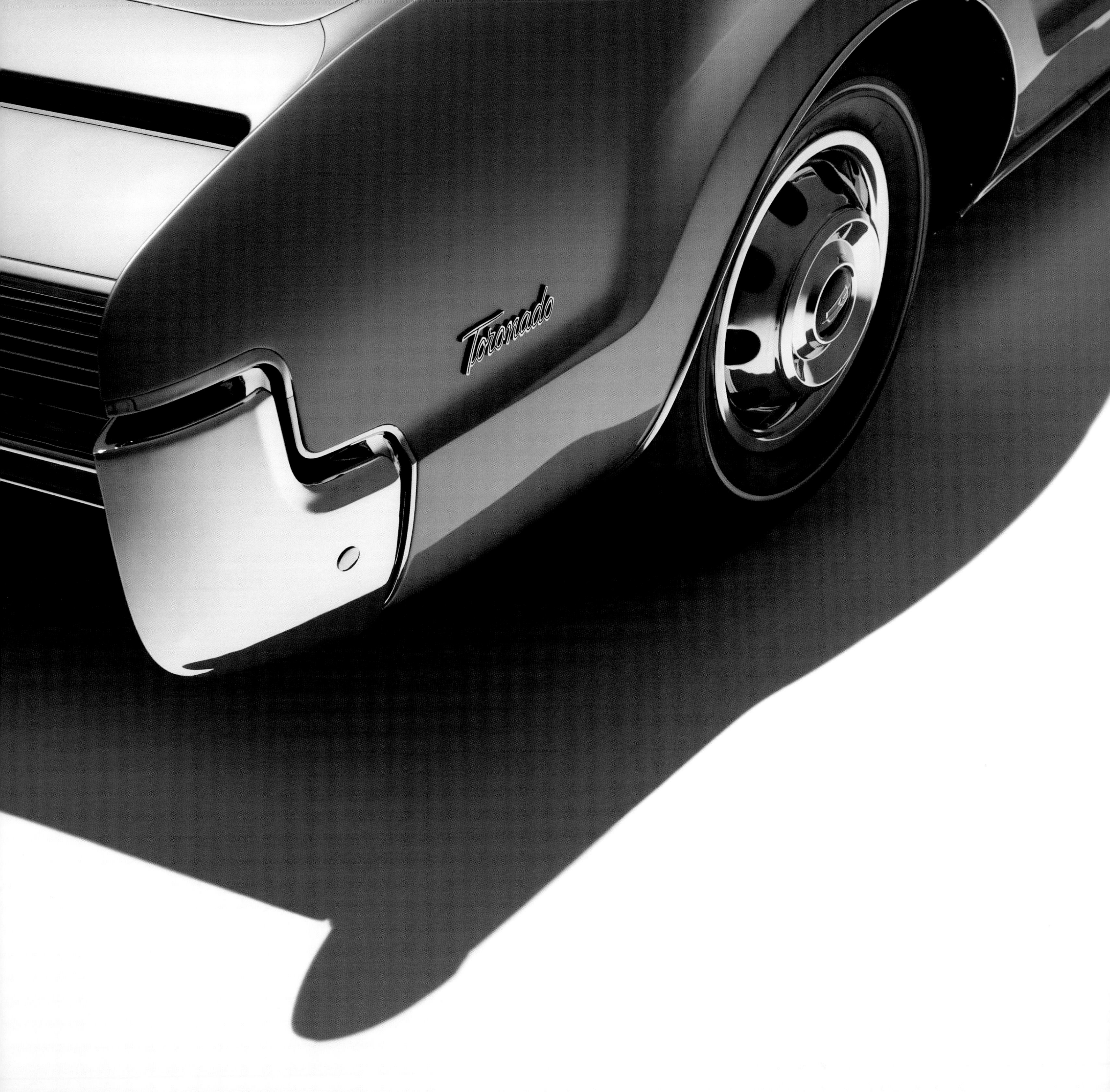
Toronado

1 9 6 6

G E N E R A L M O T O R S

O L D S M O B I L E

T O R O N A D O

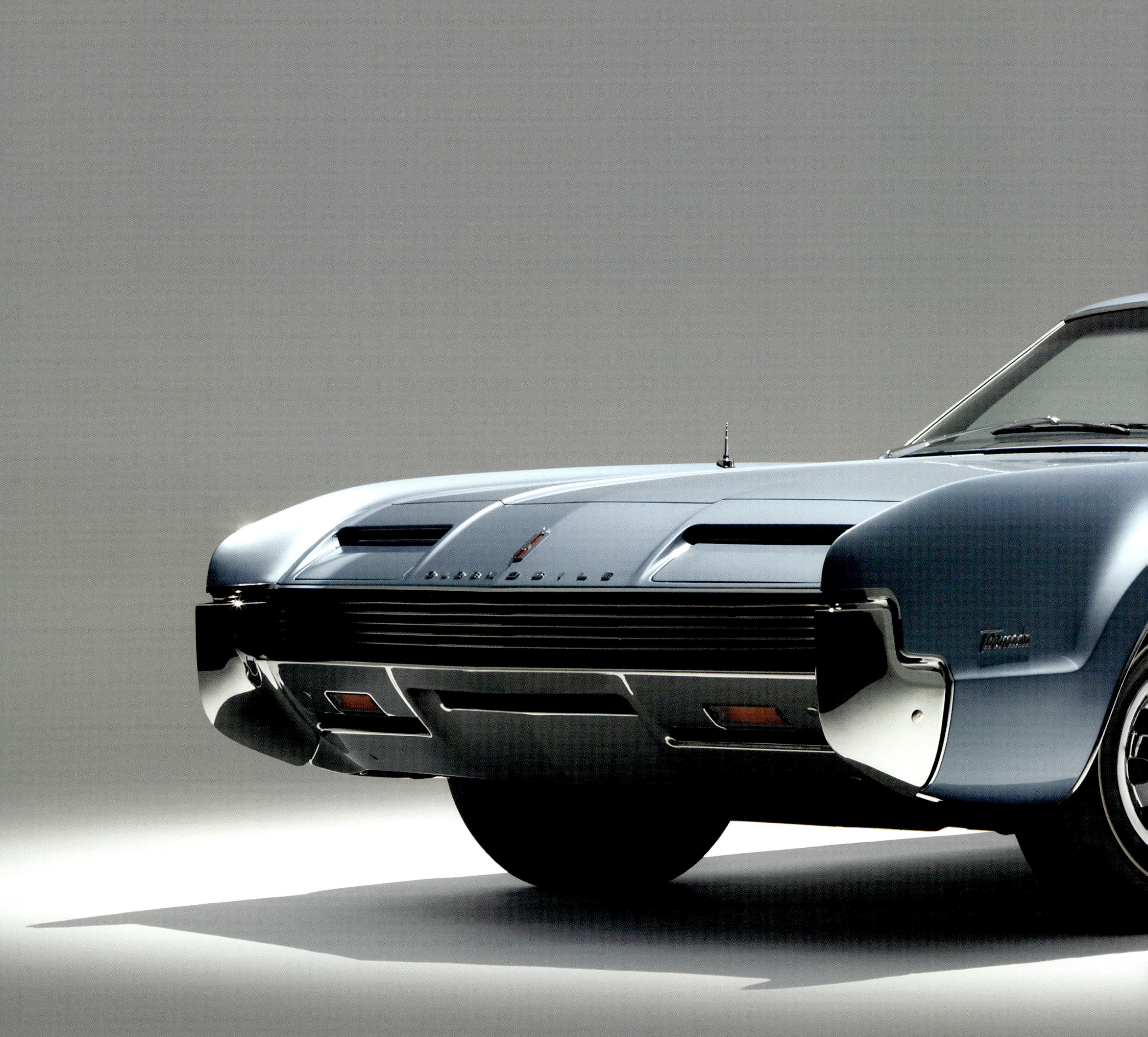

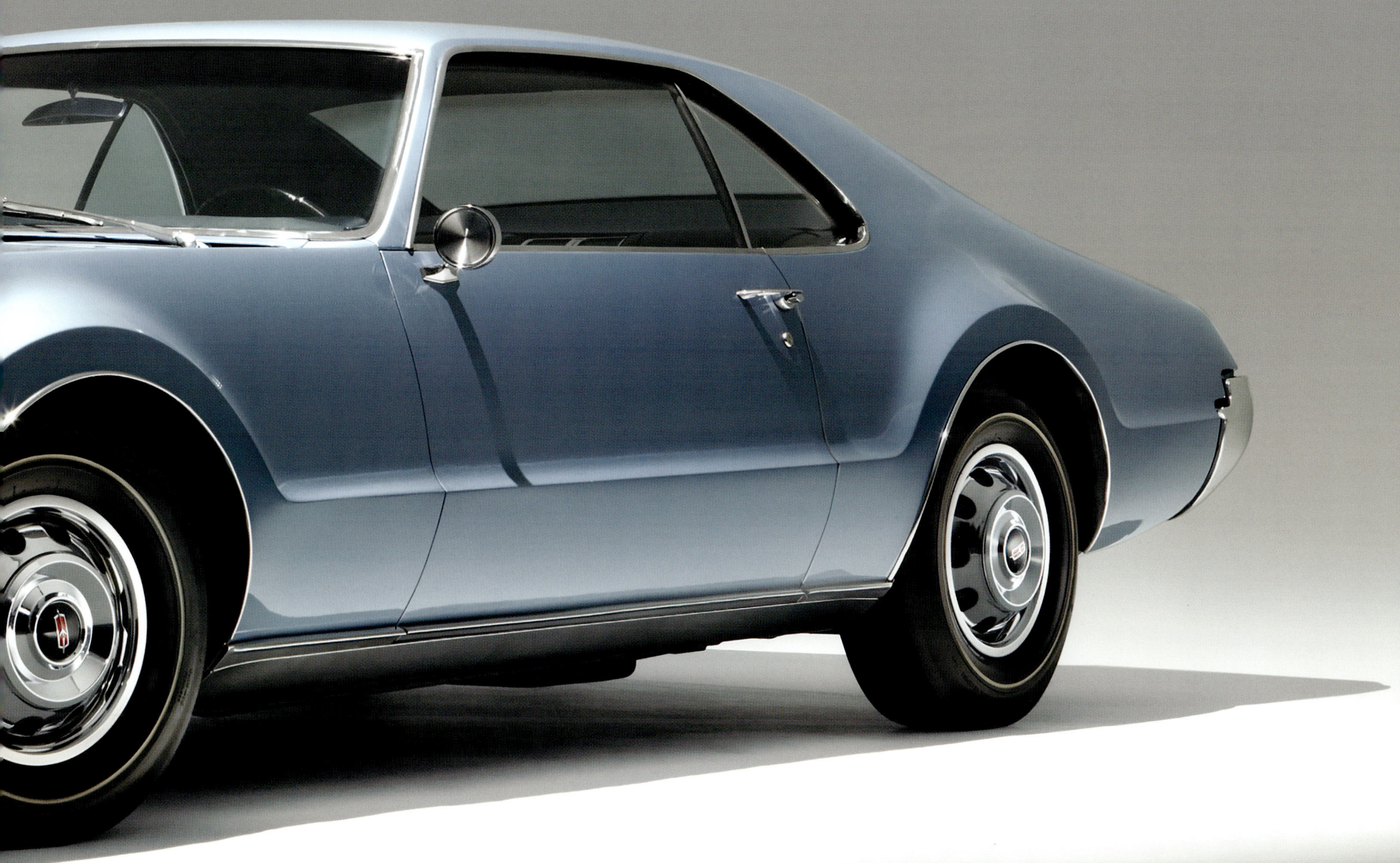

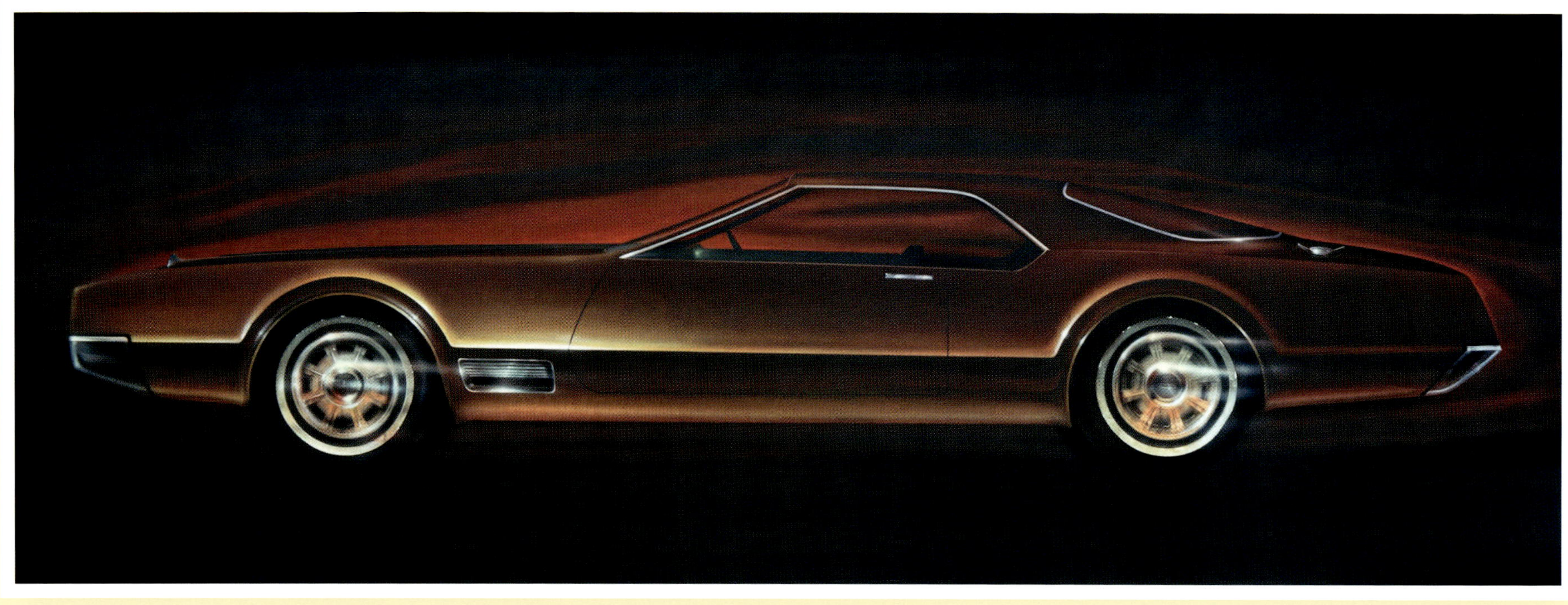

Photograph of David North's flame-red car proposal from the General Motors Design Archives.

The 1966 Oldsmobile Toronado surprised the public at its October 1965 introduction. A boldly styled luxury model, it entered the market as the first American car with a front-wheel drive system in three decades. This engineering innovation inspired the designers at General Motors to create a sleekly modern exterior punctuated with graphic lines that helped define a new formal vocabulary for car styling.

The Toronado began its life in October 1962 as a GM styling project named XP-784 shared by the Pontiac, Oldsmobile, and Buick studios. The goal was to create a new model using the so-called E-body car platform. This system, in which different types of cars had a common set of structural and functional elements, allowed companies like GM to distribute tooling and engineering costs among brands while investing in the styling and design of more visible features to attract customers. By February 1963 Pontiac was no longer involved in the project, but Cadillac had come onboard. Using design drawings, modelers created a scale model for wind tunnel testing. In August 1963 executives decided to move forward with the Oldsmobile and Buick E-body designs that would become the Toronado and Buick Riviera for the 1966 model year. Tooling for body production had already begun in late December 1963, and full-scale fiberglass models of both cars were finished in August 1964.[1]

Most American rear-wheel driving cars have an engine in the front connected to the back wheels by a driveshaft. To accommodate the driveshaft, a large hump often runs along the floor, making the interior uncomfortable for anyone sitting in the middle of the bench seats popular in car designs of that period. This hump can be eliminated in front-wheel driving cars. According to William Mitchell, then the vice president for styling at GM, "the resultant low flat floor opened entirely new possibilities for vehicle architecture and provided the opportunity for styling designers and engineers to come up with a completely fresh design approach" for the Toronado.[2] If the interior took advantage of the car's front-wheel drive mechanics, the exterior was meant to emphasize the powerful engine roaring under its hood. As one observer wrote: "it's a sleek, brutal-looking machine. Even when it's parked, it looks like it's crouching."[3] In addition to the much-touted styling, the car had features such as air conditioning, an auto-tuning radio, and power windows. It was introduced with a high-end base price of $4,617.

According to Mitchell, the initial concept for the Toronado came from a prompt given in the advanced studio. The designers were shown "a flame-red illustration of a low, four-passenger car" and challenged "to apply their creative efforts to the design of a dream car that they themselves would like to own and drive" (opposite).[4] That flame-red illustration by designer David North (born 1936), who worked in the Pontiac studio before moving to the advanced studio at GM, was an idea for a future GTO, a smaller sedan than the Toronado that went into production. Using a luminous red ink on black paper, the drawing was intended to wow company executives with its dramatic silhouette. Within the advanced studio, North's concept was refined with designers Edward Taylor and Wayne Cherry, and the car was selected to move forward—but not as a GTO. Oldsmobile executives were eager for a new marquee car and the Toronado fit the bill.[5] The round wheel surround arches, which the designer created to add visual interest to the broad plane of the side and emphasize the power and speed of the car, recalled the round wheel wells associated with Oldsmobile during Harley Earl's tenure.

The Toronado was adapted, with notable changes to the front-end proportions, to suit the E-body platform that GM used for the Buick Riviera. The group of designers working to refine the concept and forms included Donald Logerquist, Richard Ruzzin, and Stanley Wilen, Oldsmobile chief designer from 1962 to 1968. Many of the features from North's drawing are evident in the production model, including the sharp angle of the front fenders, for which the designer found inspiration in the punctuated fuselage of a recently designed supersonic jet. The broad bands of the front grille were styled as a nod to the wraparound grille of the last front-wheel driving American car—the Auburn Cord 812, which had gone out of production in the 1930s.[6] Good timing helped the Toronado make its mark upon debut. It was the only new model introduced by any of the Detroit companies for 1966, making it doubly notable as a departure from the standard engineering of Detroit cars.

Ultimately the Toronado reflects a move toward the monocoque style of car design, in which the exterior body shape reflects the structural frame of the car. Instead of applying ornaments and forms, it is designed to emphasize the invisible chassis and engine. ❖

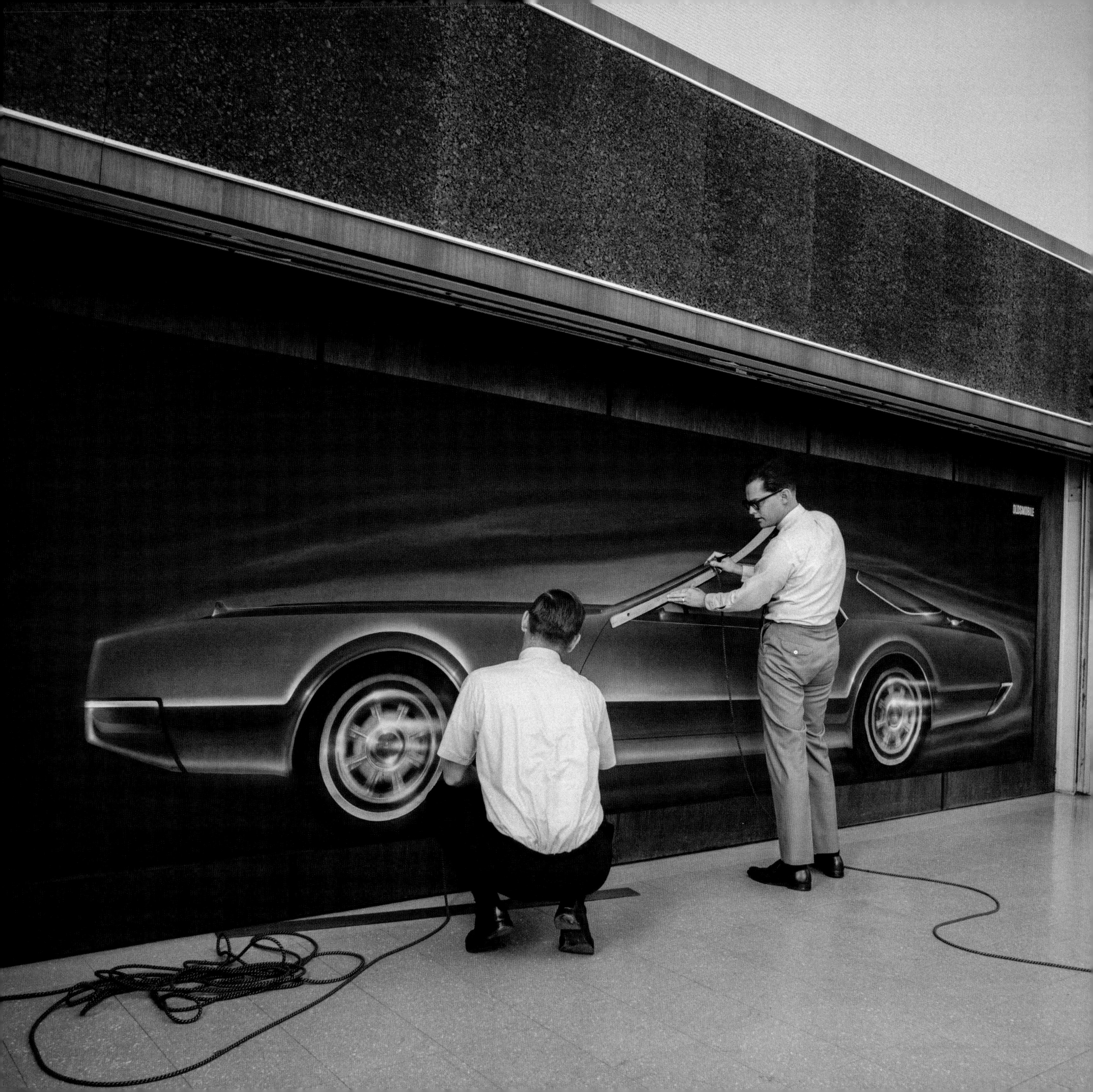

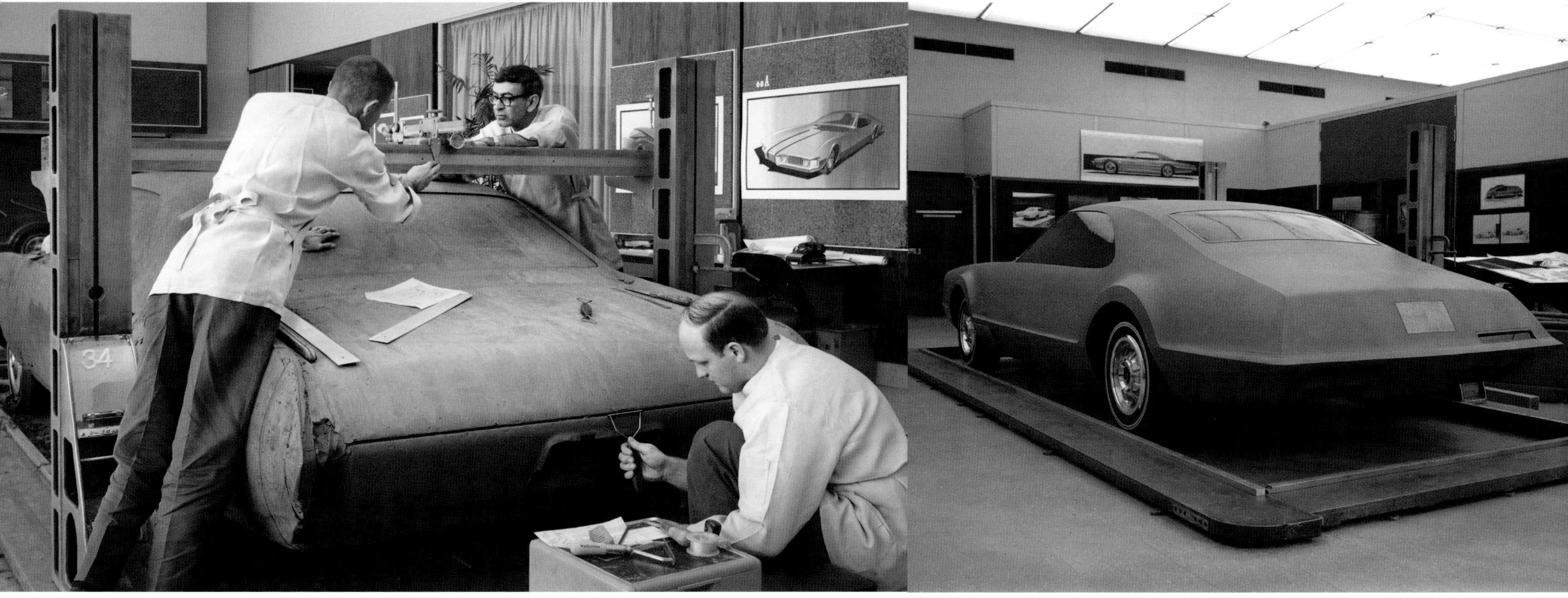

General Motors, Oldsmobile Toronado, 1966. *p. 60:* Front end (detail); *pp. 62–63:* Front three-quarter view; *opposite:* Designers refining David North's flame-red car proposal, circa 1962; *above left:* Creating clay model of 1966 Oldsmobile Toronado, 1963; *above right:* Clay model of 1966 Oldsmobile Toronado, 1963.

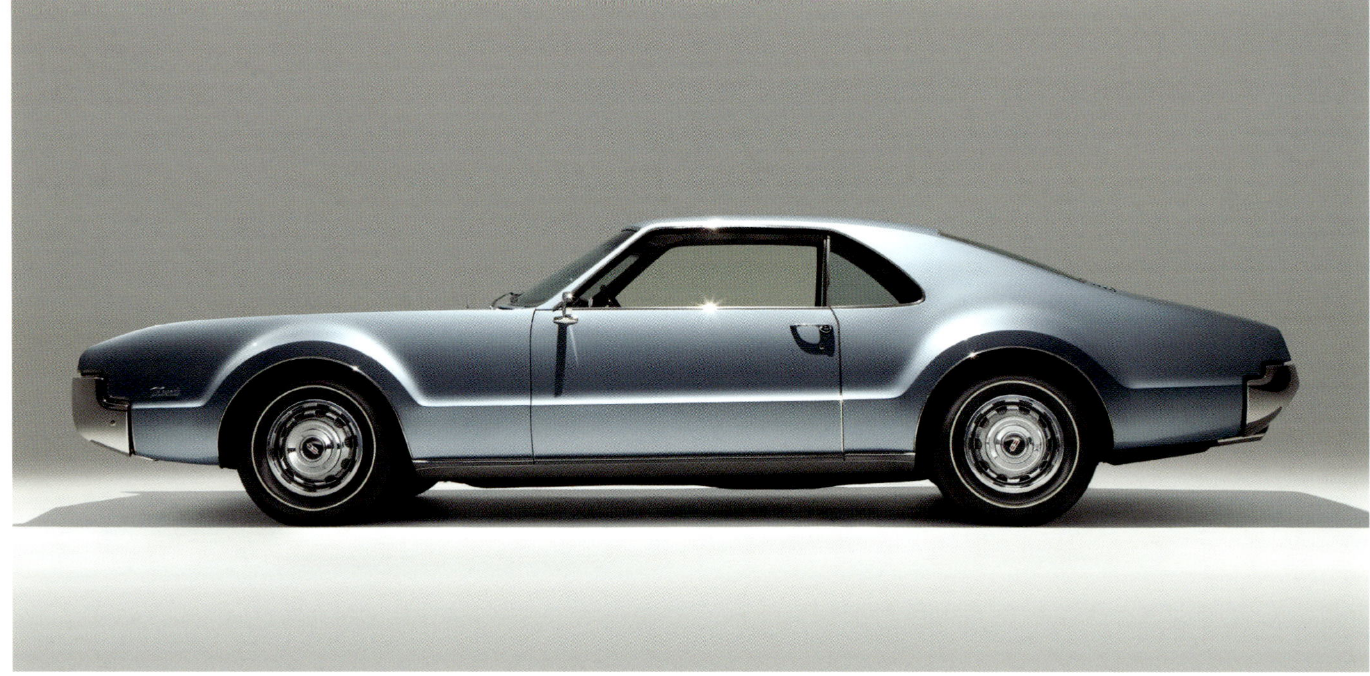

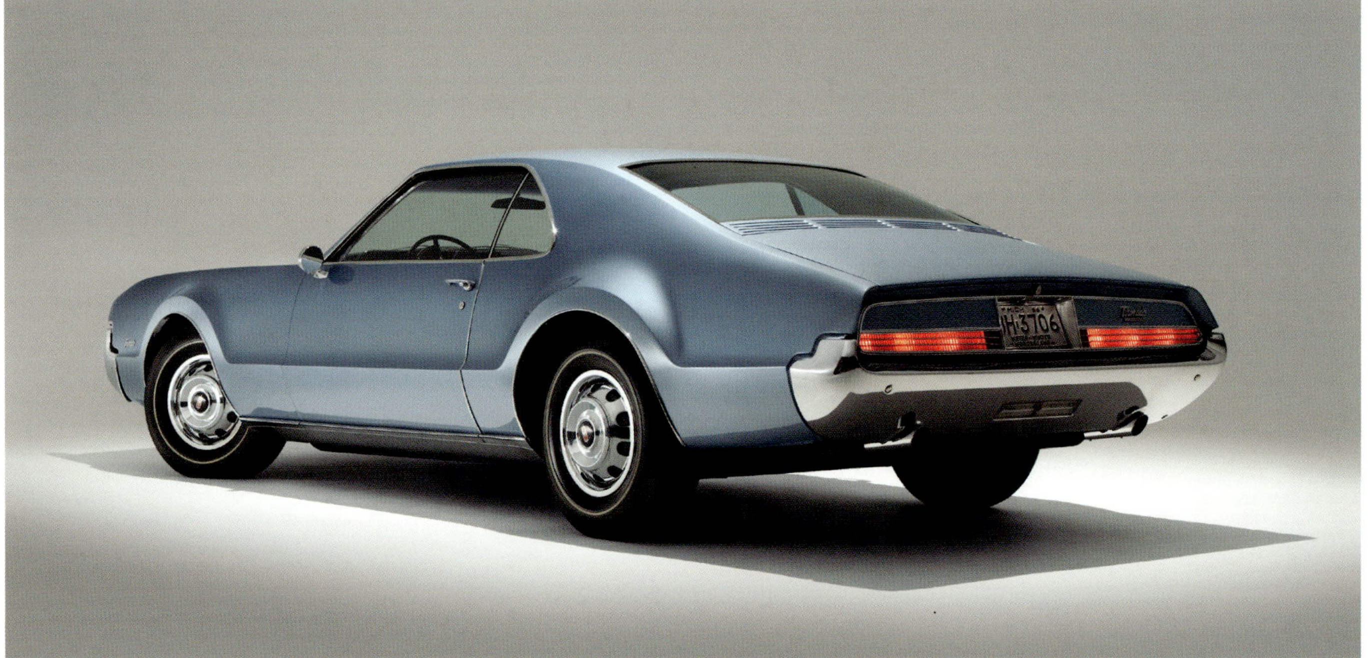

General Motors, Oldsmobile Toronado, 1966. *above:* Left side profile view showing arched wheel surrounds; *below:* Rear three-quarter view showing fastback roofline; *opposite:* Front end view showing horizontal grille and concealed rotating headlamps.

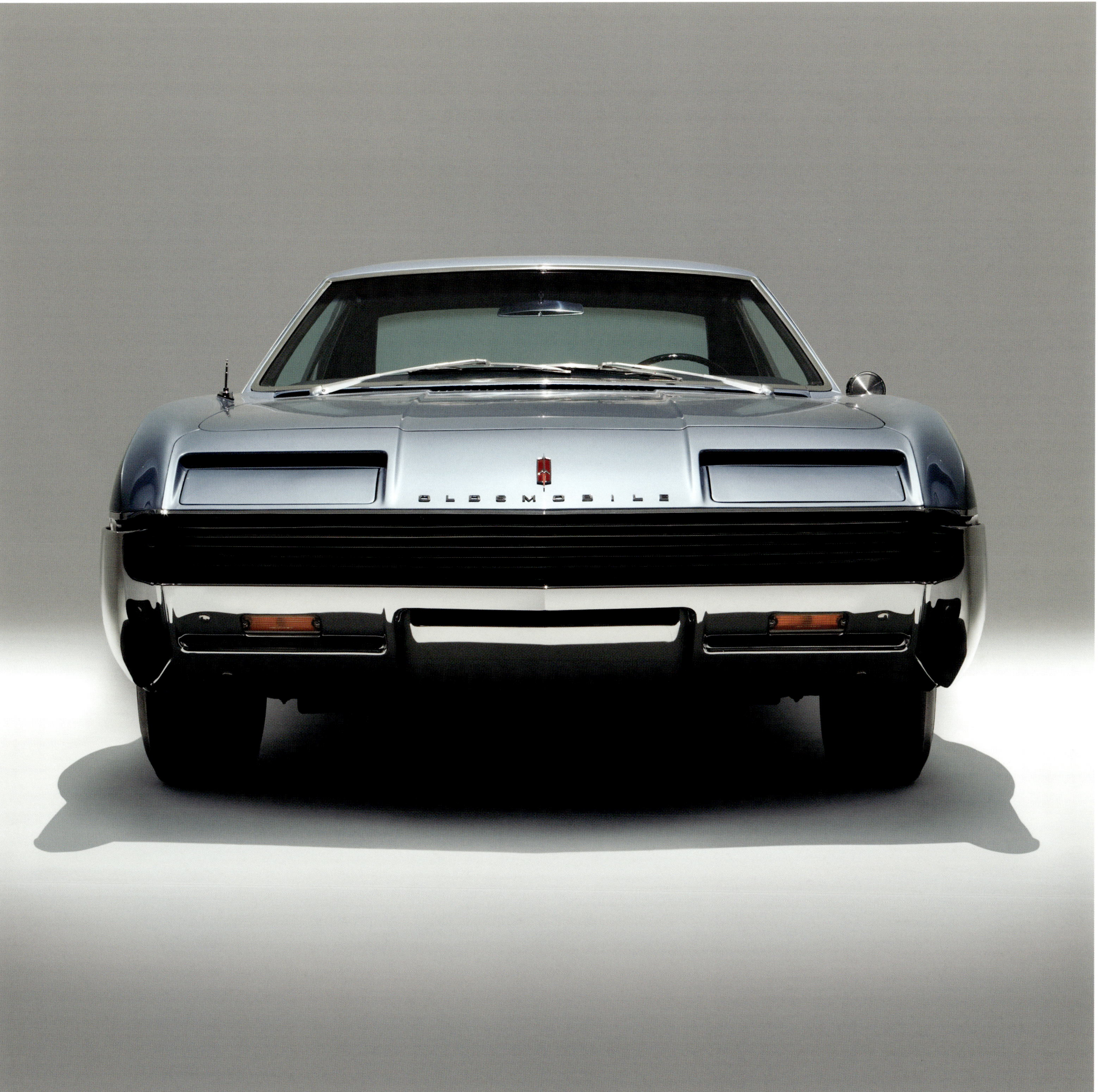
OLDSMOBILE

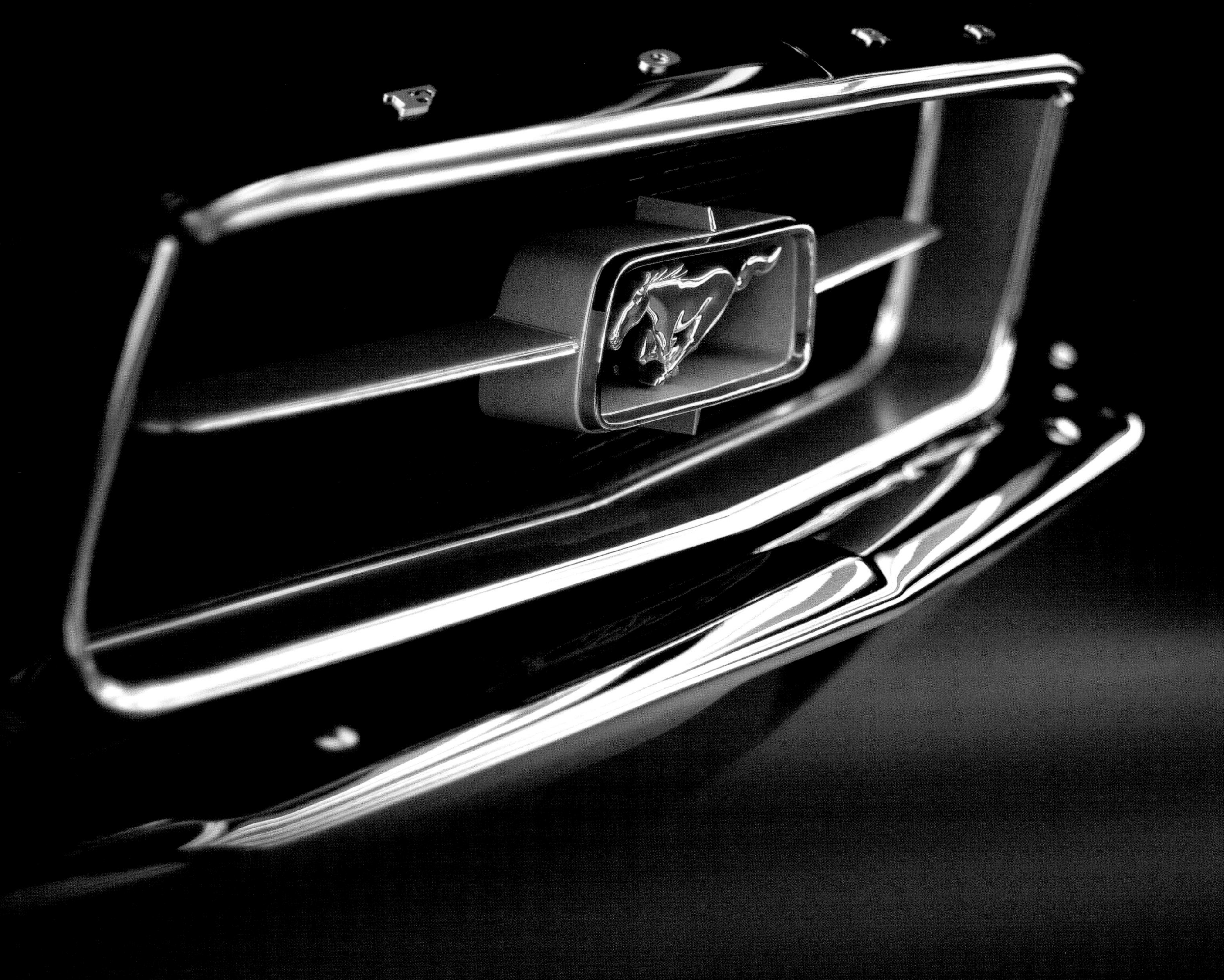

1 9 6 7
F O R D
M U S T A N G

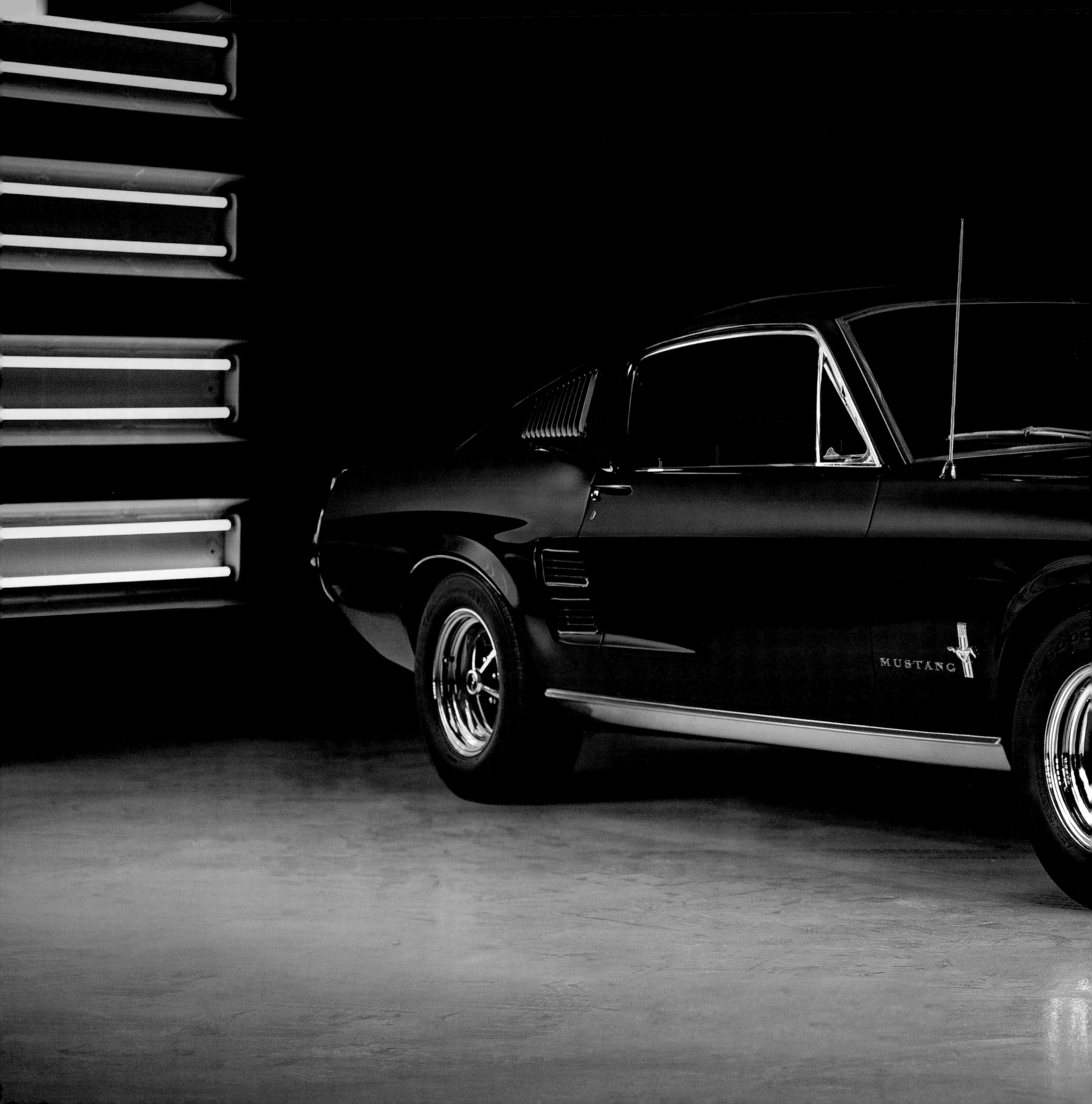
MUSTANG

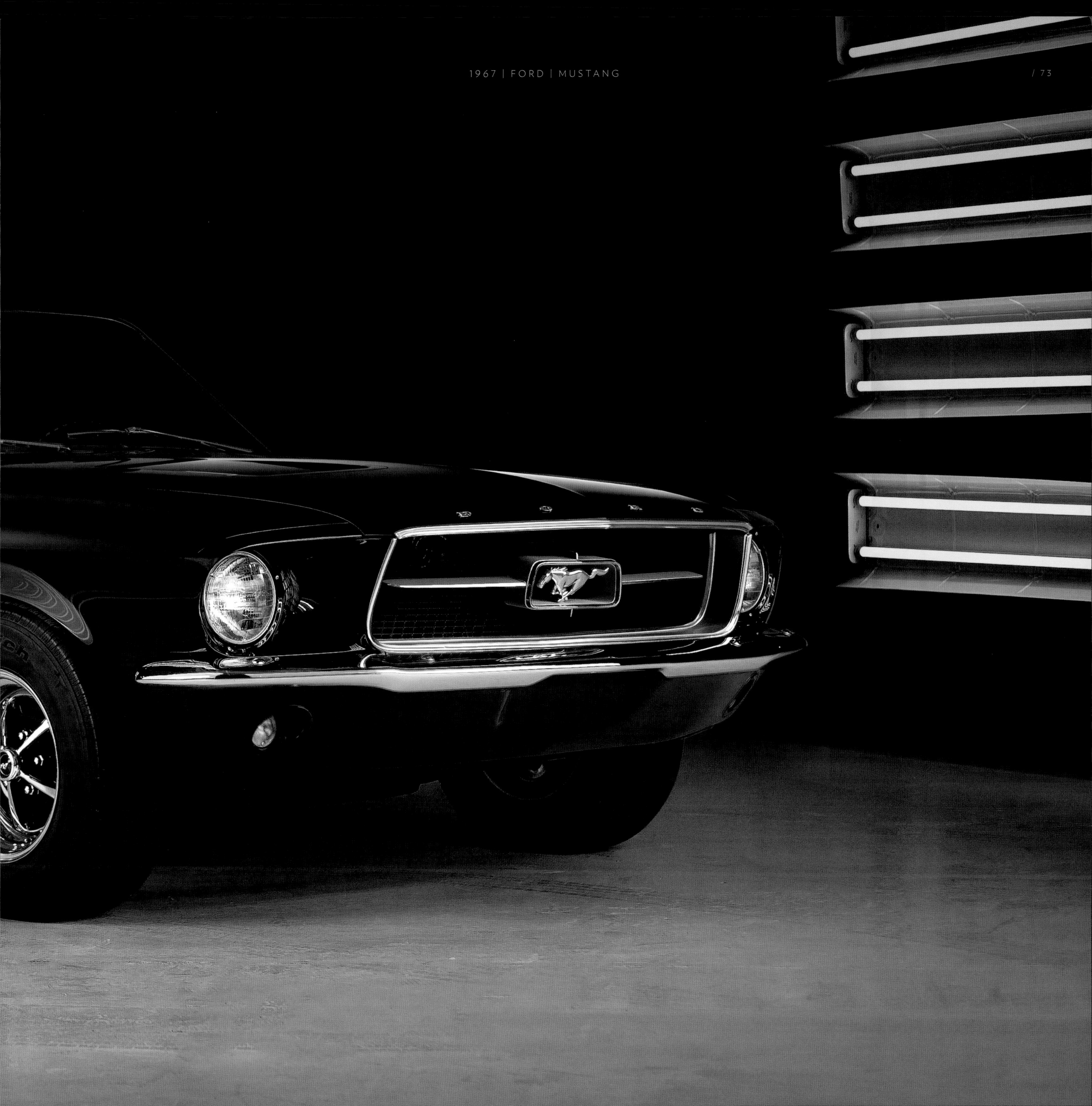

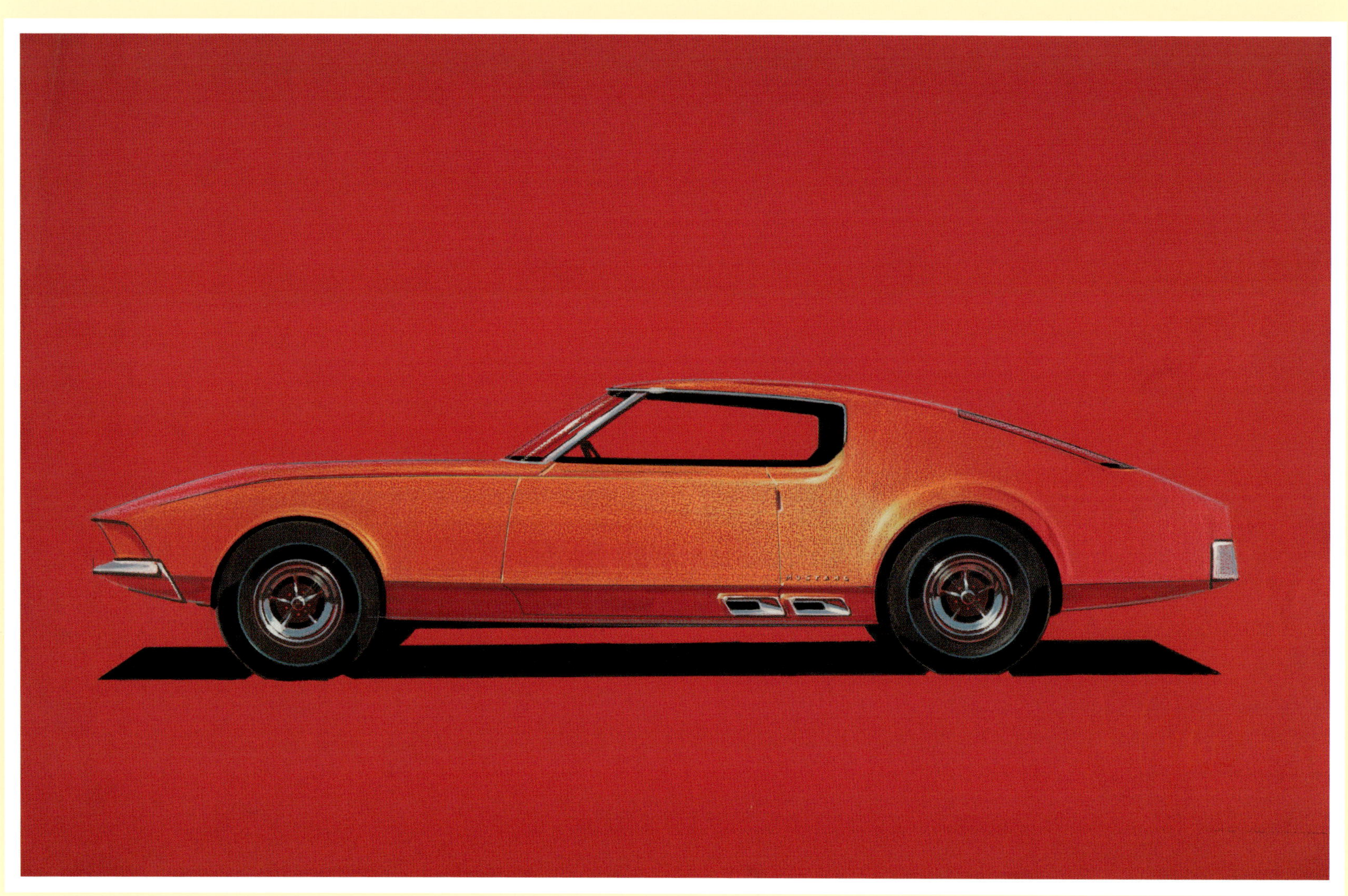

HOWARD PAYNE

Ford Mustang, 1965, Prismacolor and gouache on red charcoal paper

Ford's introduction of the Mustang in 1964 revolutionized American cars and defined a new genre of so-called pony cars that adopted the styling and racing affect of their muscle car contemporaries, but with modest engines geared toward everyday driving.

The birth of the Mustang indicates a number of new influences on the look of Detroit cars. As the postwar years began to wane, strategic plans for marketing new cars to the maturing generation of baby boomers took on increasing significance. Ford Divisional General Manager Lee Iacocca imagined a "sporty personal car" at a modest price that would appeal to the youthful spirit of the day and to both male and female drivers. After a series of preliminary concept cars defined a general direction for the still unnamed car, Eugene Bordinat (1920–87), recently appointed vice president for styling at Ford, initiated a contest inviting proposals from teams in the company's design studios. The winner was a clay model created largely from proposals drawn by Gale Halderman and Joseph Oros (1916–2012) in the Ford design studio. The team that contributed to the design in production included L. David Ash, Charles Phaneuf, Damon C. Woods (died 1968), John Najjar (1918–2011), and John B. Foster.[1]

The design process took place against the backdrop of a promotional book published in 1963 by the Ford Motor Company called *The Ford Book of Styling*. By describing the tools and processes of the car designer, this book celebrated a transition in the way important works of design come to be. While the past was illustrated with exquisite examples of rarified craftsmanship and artistry produced for royal or aristocratic patrons, the modern era was characterized by mass-produced industrial design. A beautiful and functional machine would capture the style and ambitions of the 1960s.[2] The Mustang did just that. With proportions defined by a long hood and short rear deck, the two-door, four-seat car was styled to convey speed and power. Its angled front end, recessed panel below the side beltline, applied chrome simulated side air intake, and curved rear fender all suggest the dynamic energy of a machine in motion.

When the Mustang first went on view in April 1964, it was described as "a cross between a sports car and a family sedan" and offered at prices ranging from $2,368 for the base model, to $4,000 for a higher-powered engine and luxury options. Sleek, adaptable, versatile, aspirational, and within reach for a middle-class buyer, it stood in marked contrast to the reputation Ford earned in the 1950s for affordable and functional cars with modest styling. The mustang on the front grille, an addition to the design after a name was applied to the project, conjured romantic associations of a wild horse galloping across the American West. The company touted in ads, "This is the car you never expected from Detroit."[3] The Mustang's timely look and price were perfectly suited to the maturing generation of drivers Ford was courting. It was an instant success when it launched, becoming the model for a spate of competing pony cars.

By 1967 this new segment of the market had become a powerful force in the American auto industry despite falling sales that year. Between April 1964 and May 1967, Ford sold 1.5 million Mustangs, accounting for more than 5 percent of American auto sales.[4] This success created a challenge when Ford's designers set out to modestly update its styling for 1967. With increased competition from General Motors and Chrysler, the new Mustang needed to appear both updated and instantly recognizable. Asking, "How do you improve on a classic?" the ad copy proudly answered: "with subtle body changes and interior improvements. The result is a rare combination that says Mustang for '67 is undeniably new—without taking away the flair and flavor of the classic design."[5]

While preserving the Mustang's instantly recognizable profile and front end, the stylists updated its proportions and lines to emphasize its power and speed. Its original theme and most identifiable features were retained, but the car became wider, longer, and slightly taller. This made it appear lower to the ground, in keeping with a new emphasis on speed and power. The car was also offered as a fastback and a convertible. For the fastback version, the tapering roofline extended to the rear end of the car, creating a unified form from windshield to rear bumper that suggested aerodynamic efficiency. These subtle refinements to the original design created an elegant and powerful-looking car that felt new but was still a Mustang. ❖

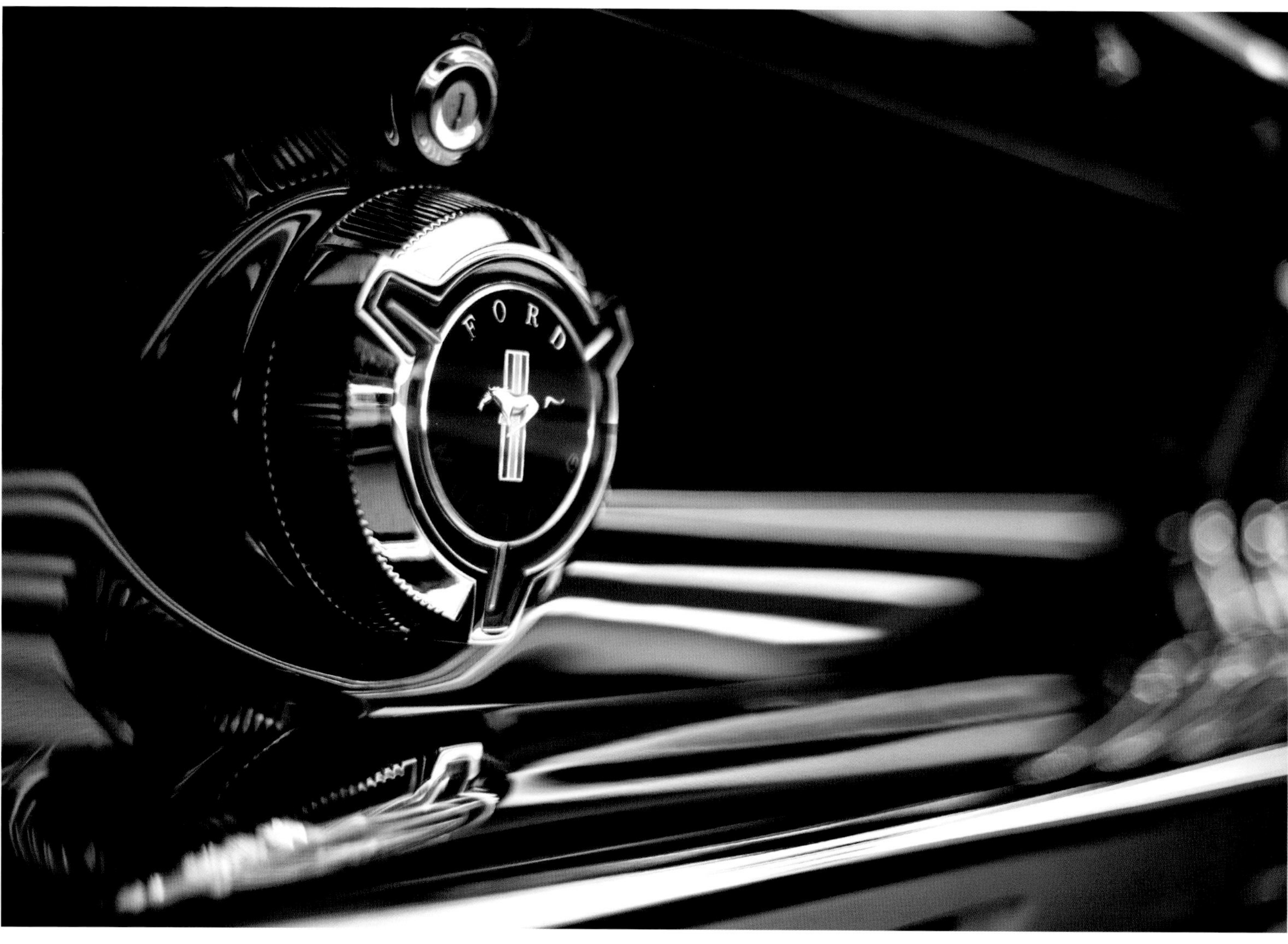

Ford Motor Company, Mustang, 1967. *p. 70:* Front end (detail); *pp. 72–73:* Front three-quarter view; *above:* Gas tank cap; *opposite:* Front end view showing Mustang insignia.

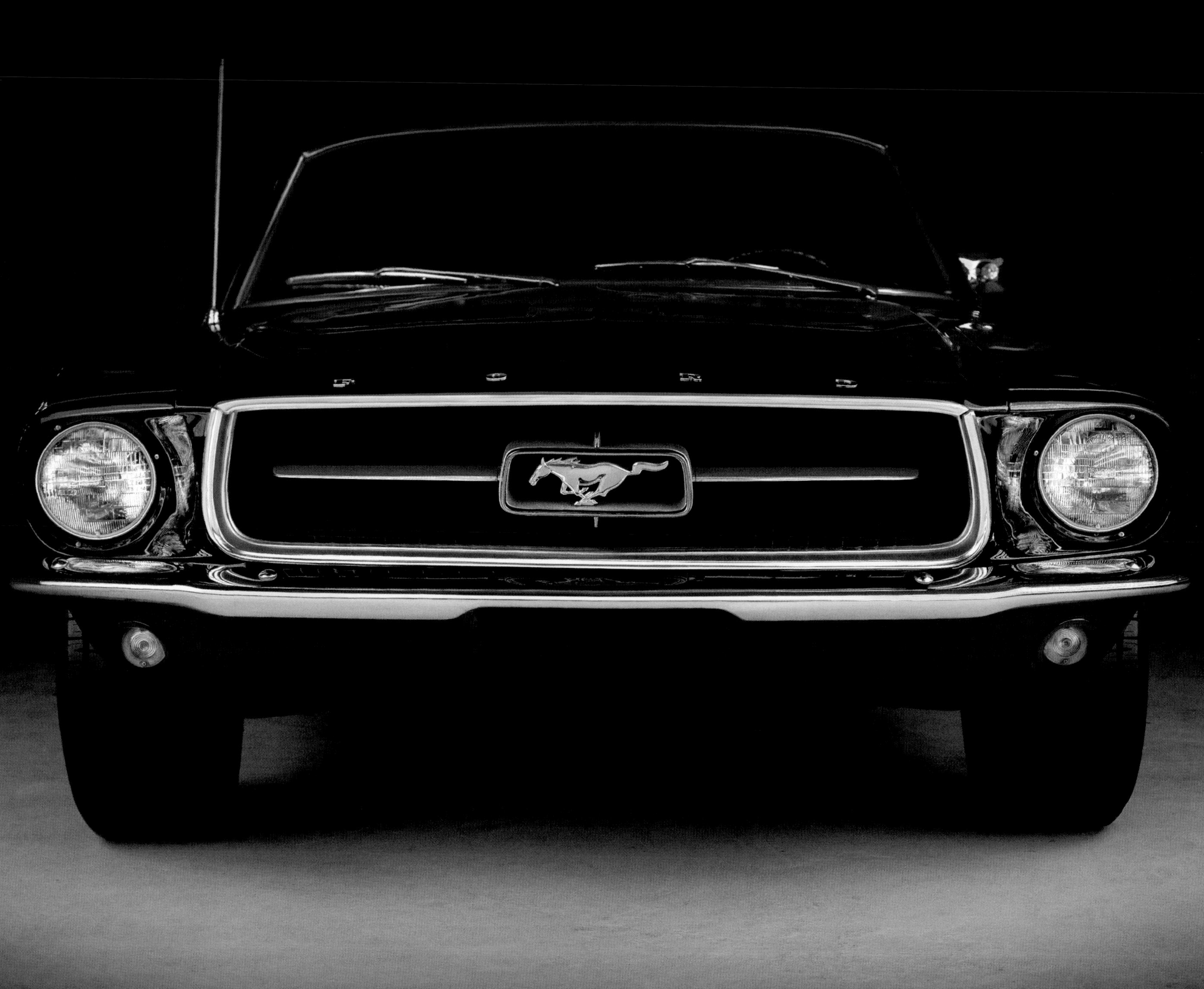

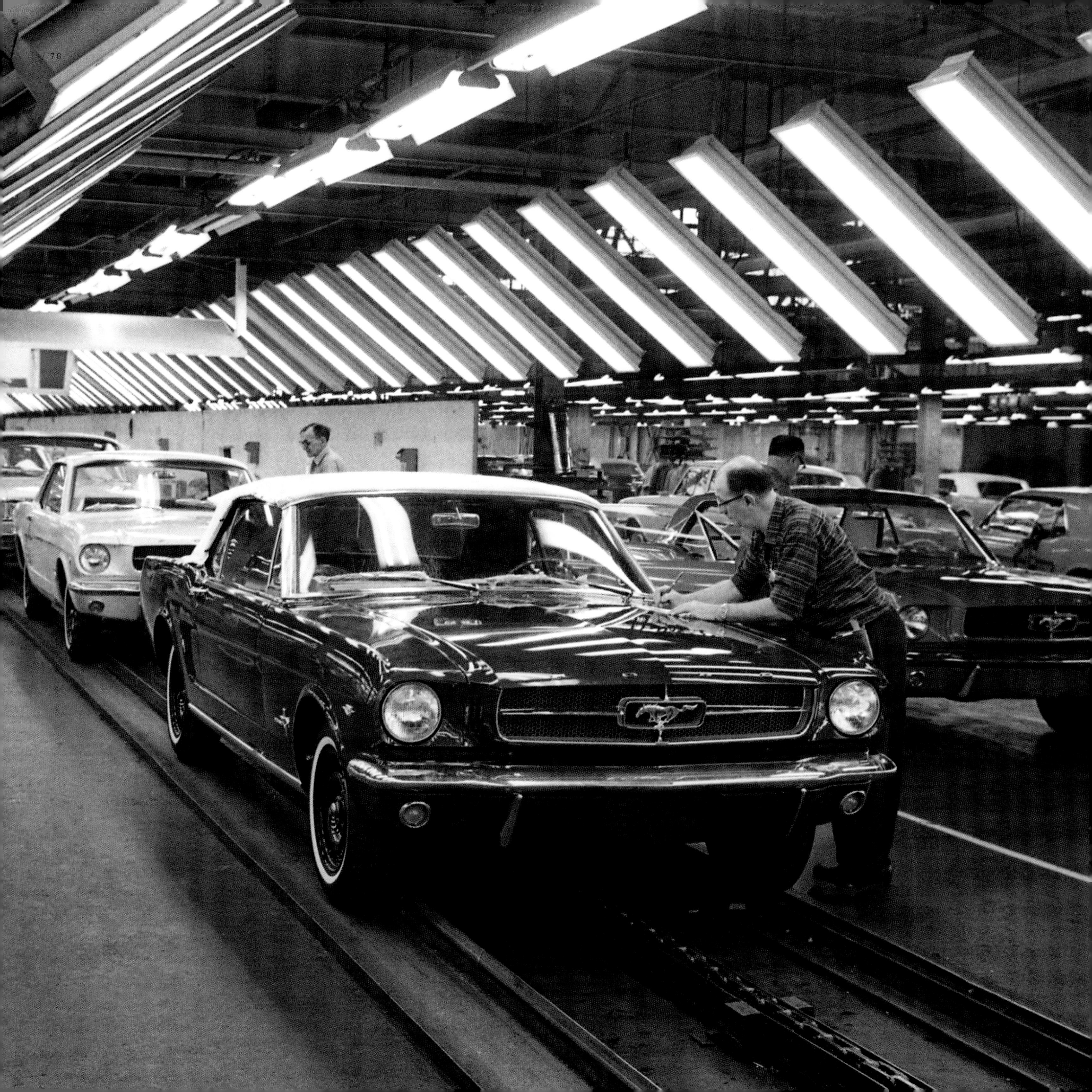

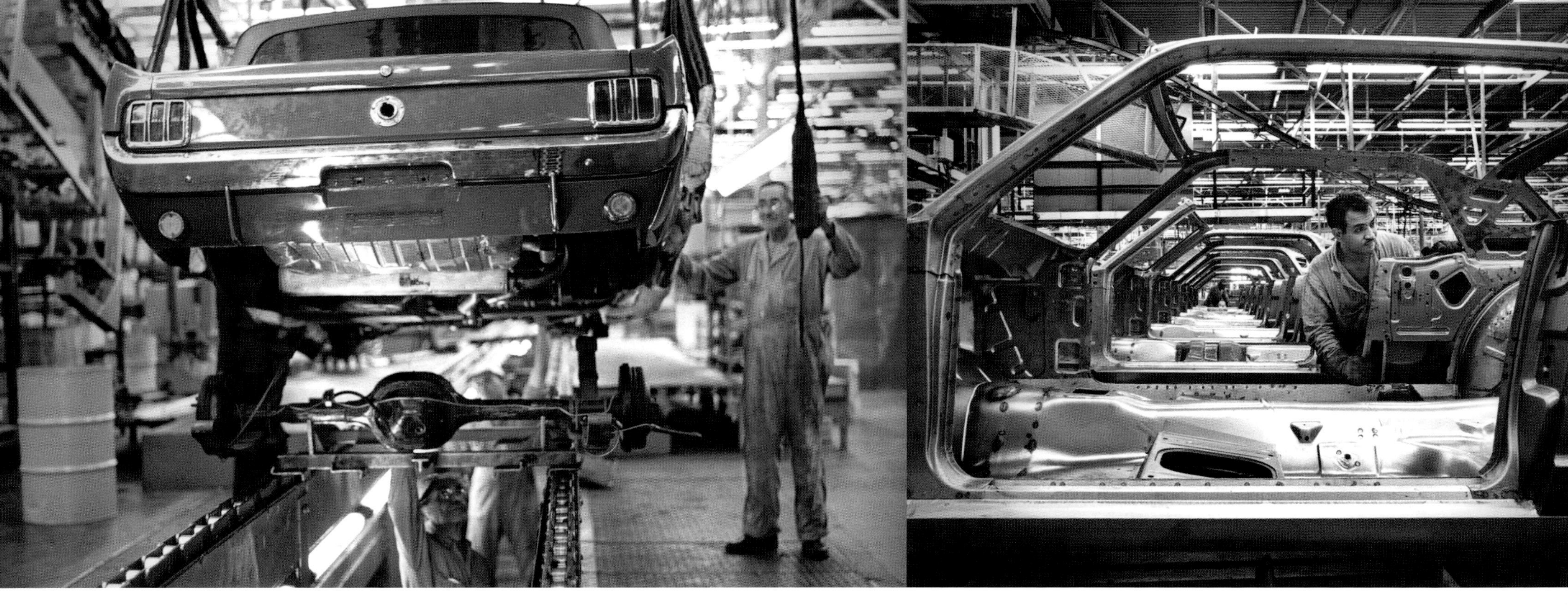

opposite: Ford Mustang final inspection at Dearborn assembly plant, 1965; *above left and right:* Ford Mustang at the San Jose assembly plant, 1964.

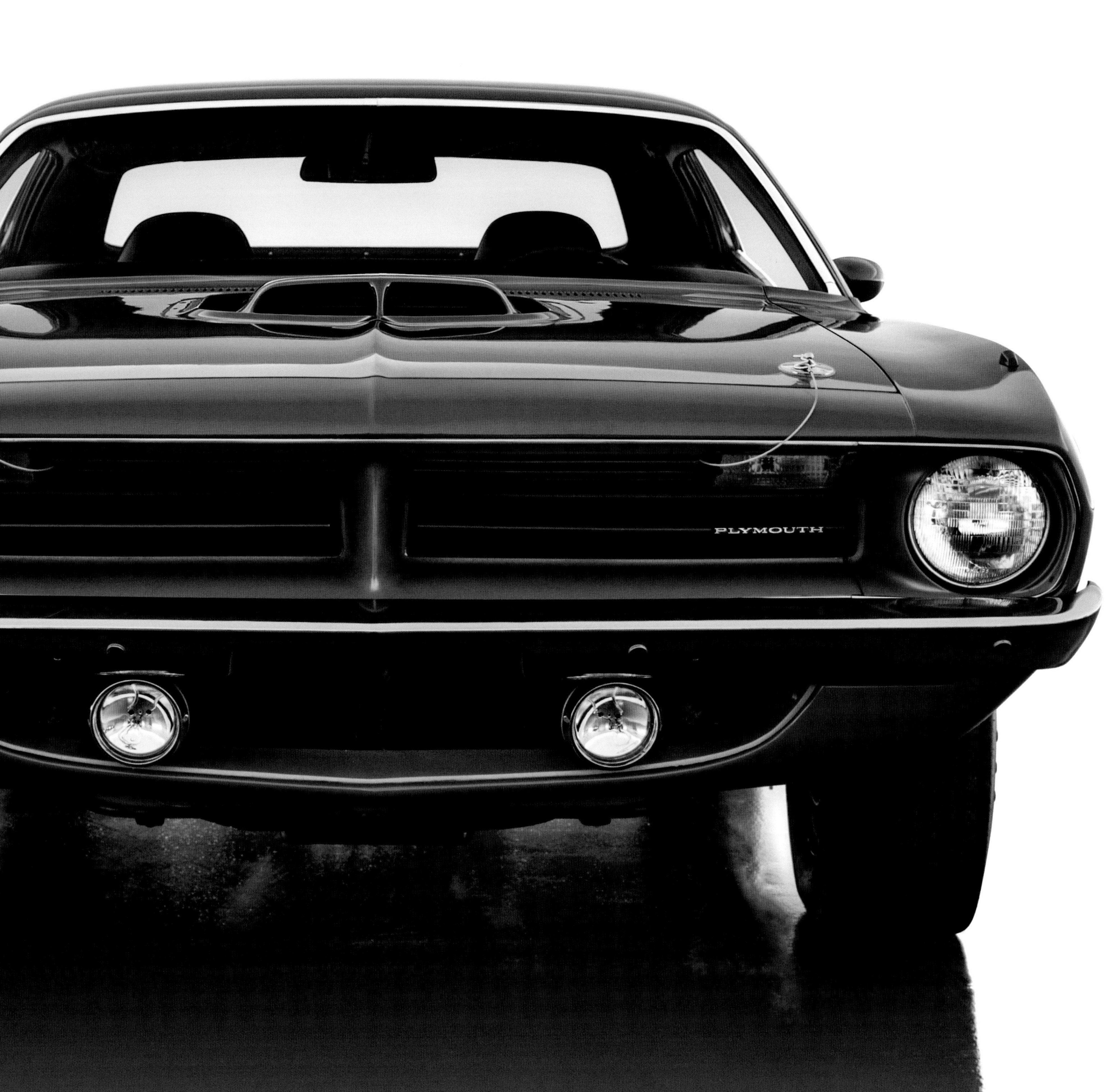
PLYMOUTH

1970 CHRYSLER PLYMOUTH BARRACUDA

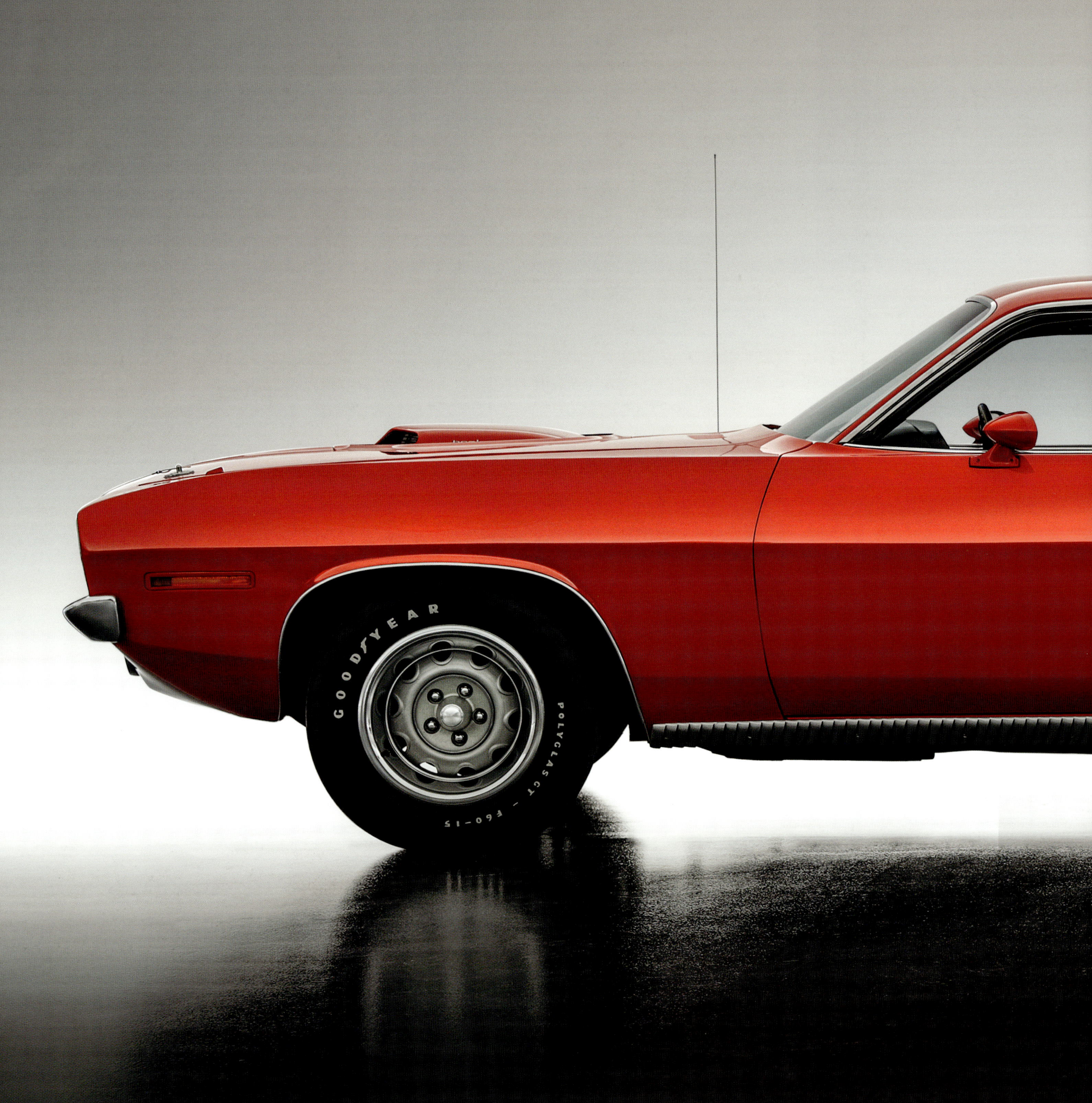
GOODYEAR
POLYGLAS GT – F60-15

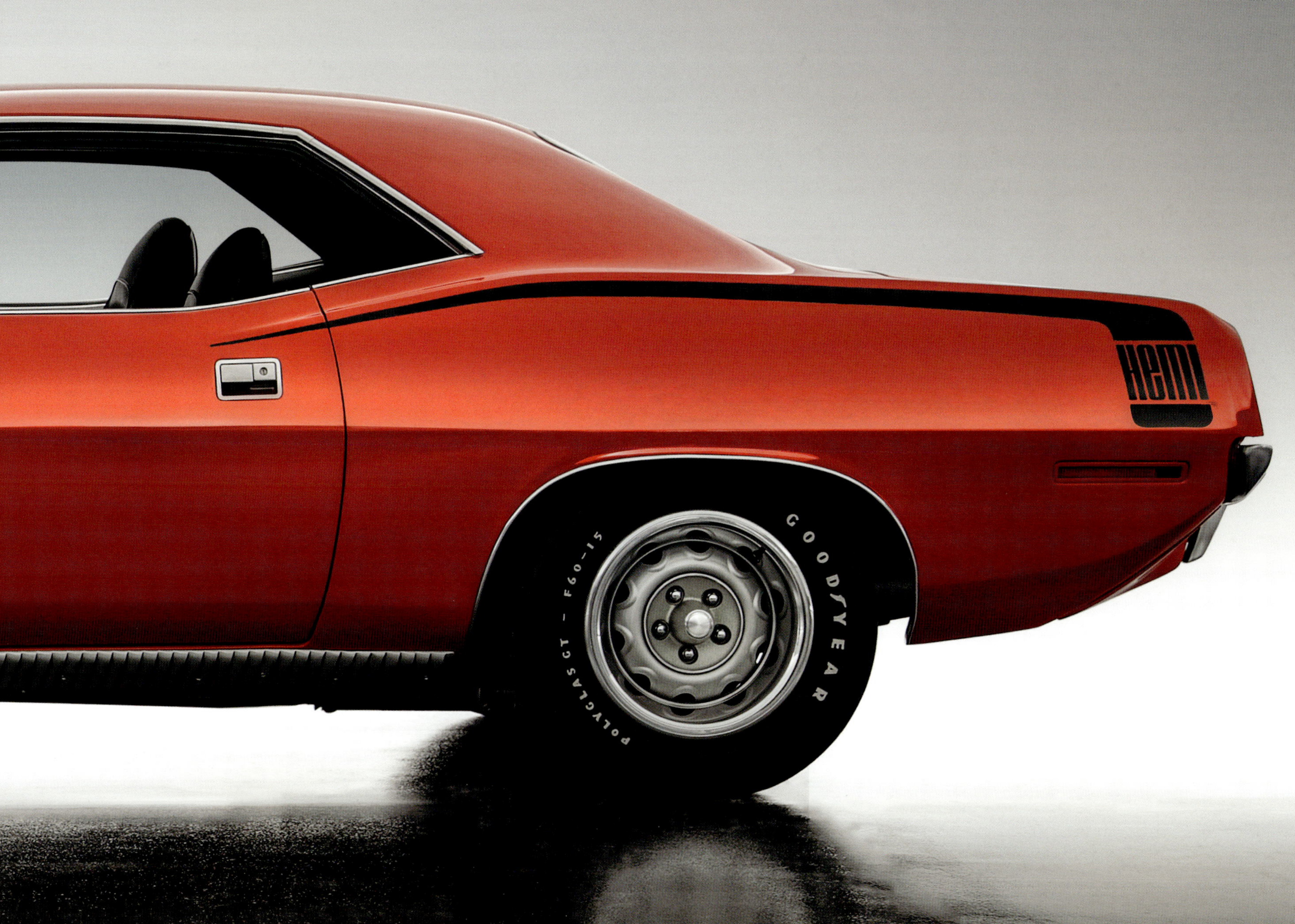
HEMI
GOODYEAR
POLYGLAS GT – F60-15

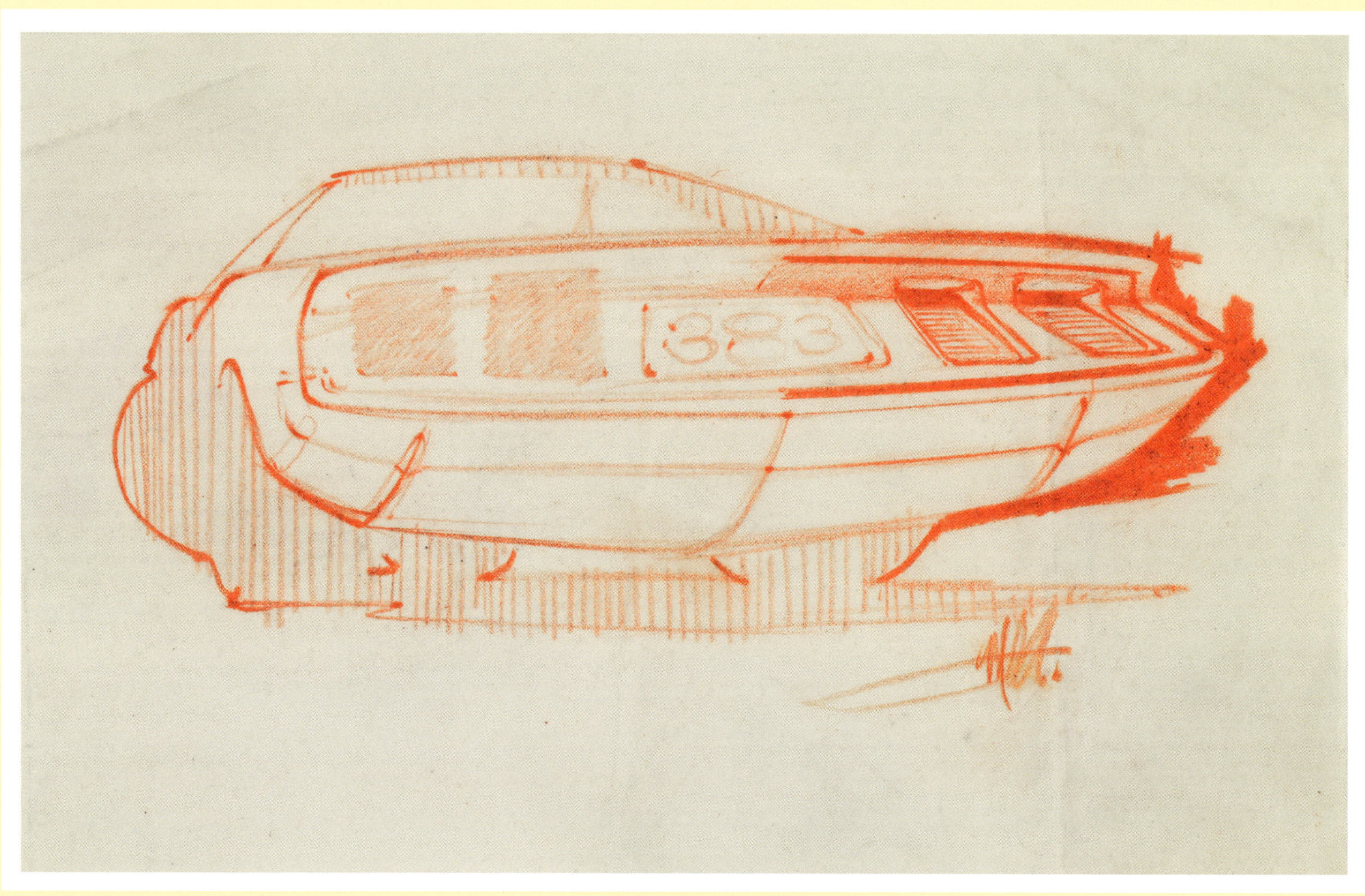

MILTON ANTONICK

Barracuda Rear Form Sketch for Clay Development, 1967, orange Prismacolor on vellum

The 1970 Plymouth Barracuda reflects a changing vocabulary in Detroit design studios. Inspired in part by the runaway success of Ford's Mustang, the redesigned Barracuda evolved from its compact roots into a snarling machine meant to convey the horsepower under its hood.

The original Barracuda, launched in the 1964 model year, built on Chrysler's success with the sporty, compact Plymouth Valiant introduced in 1960. As Ford began the drawn-out campaign leading to the debut of the Mustang, known widely as the sporty successor to the Falcon, Chrysler looked to position an updated Valiant as a market rival. The Barracuda debuted in 1964, largely as a modified Valiant with a fastback roof.[1] It was followed by the second-generation Barracuda, produced from 1967 to 1969, which adopted the look and proportions of the muscle cars that were becoming an increasingly powerful segment of the American market. With a curved form and taut surfaces, it was styled to suggest a muscular armature under the molded metal skin.[2]

Produced with slight changes from 1970 to 1974, the third-generation Barracuda was designed under Chrysler chief stylist Elwood Engel (1917–86) and Plymouth chief stylist Richard Macadam. The designers who contributed to the project included John E. Herlitz (1932–2008), Gerry Thorley, John Samsen, Milton Antonick, Don Hood, and Fred Schimmel. It was built on a specialized E-body platform shared with the Dodge Challenger, developed by Clifford Voss. Growing into its own, the third-generation Barracuda also embraced a series of contrasts between the curved musculature of the previous model and its own boldly angular features emphasizing brute mechanical force.[3] A straight beltline crease punctuates the side of the 1970 Barracuda from headlamp to taillight. Optional decals articulate the undulating surface of the rear fender. The smooth curves of the front end terminate in a flat nose pierced by two rectangular inset openings. A number of features reference elements of race cars, such as hood scoops to bring cool air to the engine and pins to secure the hood at high speeds.

The 1970 Barracuda was designed simultaneously with, and in parallel studios to, the Dodge Challenger pony car of the same year. The advanced styling studio developed specifications for each car, beginning work in February 1967. The Barracuda studio, managed by Milton Antonick, then refined the design. A number of important decisions happened quickly to accommodate a tight schedule once the design had progressed from sketches on paper to full-scale clay model. Over the course of a weekend, Engel, Antonick, and a group of modelers created the form that would go into production.[4]

Speeding cars and open roads were potent metaphors in American popular culture. The flourishing of the muscle car in the 1960s and 1970s coincided with a proliferation of road movies from Hollywood. In these films the protagonist or a tragic hero takes to the road to find freedom or to escape the demands of everyday life.[5] "Speed means freedom of the soul," says a radio DJ in the 1971 road movie *Vanishing Point* following a high-speed chase between a 1970 Dodge Challenger and the police.

The car was also a ubiquitous part of the American scene. While some celebrated or criticized the effect it had on daily life, others found new ways to examine its form. For the sculptor John Chamberlain (1927–2011), crushed and contorted car parts were raw materials he used for their formal and gestural qualities. For works like his 1962 sculpture *Coo Wha Zee* (p. 8), he fitted together and shaped found car parts into sculptures. Describing his adoption of car parts, the artist said, "I ran out of the materials I'd been working with before." Parts of old cars were in ready supply.[6]

Prompted by a number of cultural, economic, and political factors, some people began to question the safety and efficiency of American cars. The National Air Quality Standards Act of 1970 included a requirement that the auto industry create engines that drastically curb emissions of hydrocarbons, carbon monoxide, and nitrogen oxide by January 1, 1977.[7] Ralph Nader's best-selling book *Unsafe at Any Speed* (1965) had convinced the American public that safety should be a greater factor in car design, leading to new legislation that changed the shape of American cars. The oil embargoes, crises, and shortages of the decade that followed would further sway public taste against the powerful, fast, and fuel-inefficient muscle and pony cars that consumers had previously clamored to buy. The rising political and economic anxieties of the early 1970s compounded these concerns. The ongoing war in Vietnam destabilized a generation of young men who qualified for the draft, while inflation and economic stagnation forced Americans to question the wisdom of major purchases like a new car.

An article in the *New York Times* described the atmosphere of the car market: "the new styling war comes at a time when sporty car sales are falling." As muscle and pony cars saturated the market, the styling of models from Detroit became increasingly important. Detroit companies used updated designs to capture the eye of fickle or hesitant customers.[8] ❖

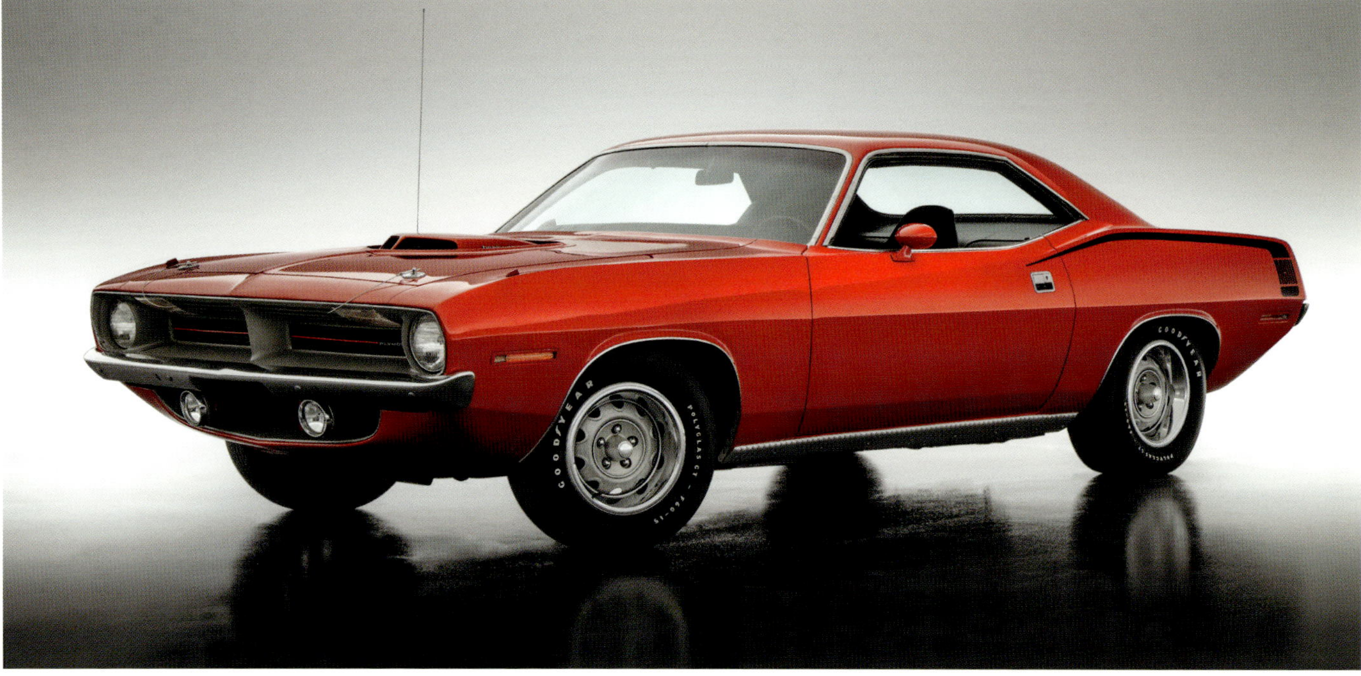

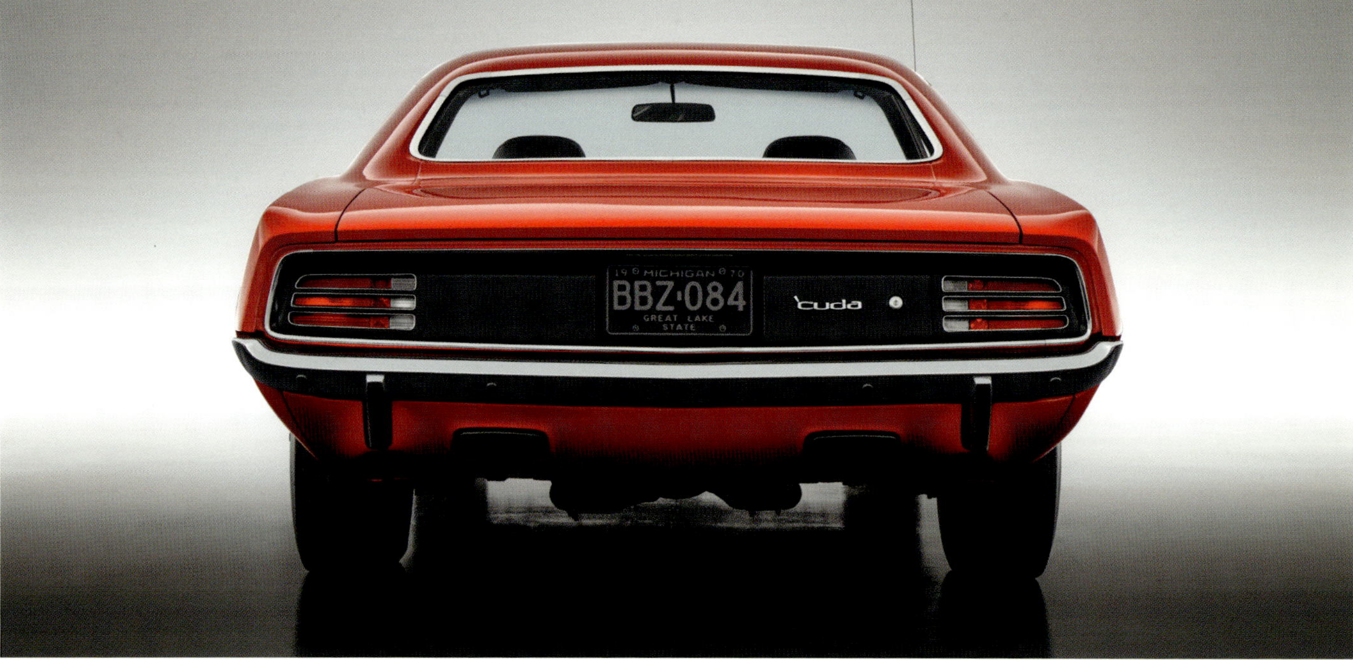

Chrysler Corporation, Plymouth Barracuda, 1970. *p. 80:* Front view (detail); *pp. 82–83:* Left side view; *above:* Three-quarter front view showing fender curves; *below:* Rear view showing forms related to Milton Antonick sketch; *opposite:* Front view showing hood scoops.

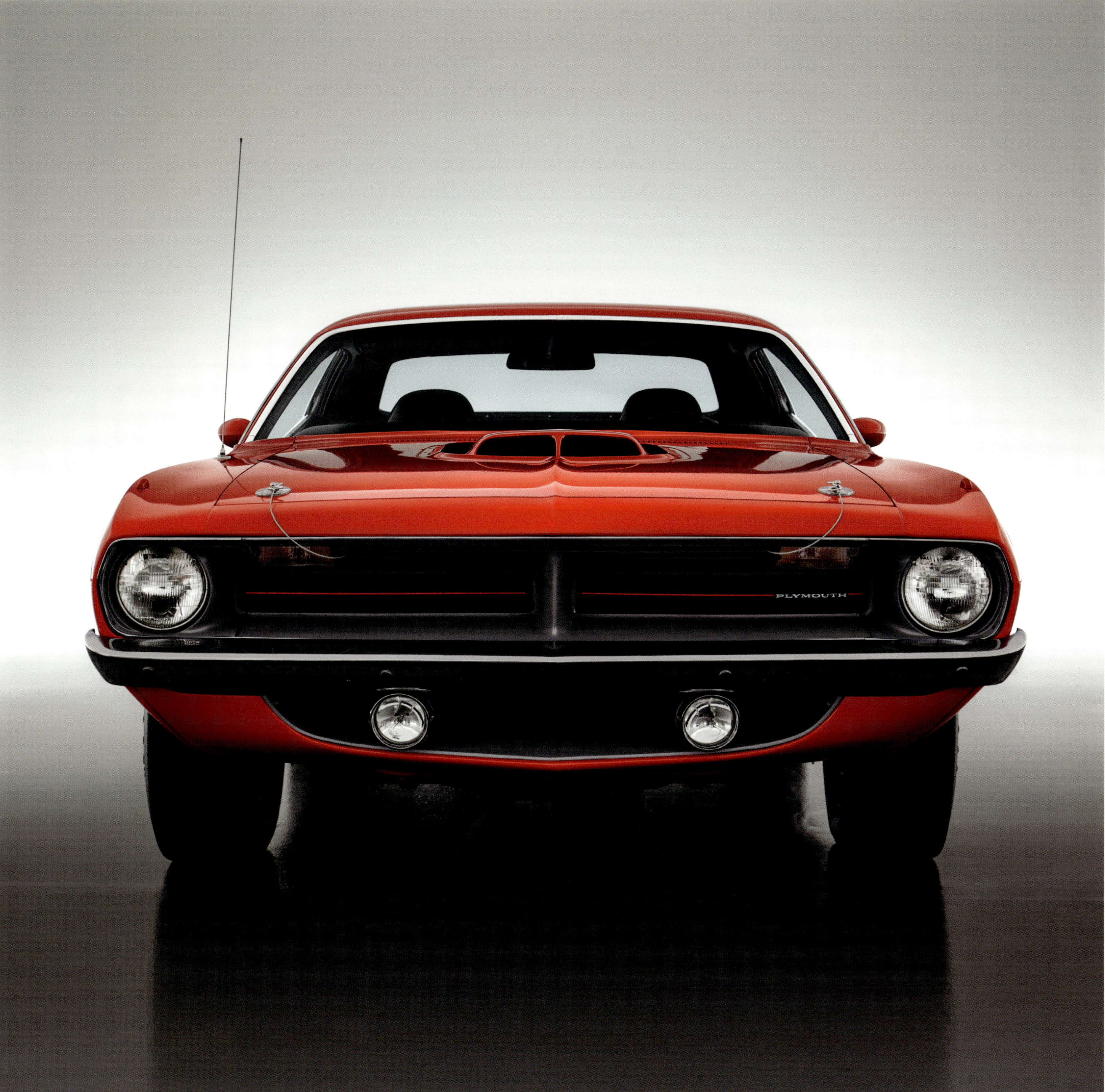
PLYMOUTH

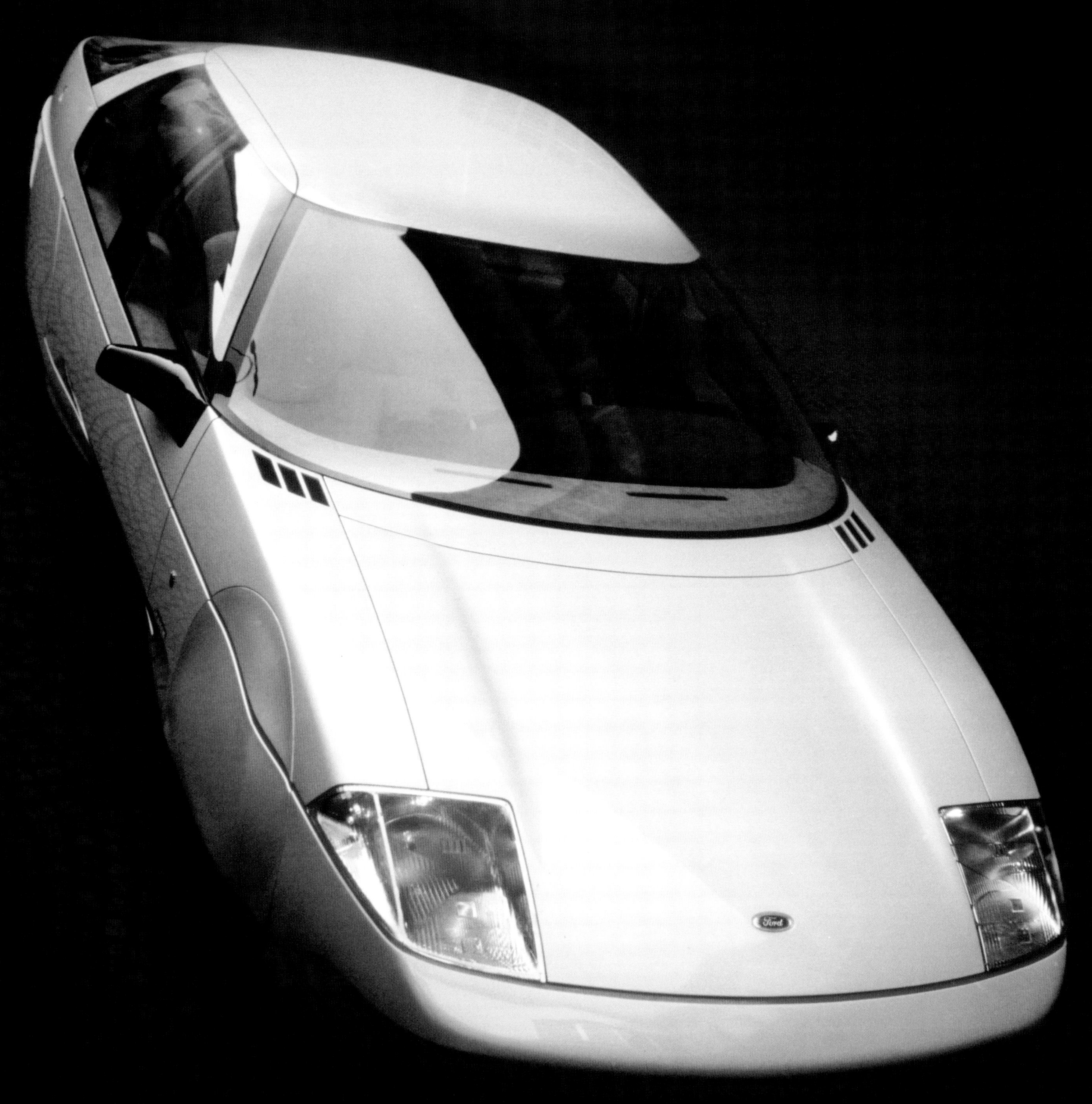

1 9 8 3

F O R D

P R O B E I V

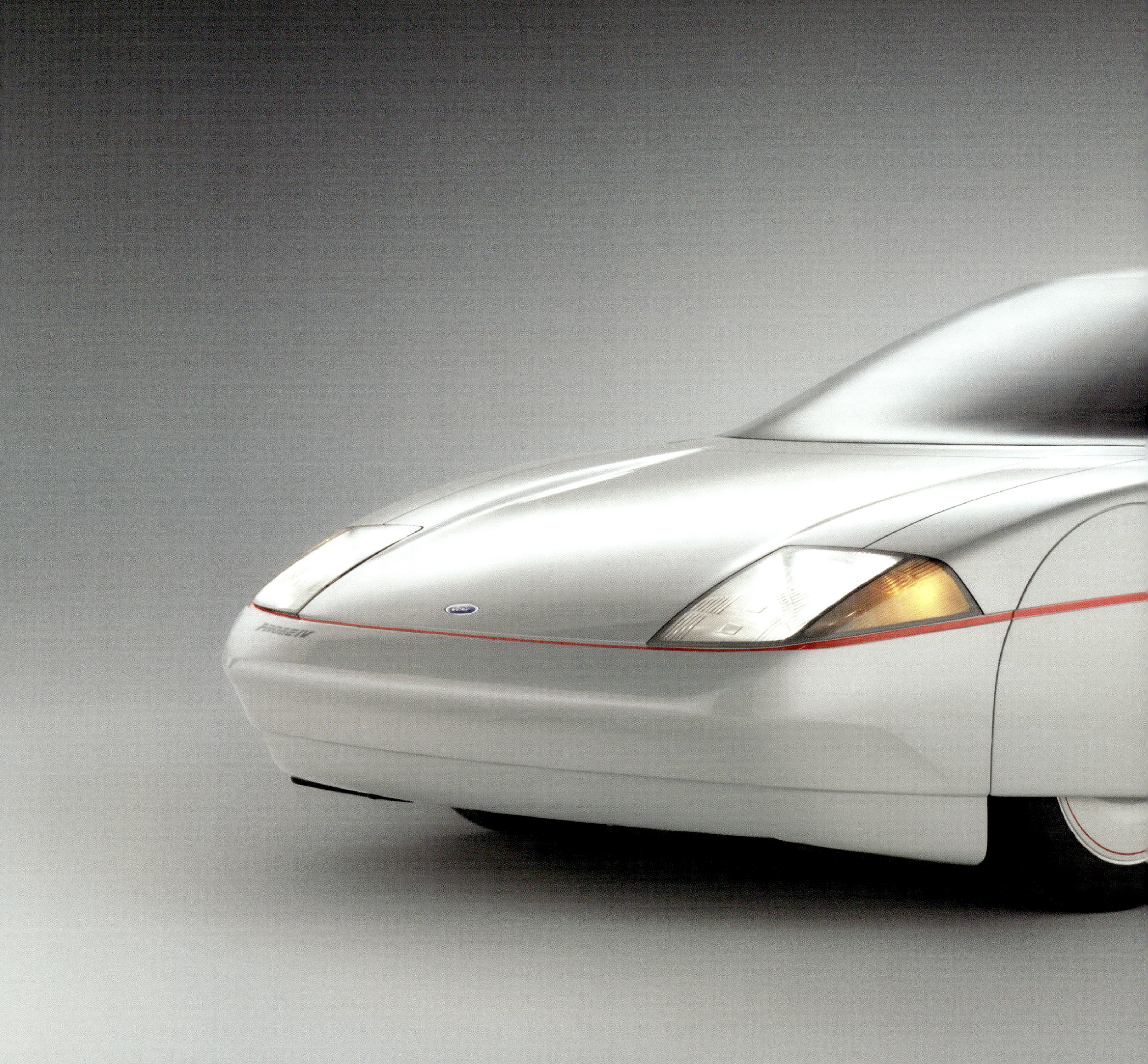

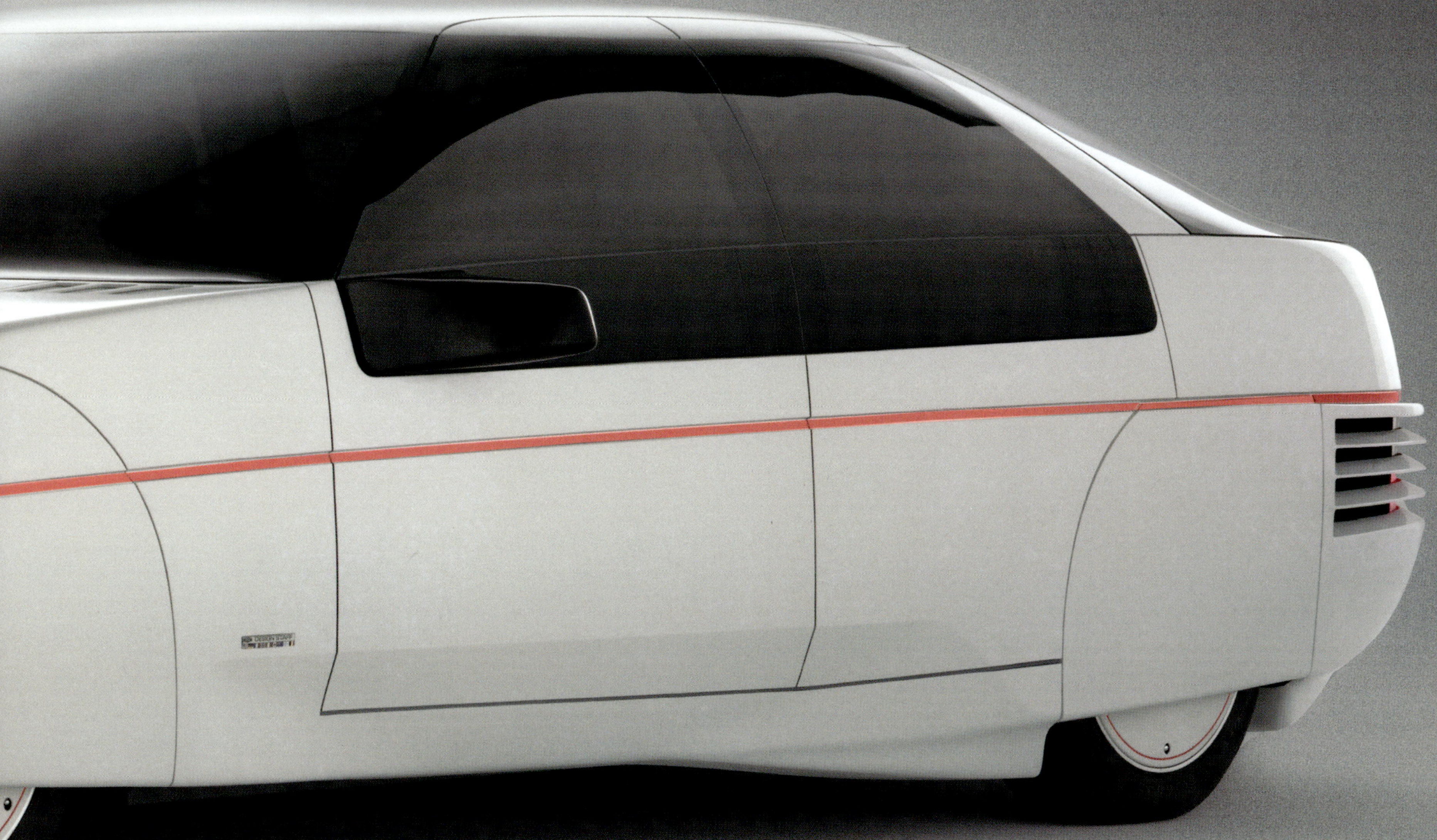

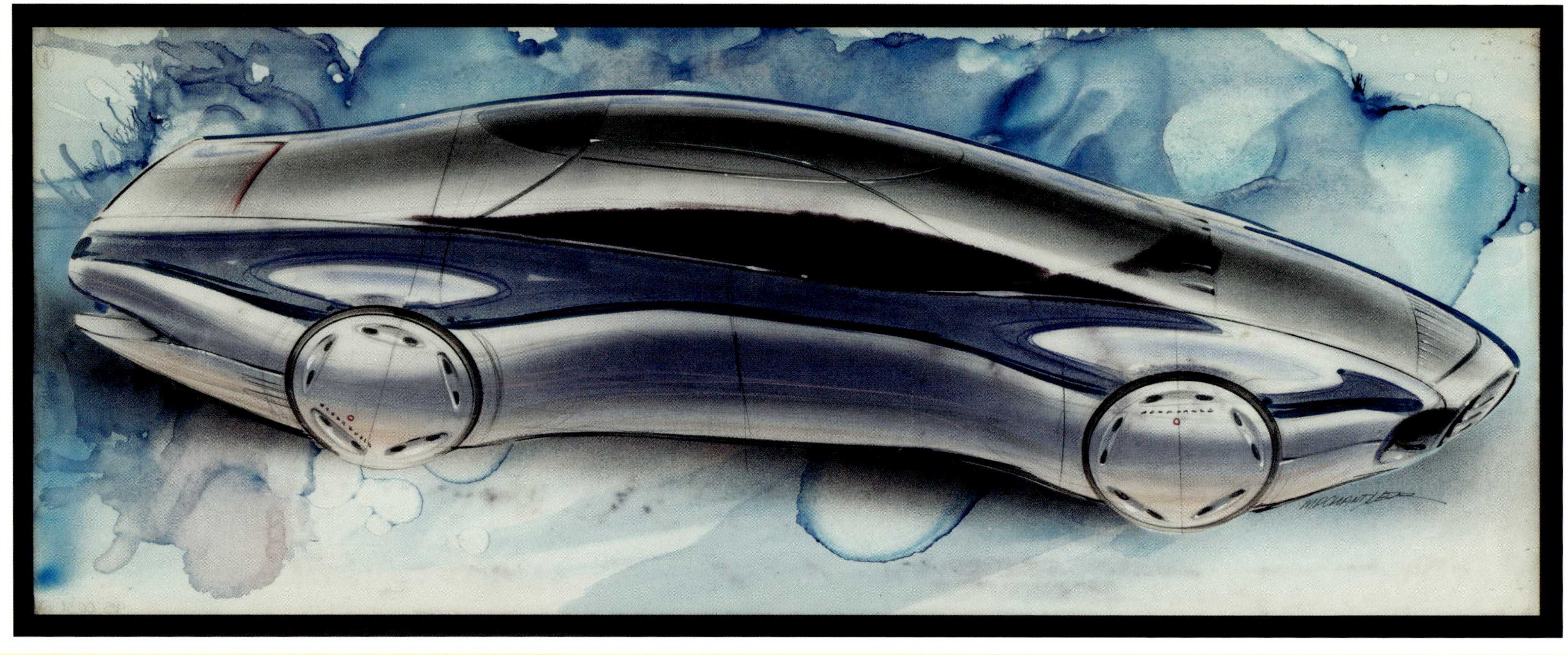

MAURICE CHANDLER

Aerodynamic Car Proposal, circa 1985, pastel, ink, Prismacolor, gouache, graphite, felt marker, and pressure-sensitive tape on vellum; collage over drawing: watercolor on vellum

New design ideas flourished in Detroit studios in the 1980s. Following the era of muscle and pony cars in the 1960s and 1970s, a number of cultural and economic forces diminished the appeal of fast-driving, sporty cars such as the Ford Mustang or Chrysler's Plymouth Barracuda. In their place, consumers were eager for elegant, high-tech cars that could deliver comfort and performance through efficiency in design and engineering.

At Ford, diminishing sales in the late 1970s and early 1980s created an atmosphere ripe for reinvention. Donald F. Kopka, vice president of design from 1980 to 1987, and Jack Telnack (born 1937), who joined Ford as a young designer and became chief of North American design before succeeding Kopka in 1987, shepherded in a new program of aerodynamic designs that challenged public perceptions of the company and its cars. In the place of fuel-inefficient muscle cars, they introduced a new vocabulary of sleek curves, rounded edges, and integrated forms. Kopka led the design programs that produced five Probe concept cars between 1979 and 1985, each testing new ideas in design and technology that could slowly make their way into production, and Telnack helped to bring key ideas from those cars to the mass market.

When the Probe IV was introduced in 1983, it set a new standard for aerodynamics in American cars. Every inch of it was meant to ensure efficiency. Kopka described it as the product of a close collaboration among aerodynamics engineers, vehicle engineers, designers, and the craftsmen at Ghia in Turin who created the prototype. The wheel wells were covered in the front with pivoting shields that moved as the wheels turned. The recessed headlamps were covered with plastic molded smoothly into the line of the front end. The hood tapered downward into a low nose capped with an integrated bumper. The side windows were fixed in place with only a small opening panel, allowing flush mounting with the body panels. The front end rose and lowered like a front air dam, calibrating the profile of the car to its speed.[1]

The aerodynamic design offered practical advantages to the driver. By 1985, Ford credited it with increasing the average fuel economy across its products by one and a half miles per gallon. When tested in a wind tunnel, the car was found to have a remarkably low drag coefficient—the measure of its air resistance in motion—of .152, and this number was emblazoned on the front and rear bumpers.[2] Commentators proclaimed it "Ford's new wind-cheating supercar" when it debuted at the Detroit Auto Show in Cobo Hall in January 1983. Reduced drag also translated into smoother handling of the car and reduced interior noise. As Telnack wryly suggested in 1987, this provided added value for the car buyer without exorbitant investment by the company: "you have to shape the metal anyway. So why not shape it right?"[3]

The Probe's radical departure from the cars immediately preceding it was deliberate. If the company wanted to change its popular reputation, it needed to take a bold new direction in the design of its cars. As Telnack observed: "The design is no good if you don't feel uncomfortable with it at first. If you feel right away in the showroom that the car is as familiar as an old friend, it's a sign that it will lack longevity."[4] The aerodynamic look pioneered by Kopka's design studios at Ford in the 1980s was deeply influential and other companies soon introduced their own aerodynamic cars. Indeed, Ford's impact in the 1980s was sometimes compared to that of General Motors under Harley Earl in the 1950s.[5]

The new look at Ford was partially the result of using a new set of tools in car design. If the futuristic cars produced in Detroit in the 1950s looked to the stars, those of the 1980s looked to the computer. According to Kopka, the Probe IV was the first car at Ford designed using a computer—its exterior surface was developed using computer-aided design programs, and it was then modeled by hand from those dimensions—and its high-tech form suggests the sleek cladding of a complex digital tool. The computerization of the design process at Ford continued through the decade, and by 1987 designers were able to render a car in three dimensions on a computer and then translate those designs to a clay model using automated carving machines.[6]

The turn to aero styling at Ford came at a transitional moment. When the Probe IV was introduced in 1983, Detroit companies had realized they were losing a share of the American market to European and Asian cars. To combat that shift, executives began appealing to style. The aero look pioneered at Ford in concept cars like the Probe IV found its way to the mass market in models like the Ford Taurus, which became the best-selling car in the country.[7] Instead of designing the car around a powerful engine, the Ford international design studio under Donald Kopka pioneered a new vocabulary in concept cars that would influence a generation of wildly popular production models. If in the 1970s, quality manufacturing and finish were considered the most important factors in a car purchase after price, by the late 1980s, design occupied that position. ❖

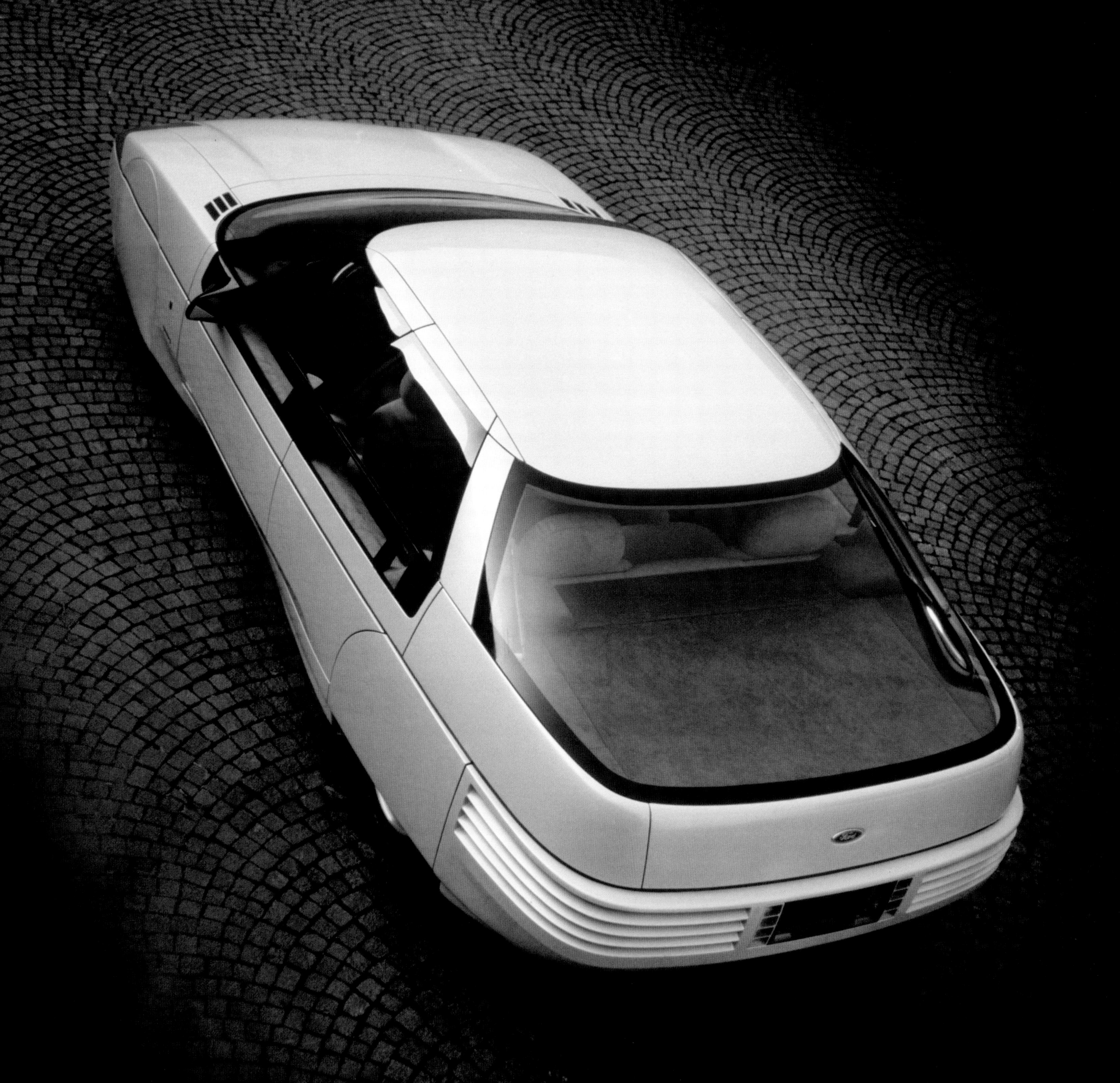

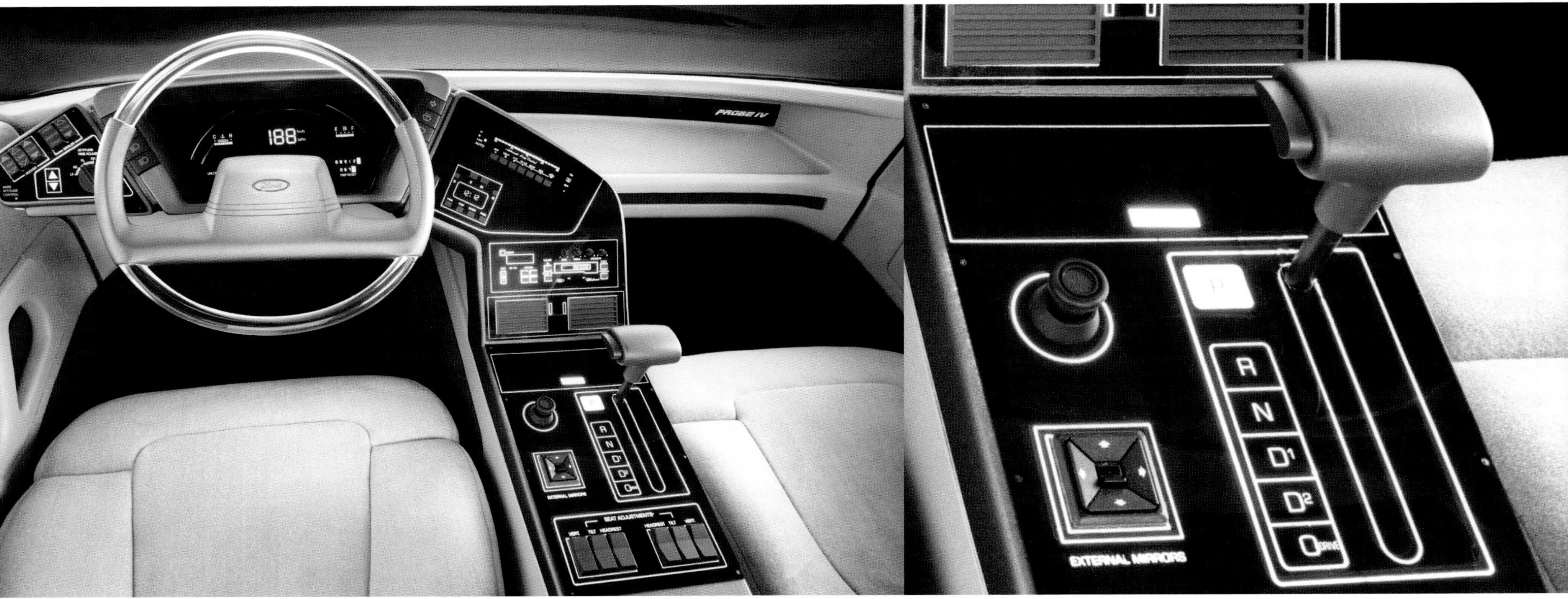

Ford Motor Company, Probe IV, 1983. *p. 88:* Front three-quarter view, right side; *pp. 90–91:* Front three-quarter view, left side; *opposite:* Rear three-quarter view; *above left:* Interior view showing instrument panel and steering wheel; *above right:* Gear shift.

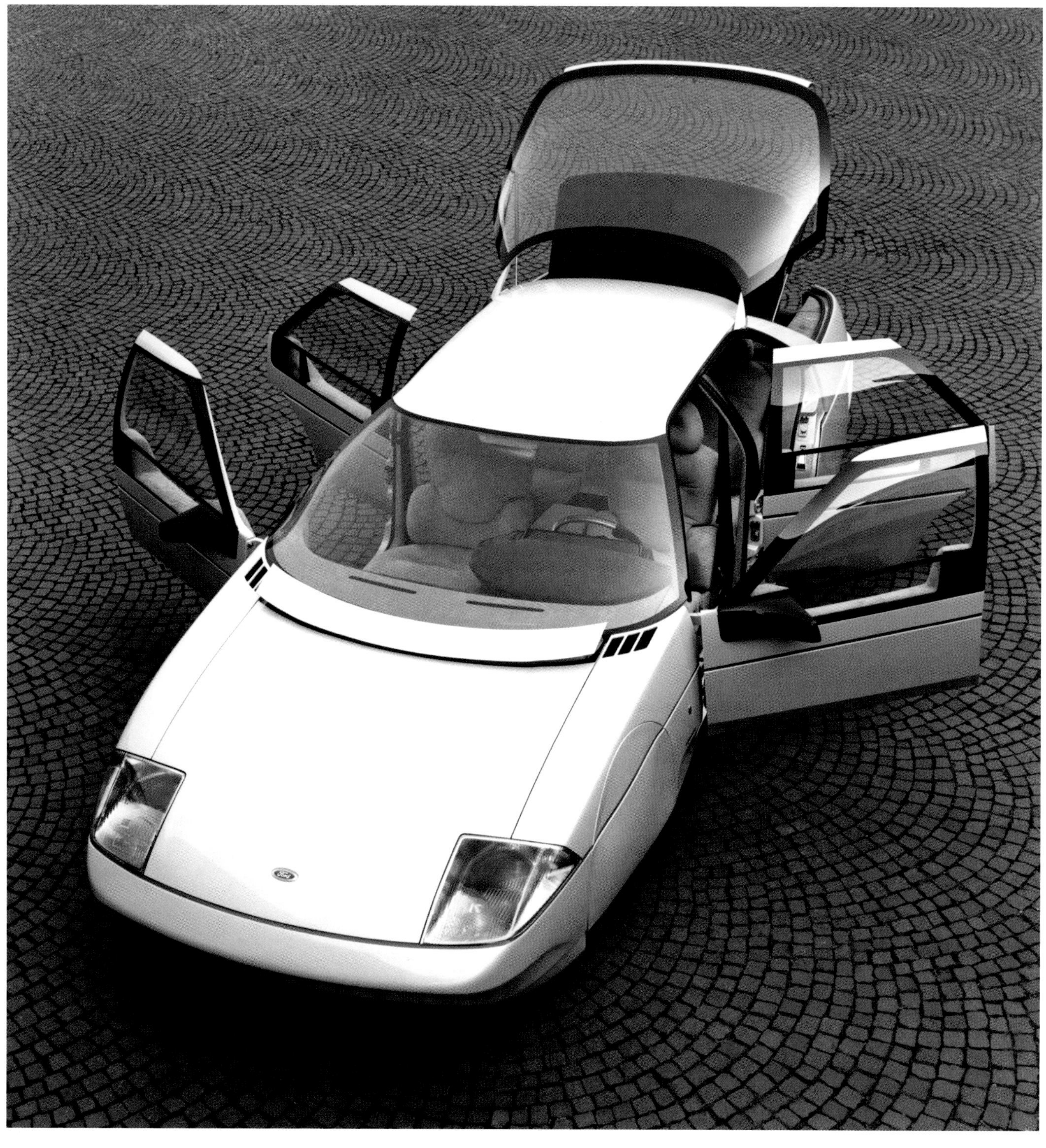

Ford Motor Company, Probe IV, 1983. *above:* Front three-quarter view with doors open; *opposite:* Left side view.

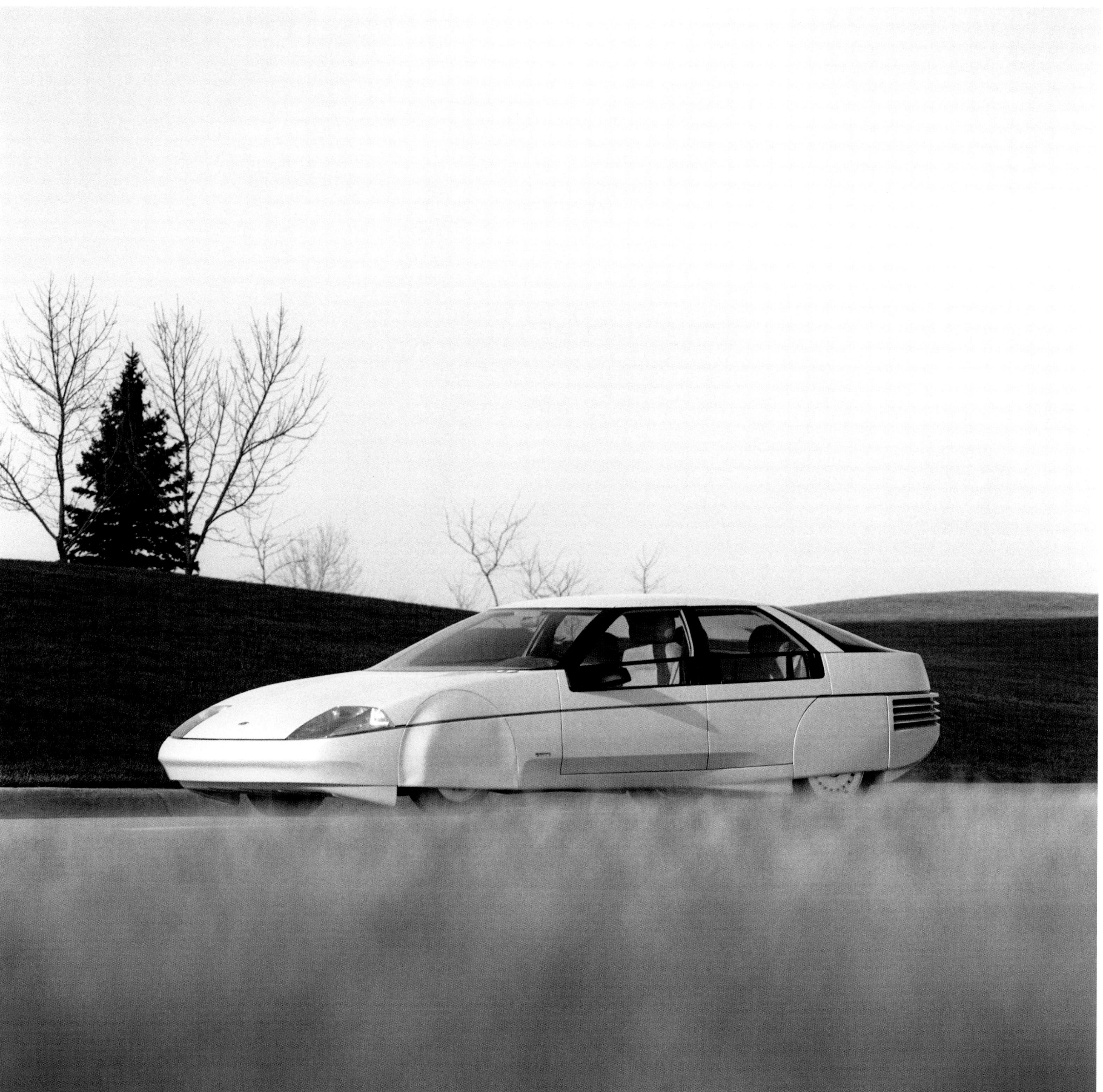

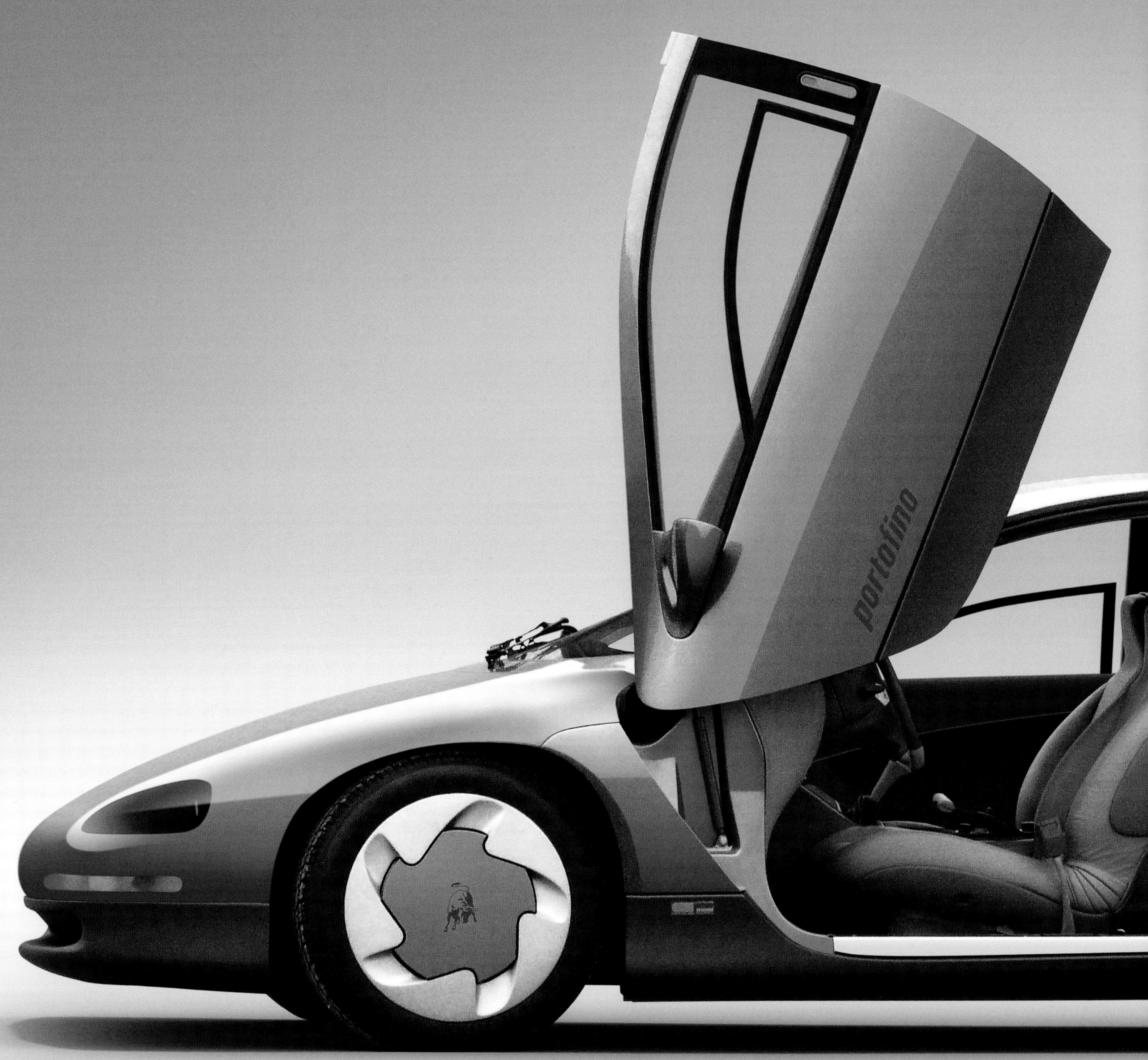
portofino

1987 CHRYSLER PORTOFINO

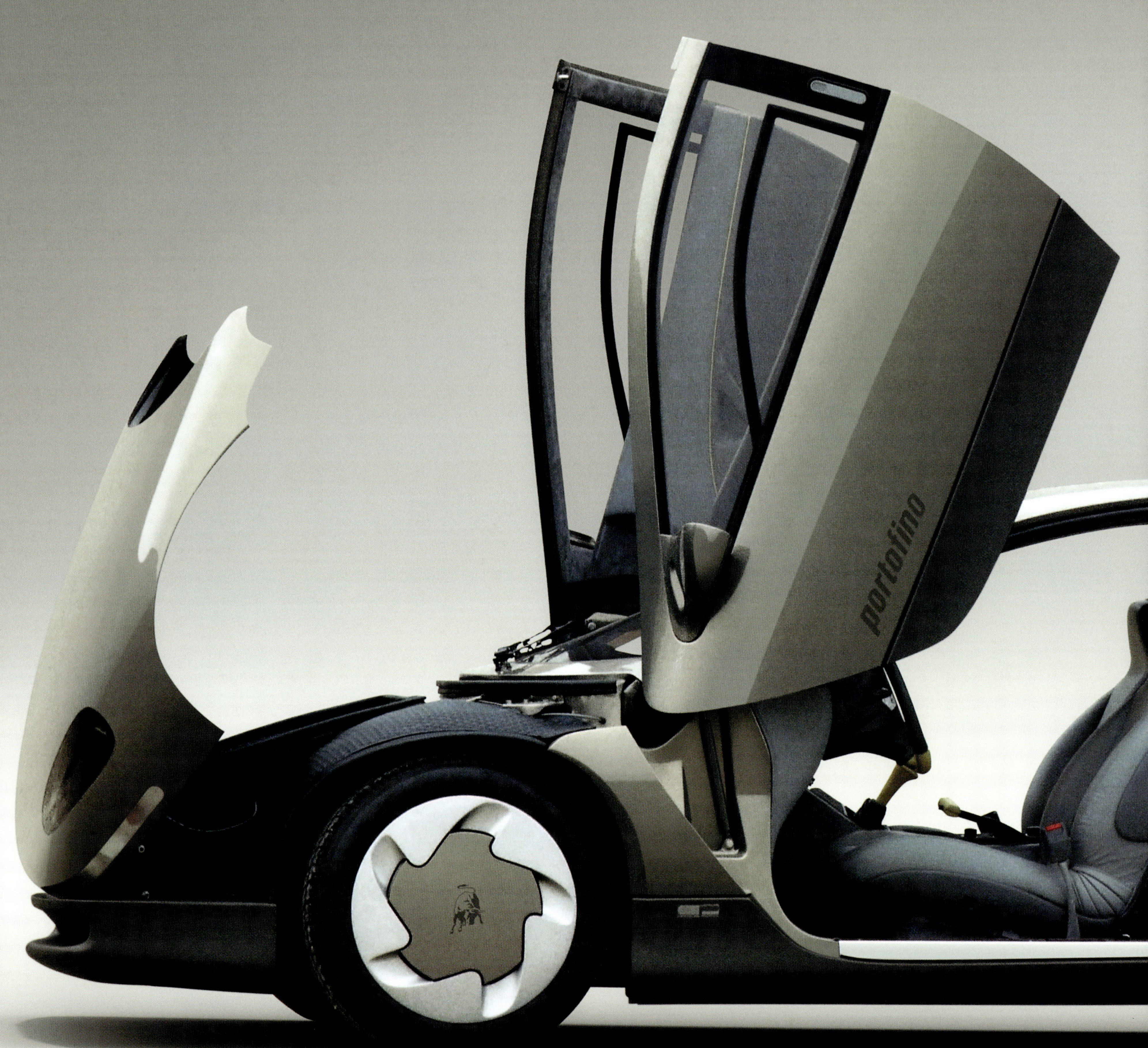
portofino

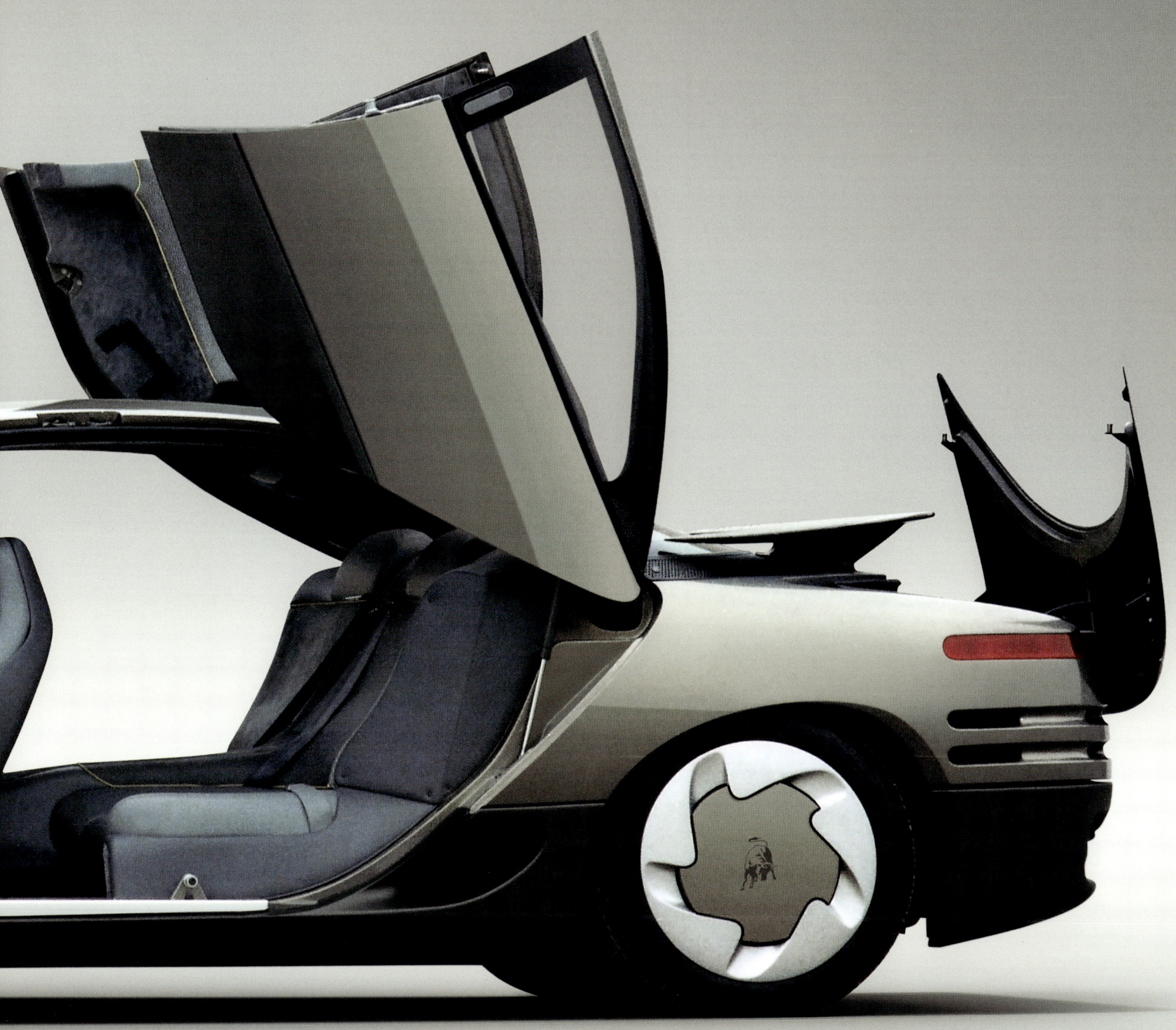

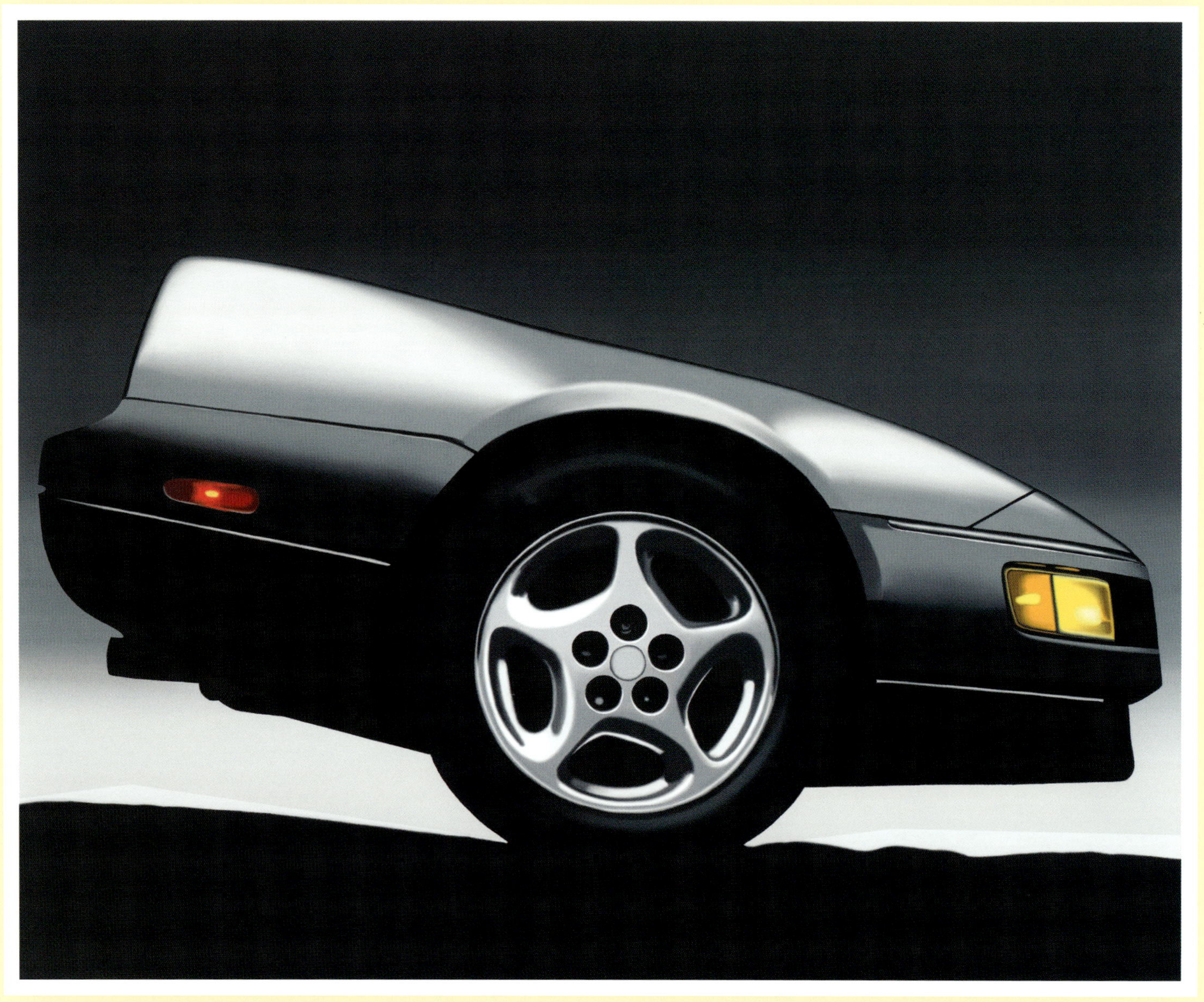

PETER CAIN

Z, 1989, oil on canvas

The introduction of the Lamborghini Portofino in 1987 marked a shift in design strategy at Chrysler. Its purchase of Nuova Automobili F. Lamborghini in April 1987 was part of a trend among Detroit automakers to associate themselves with the global reputations of high-performance European luxury carmakers.

Chrysler already owned a stake in the Italian carmaker Maserati. General Motors owned a majority share of the British racing company Group Lotus. Ford purchased the Turin-based coachbuilder Ghia in 1973, and the Ghia studio provided meticulous craftsmanship for the prototyping of concept cars like the Probe IV. For Detroit companies, an ownership stake in a European luxury sports carmaker provided access to new ideas in engineering and design, while also increasing the market appeal of an American-made car. A consumer who could not afford to pay $127,000 for Lamborghini's most popular model could buy a Chrysler—burnished by its association with Italian design and performance engineering.[1] Through its relationship with the Italian luxury carmaker, the company experimented with a new design vocabulary that would reshape its production sedans in the 1990s.

The car that became the Portofino began its life at Chrysler in the hands of designer Kevin Verduyn under the name Navajo. With its gentle curves and unified exterior styling with minimal ornamentation, the Navajo reflected the turn to aerodynamic design in the 1980s. The proportions of the four-door sedan are dominated by its long cabin, and the front end of the car is a slender, short, and tapered nose with a low-slung grille integrated into the front bumper. A large, gently sloping windshield leads to a spacious cabin. One of the car's most distinctive features is the orientation of its doors. Both front and rear doors rotate upward—the front counterclockwise and the rear clockwise—revealing the large, open cabin uninterrupted by the structural pillar that generally separates front and rear doors. Verduyn's design progressed to the clay model stage as the Chrysler Navajo. It was completed as the Lamborghini Portofino, powered by a Lamborghini engine, for debut at the Frankfurt Auto Show in 1988. The sole prototype for this design was crafted by Sergio Coggiolo at his Carrozzeria Coggiola near Turin.[2]

When the Portofino was singled out for praise by the Industrial Designers Society of America's Industrial Design Excellence Award in 1988, the jurors suggested that it connected "the truly futuristic and unachievable and the near-term production automobile."[3] The lure of the future created a fruitful new terrain for both designers and artists in the late 1980s. The New York artist Peter Cain (1959-97), for example, created a group of paintings based on the unfamiliar curves and forms of recent cars, inventing sleek profiles for otherworldly vehicles. In works like his 1989 *Z* (opposite), he modified and contorted familiar images of cars to create compositions that he later developed into paintings. The improbable machine he painted has recognizable elements from cars on the road, but appears both futuristic and unachievable, like the curves of the Portofino when it made its debut.[4]

The Portofino was the first major concept car introduced under the leadership of Tom Gale (born 1943), Chrysler's head of design, and its radical profile and legacy reflected his ambitious vision. During Gale's tenure, Chrysler debuted a series of influential concept cars to test ideas that could be brought to the public in modified form in the near future.[5] The Portofino would influence the sleek aerodynamic exteriors of production cars. After its popular reception, a small group of Chrysler cars was introduced to the market with related proportions. Models like the Dodge Intrepid, introduced in the 1993 model year, and the Neon, introduced in the 1995 model year, recalled the Portofino's low-slung, curved profile and minimal ornamentation.

Portofino's influence was most directly seen in a new interior design scheme called the "cab forward" look, introduced by Chrysler in the 1990s. This was a major shift in the way designers oriented the space and profile of a sedan. These cars were designed from the inside out, with exterior styling shaped by the demand for interior comfort.[6] The engine compartment was reduced in size, and a sloping windshield shifted forward. An expanded wheelbase pushed the front wheels forward as well, and the rear wheels back. The short hood contrasts with a long cabin. First seen on Kevin Verduyn's design for the Portofino, these features would come to define Chrysler's passenger cars in the 1990s. Having begun its life as a Lamborghini prototype that looked toward the future, the Portofino found its legacy in mass-produced Chrysler sedans echoing its proportions to create comfortable interiors. ❖

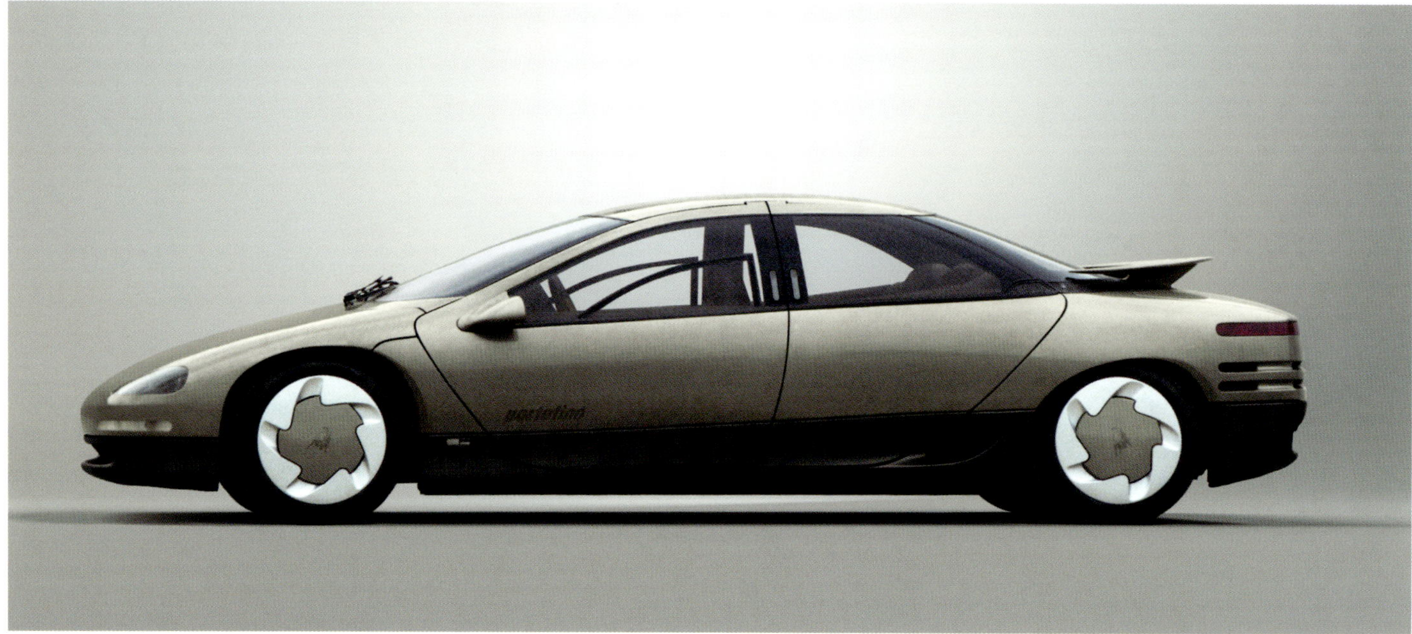

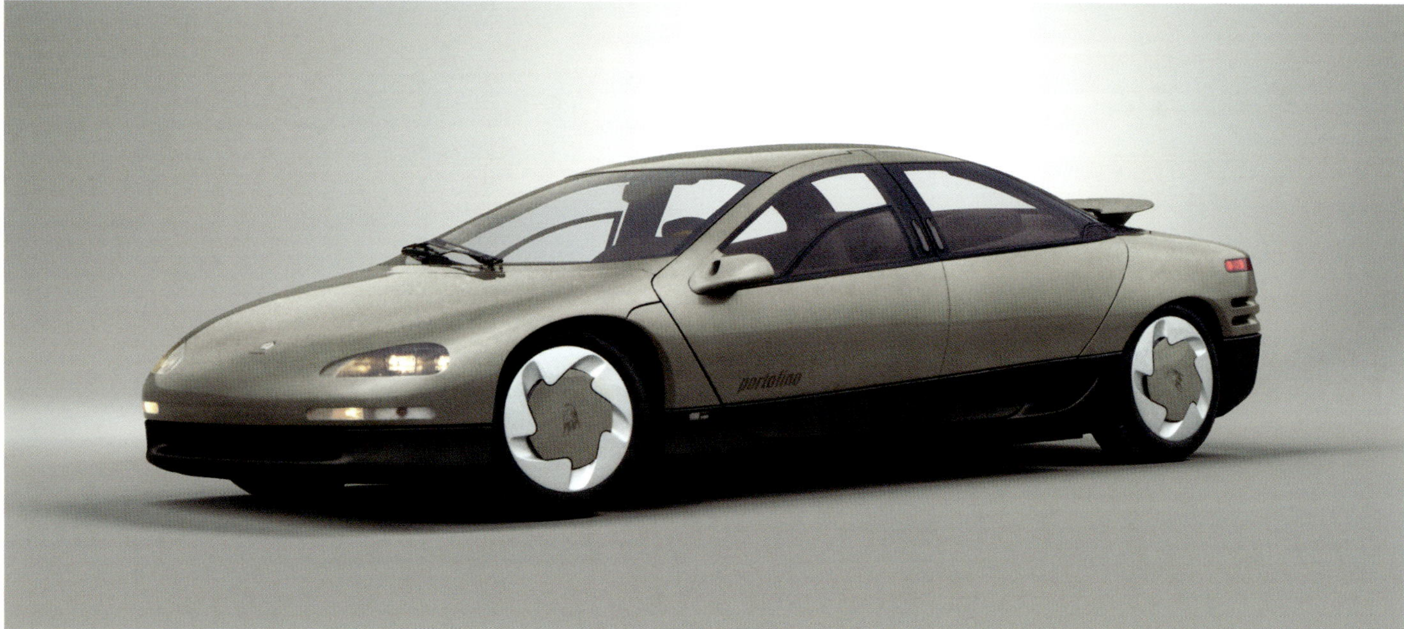

Chrysler Corporation, Lamborghini Portofino, 1987. *p. 98:* Left side view (detail); *pp. 100–101:* Left side view with doors open; *above:* Front three-quarter view showing integrated headlamp and bumper form; *below:* Left side view showing short hood proportion; *opposite:* Cabin interior.

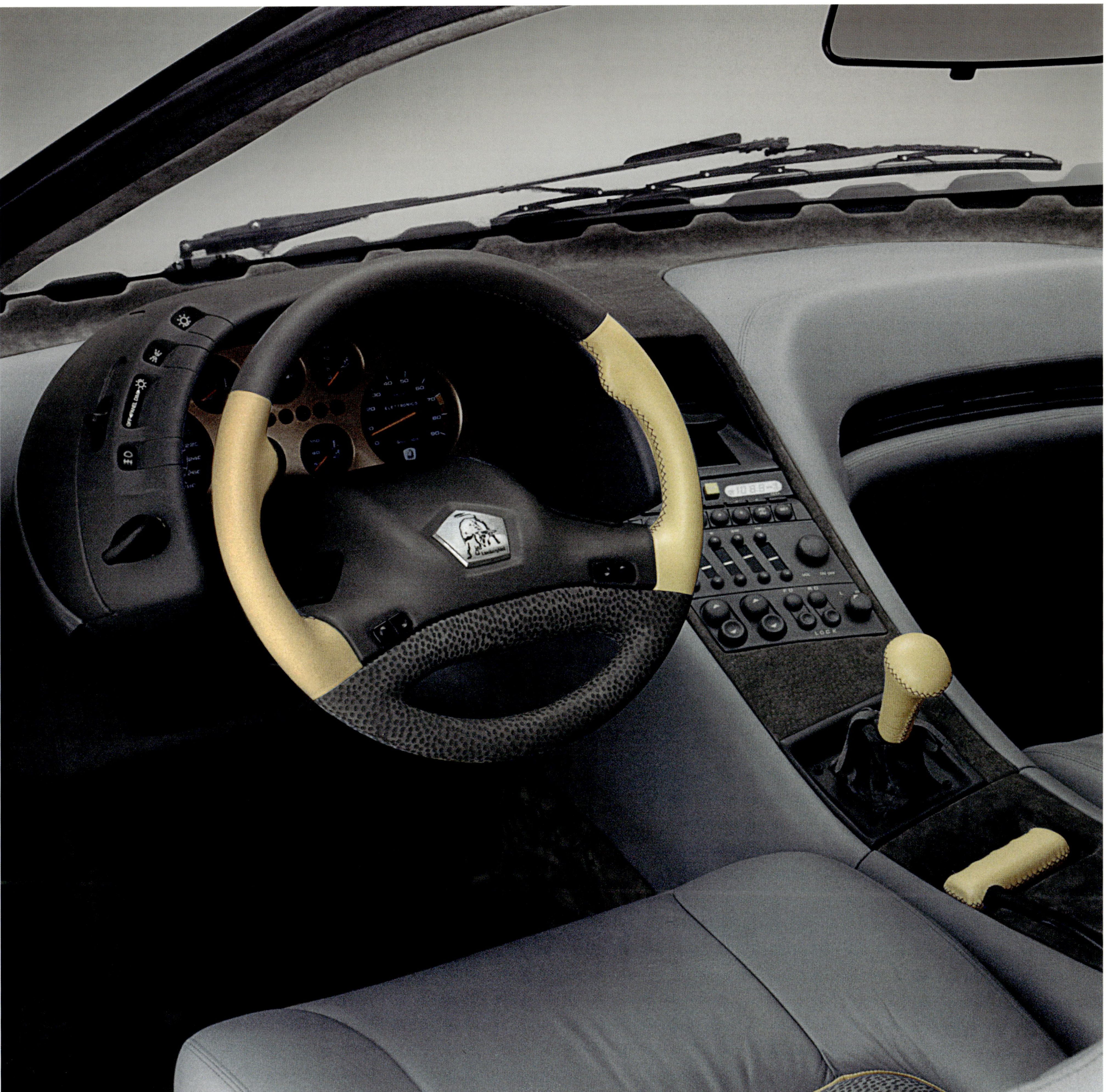

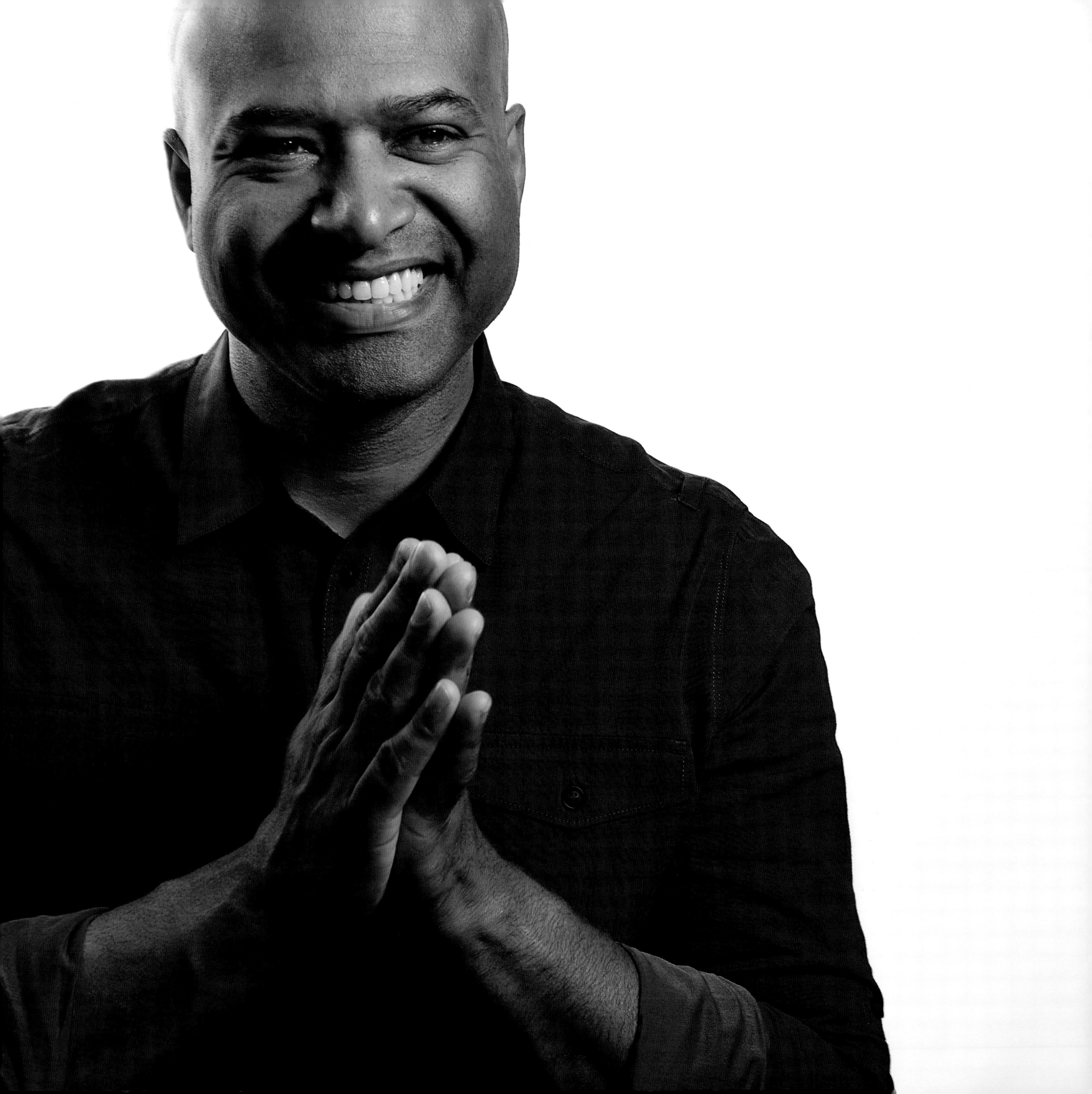

INTERVIEW WITH RALPH V. GILLES

Ralph V. Gilles began his career at Chrysler in 1992. He currently serves as the head of design for Fiat Chrysler Automobiles, a position he has held since 2015.

Benjamin W. Colman: How did you come to be interested in cars? Did you grow up in a car family?

Ralph V. Gilles: Not at all, actually, quite the opposite. I just noticed cars on my own. I consumed lots of automotive themed television as a young kid—*B.J. and the Bear, Knight Rider, The Dukes of Hazzard*—where cars were the stars. I also lived in Montreal, and Formula 1 would come to town and exotics would fill the streets.

BC: What cars were you most drawn to at that point?

RG: The pretty ones. Vintage ones. I actually loved European cars. The Porsche 911 was one of my favorites—the whale-tail, mid-1970s 911—and the Porsche 928. Anything that looked like it was designed with passion, that looked like a cohesive design. On the American side, I was really drawn to the 1969 Dodge Charger and the Barracudas from the '70s.

BC: At what point in your youth did you know you wanted to be a designer, and a car designer specifically?

RG: I used to sketch a lot and had a couple of well-intentioned aunts. One got me art lessons when I was eight or nine, but while I liked drawing, that didn't appeal to me as much as mechanical things. When I was about fifteen and a half, one of my aunts forced me to write a letter to Chrysler to find out how to be a car designer, and I did.

BC: What was the response?

RG: We actually addressed the letter to Lee Iacocca, the chief executive at the time, and he forwarded it to the design department. I got a very personal letter from the number two in design, Neil Walling. I still have the letter. I had sent him pictures I had drawn, and he was very kind and told me I showed promise and should investigate certain schools.

BC: Eventually you attended the College for Creative Studies in Detroit. What was the curriculum like at the time?

RG: Initially, you weren't allowed to go right into transportation. They wanted you to try industrial design and then you would qualify to get into the transportation program. You had to earn your way in. And you had to exercise all the disciplines: graphic art, fine arts, product design. Art history was a big part of my education. The first year was really challenging because I was a one-dimensional thinker when it came to design—I just cared about cars. The curriculum opened my mind to consider all forms of art as well as proportion, style, and beauty.

BC: At that point were you designing with pen and ink on paper, or had it moved to digital?

RG: The digital stuff was still very rudimentary. This was around 1988 to 1992. I used a mixture of pastel and air markers, which was expensive because the air markers wouldn't last very long. Some of my favorite media were newsprint and Prismacolor or black chalk.

BC: How closely were you keeping an eye on the cars on the road? Were you influenced by the aero design of the late 1980s?

RG: Not really. There was really nothing until about 1989, when Chrysler was on a roll. It really blew me away when they showed the Portofino concept car. Chrysler had an amazing run that year—the Viper show car also came out in 1989. So amazing—the proportions, the beauty, the shapes. After that, they showed the Lamborghini Diablo, which had a lot of neat, kind of exaggeratedly sporty shapes.

BC: Could you describe what was so notable about the Portofino when it debuted?

RG: This was a car like a Lamborghini Countach, in a way. It was extremely windswept and had very low, supercar proportions, but it was a four-door car with these dramatic scissor doors that opened in all directions. It made for an incredible presentation on the show stand. If you were a red-blooded anything you couldn't walk past this thing—it was that arresting. It was very clean in its design. I think if that car rolled out on the road today, it would still be something to behold.

BC: When did you join Chrysler?
RG: In the summer of 1992.

BC: I think of that as an important time in Chrysler's history, when Tom Gale was in charge of design. Two different vocabularies were popular at once. There was the cab-forward design proportion, with short hoods and spacious cabs, and a very important move to retro or heritage design with cars like the Prowler and the Viper. Could you talk about Chrysler design in those years and navigating a space between futuristic and heritage design?
RG: This was the period of the cab-forward push, and the stuff that was in the studios was making everything on the road look old to us. Design was really promoting this new look. The Stratus was being designed. At the same time, the beginnings of the PT Cruiser were underway, so you had a contrast. You had the retro-inspired but very functional vehicles and then you had fantastical cars that almost looked like movie cars. Chrysler went back-to-back-years with these great concept cars—the Chrysler 300 concept, the Chronos, the Intrepid show car. Just one after the other — either hyper cab forward, or hyper retro.

There was a lot going on. Tom Gale had a unique position where he was the head of styling and also engineering. He was quite an inspiration to all of us, teaching us that if you want to get something on the road, you have to understand how a car comes together and you have to be able to speak the language of the engineers. It was an important lesson. We could design pretty cars, but getting them into production is a lot harder.

BC: As a young designer, what was your relationship to brand history and heritage? Did you set out to study Chrysler's past?
RG: I believe that to carry a brand forward you have to understand where it came from, respect its heritage, and build on it if you can. It's like a pair of Levi's, in a way. There's always a certain classic thing that gives people comfort when they see it, especially Americans. Nostalgic memories are burned into your subconscious because of the cars you or your parents grew up with.

BC: What was the impetus behind the turn to retro design in the 1990s?
RG: A lot of it was a test, to see if the public would be turned on by the same things that brought happy memories to our leadership. A lot of the concept cars shown in the mid-'90s were about testing the waters to see how far we could take the brand and if there was a nostalgic tug on the heartstrings.

BC: When did you first realize you had a major role in shaping a car you saw out on the road?
RG: The very first project I was proud of was the 2002 Jeep Liberty. I had designed the interior. Then the Chrysler 300 series was introduced in 2005. It was started by Bob Hubbach, but I got to take the cars to production, which was very challenging. We had promised the world a retro theme, but we had never actually done a production retro car other than the PT Cruiser.

BC: What was your philosophy or concept for the 300 series?
RG: The philosophy was to find the sweet spot between something very modern and a kind of comfortable Americana. People felt very familiar with it. It brought back great memories. We did archetypal research and people would talk about going to the drive-in with their parents, going to get ice cream. It was always about these wonderful, positive images of the vehicle in American culture.

BC: How would you characterize Detroit design in 2019?
RG: I would say the best of American design is in your face. There's a certain presence, an outsize personality, that the vehicles have. Not in a garish way, but in a confident way. You cannot walk past a Challenger Redeye and not turn back to look at it. It has this arresting, shameless presence to it, which gives it personality and attitude. Designing vehicles with a certain demeanor goes back to the heyday of the 1950s with the Forward Look introduced by Chrysler designer Virgil Exner and its oversize wings and fins.

I know that when my guys set out to design a car, they don't want it to blend in. They want to make a statement. They are not just wrapping an engineering solution, they are creating a personality. They are trying to create an icon.

This April 29, 2019, interview has been edited and condensed.

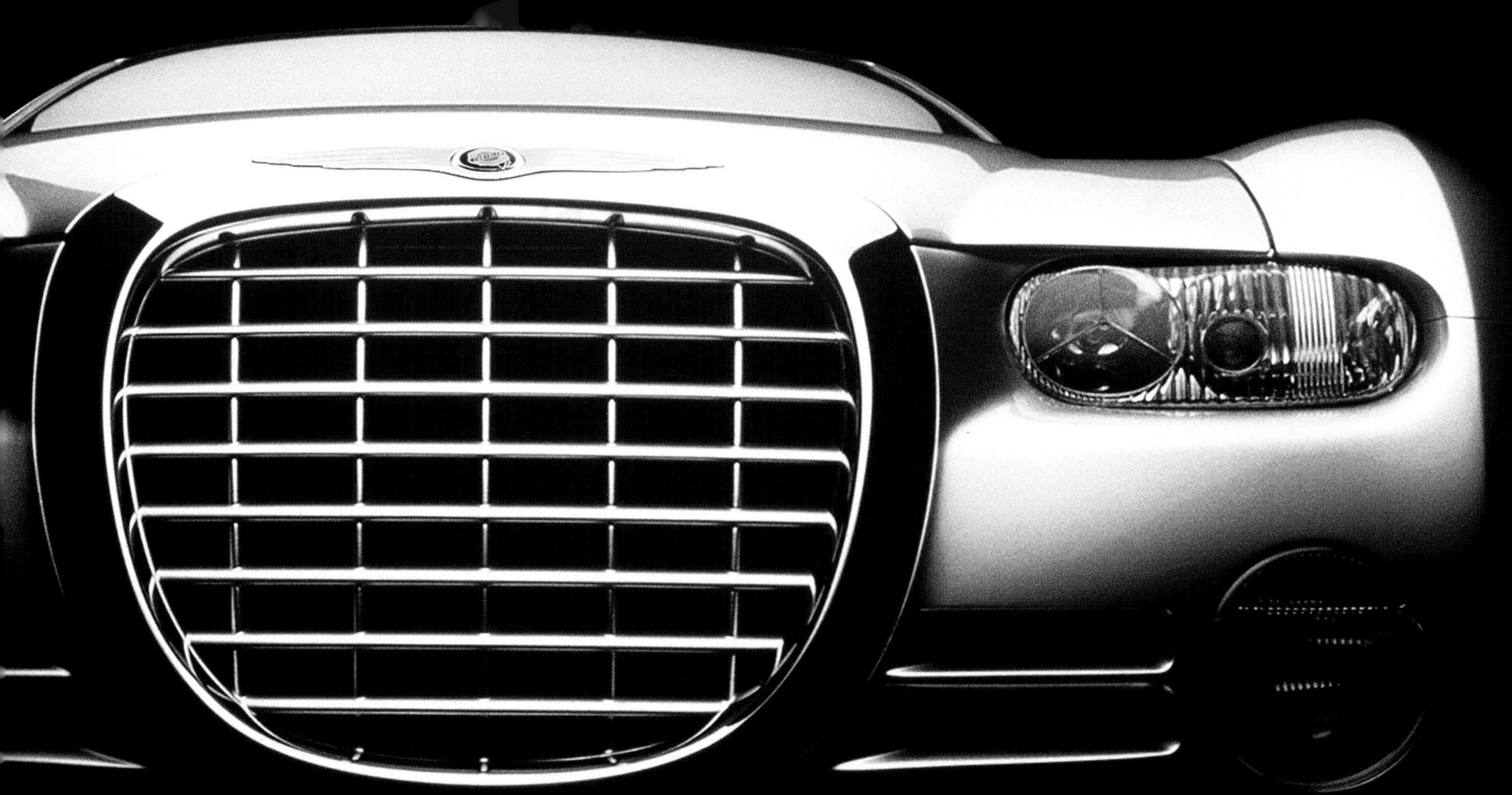

1998 CHRYSLER CHRONOS

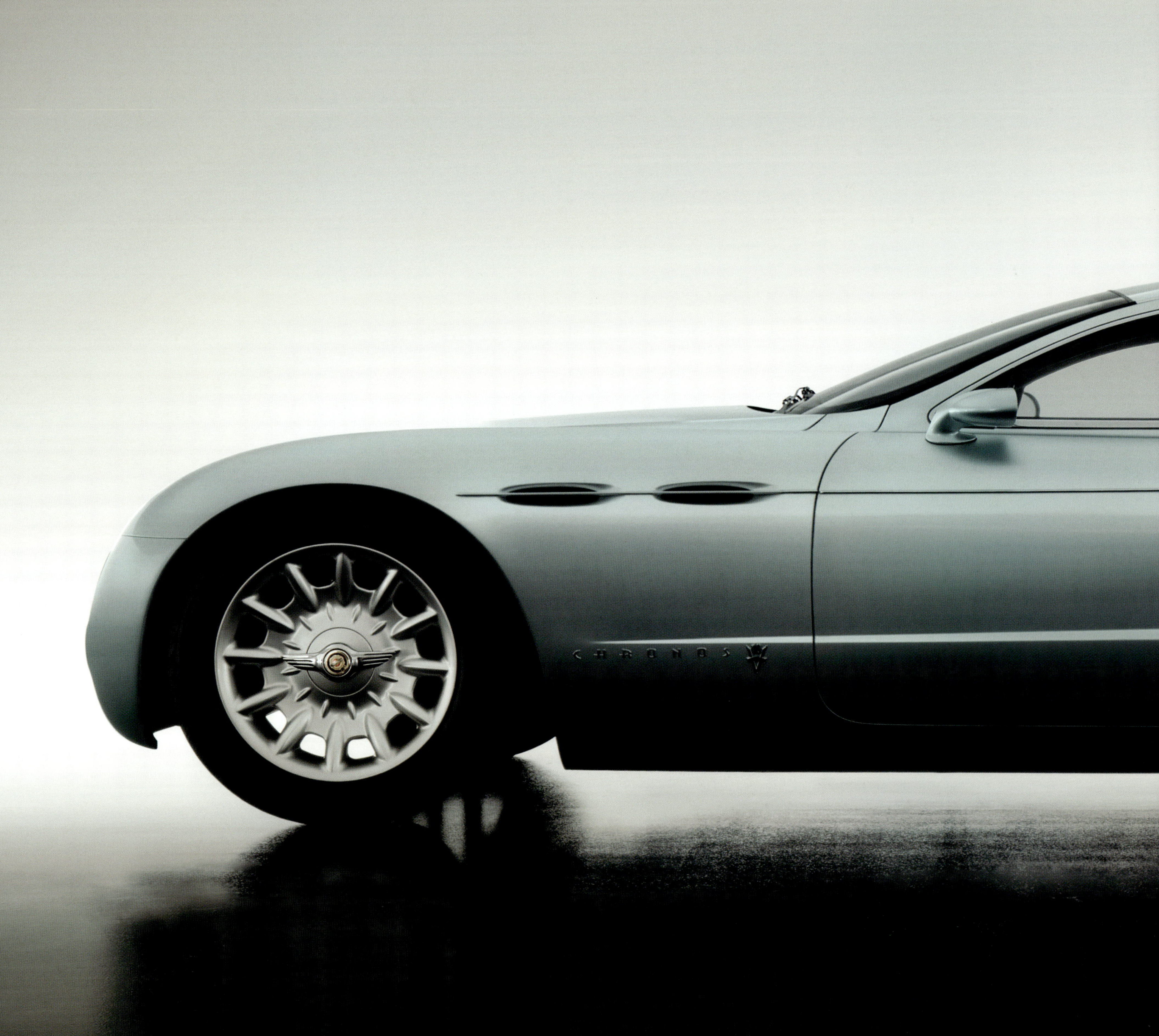
CHRONOS

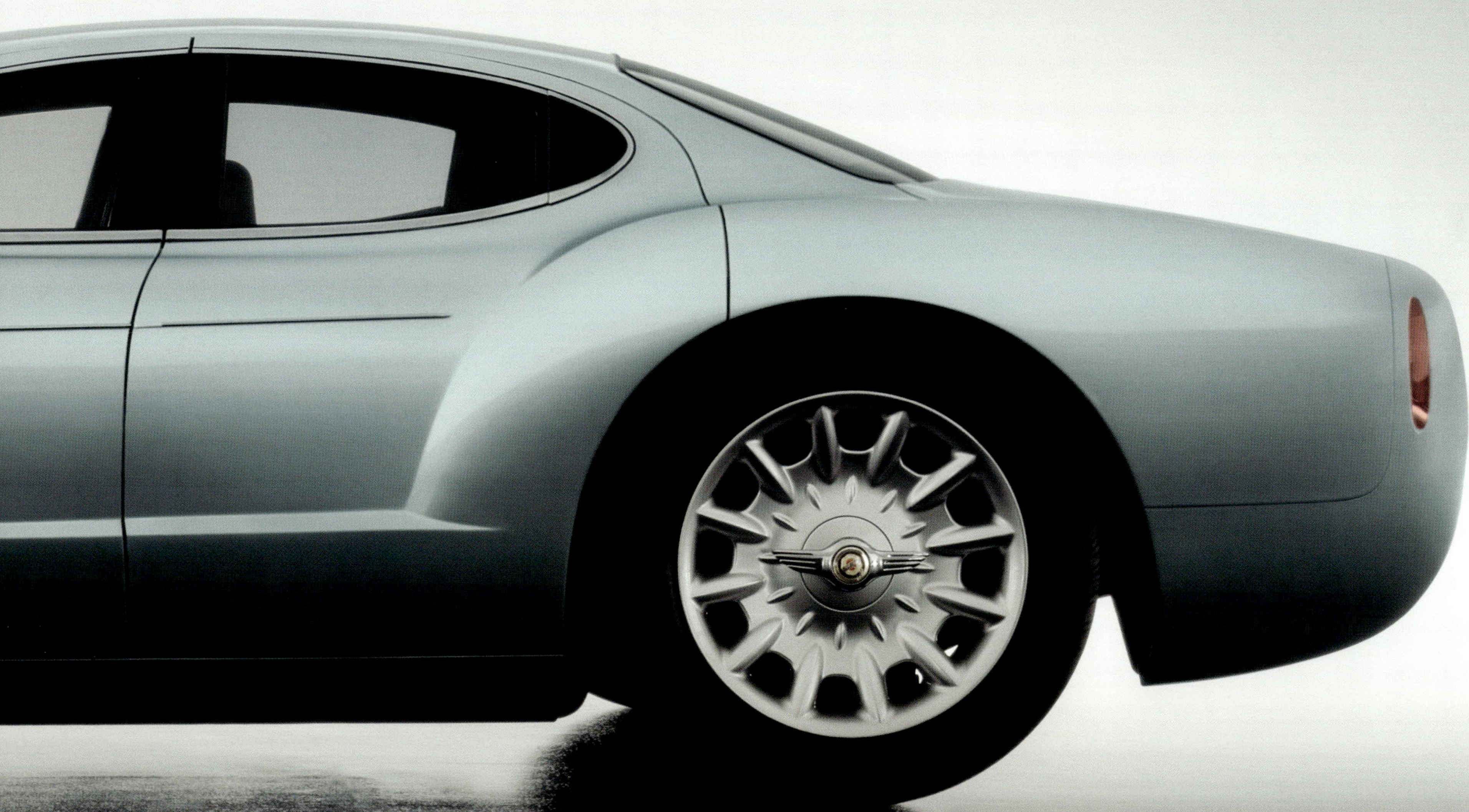

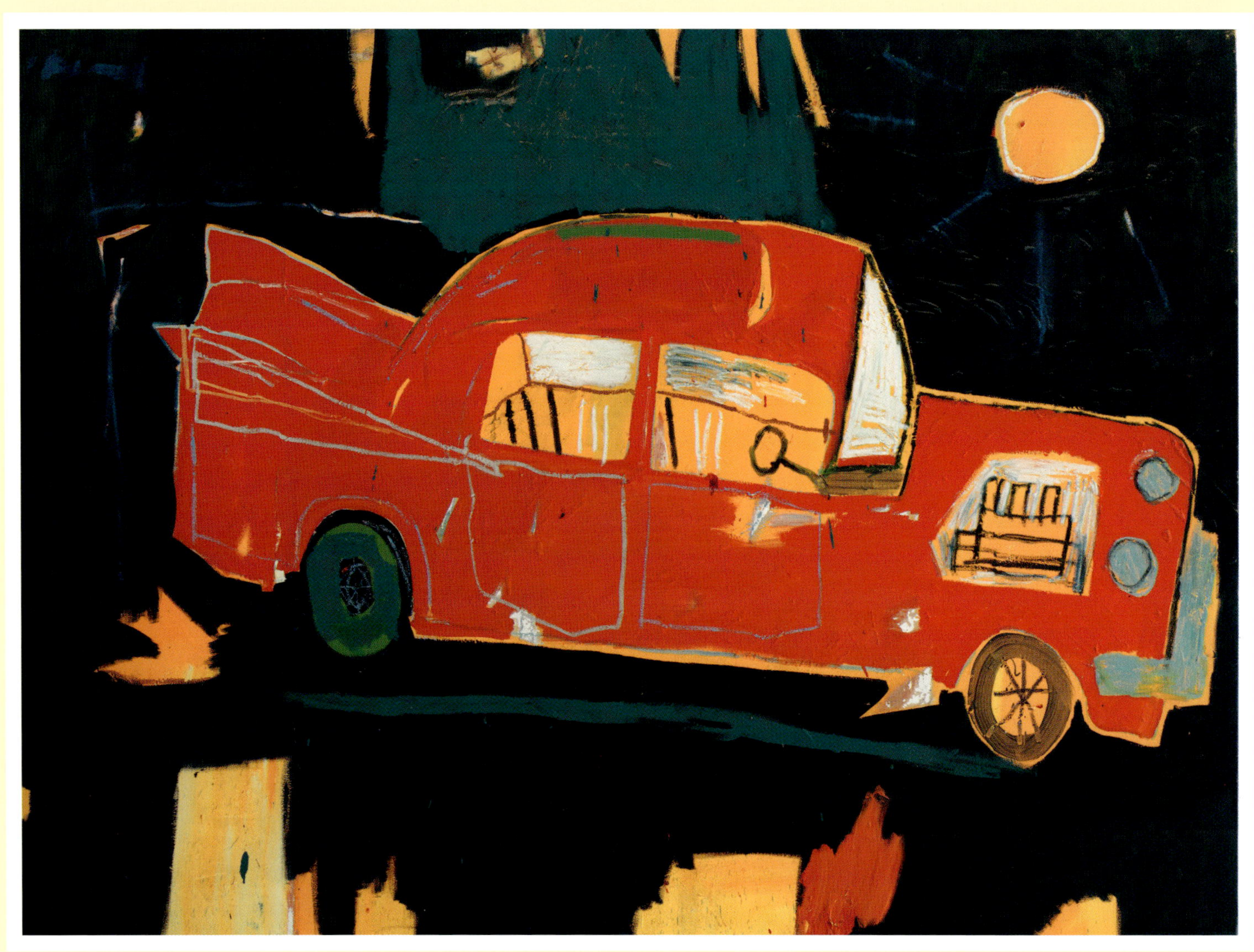

JEAN-MICHEL BASQUIAT

Rusting Red Car in Kuau, 1984, oil stick and oil on canvas. Courtesy of Vito Schnabel Gallery

The 1998 Chrysler Chronos concept car was produced amid an eclectic flourishing of design. In a period when multiple automotive vocabularies vied to capture the popular imagination, it harnessed the power of history.

The Chronos's elegant silhouette recalls Chrysler's experimental, Italian-inflected cars of the 1950s. The exterior styling was developed by Osamu Shikado, a Japanese designer who worked for the Toyota Motor Company before coming to Chrysler in 1994. His sketches show the influence of the 1953 Chrysler D'Elegance, which was the result of a collaboration between the legendary Chrysler designer Virgil Exner and the firm Carrozzeria Ghia in Turin.[1] Beginning in 1950 Exner looked to Ghia for the production of custom show cars based on drawings and clay models developed in a studio attached to his home in Birmingham, Michigan. The sumptuous curves and swept-back proportions of the cars created by Chrysler and Ghia in the early 1950s contrast with the muscular angularity of Exner's Forward Look cars from the same period, such as the 1957 300C.[2]

The Chronos also marked a departure from the unornamented, rounded, cab-forward designs pioneered at Chrysler in the 1980s and popularized for the mass market in the 1990s. Instead of the short hood and long cabin proportions of cars like the 1987 Lamborghini Portofino, the Chronos returned to earlier signals of power and strength. A long hood and curved front fenders surround the wheel well. The front end, with its integrated bumper punctuated by a rounded central grille, softens the pronounced lines of its predecessor. The curved, projecting rear fenders terminate in a low beltline running along the cabin that echoes an applied chrome line above, both emphasizing the dramatic length of the car. Together these features suggest the speed and strength of the machine.

The invocation of Exner's D'Elegance was tactical in the 1990s, as Chrysler looked to design to establish its credibility and heritage during a period of corporate uncertainty. Tom Gale, a designer who became executive vice president of Chrysler during the 1990s, used an ambitious program of concept cars to bolster the company's bona fides in the public eye.[3] John Herlitz, then Chrysler's vice president for product design, succinctly described the intent of the Chronos concept car: It was to be "a consummate design icon for the Chrysler brand."[4] Recalling historic design icons, it hinted at a direction the company would take in the future.

While the Chronos never went into production, retro design flourished at Chrysler in the 1990s with cars like the PT Cruiser (2001–10), Dodge Viper (concept debuted 1989, produced 1991–2017), and the Plymouth Prowler (concept debuted 1993, produced 1997, 1999–2002). The low cost of creating a concept car, compared with the tooling and scale required for a production car, had freed designers to play with radical ideas from eclectic sources. The Plymouth Prowler, for instance, began its life as a 1993 concept car experimenting with design motifs inspired by hot rods—vintage cars modified by drivers to create powerful and speedy machines with a menacing appearance; Gale himself, who had an affinity for classic American car culture, owned a custom hot rod based on a 1933 Ford. Its projecting front wheels reference the fenderless modifications made to early 1930s model cars.[5]

The Chronos and its peers reflect the powerful pull of nostalgic designs for consumers in the 1990s. Gale argued that "today, people want some kind of grounding, some heritage, a familiarity, even though things are changing."[6] This points to an ambivalence among the competing design vocabularies popular in Detroit studios during this period. A slate of new technologies, both inside and outside the studio, created the potential for a radical reimagining of automotive forms. New computer design tools, for example, made it faster and easier for a car to move from digital sketch to a mechanically milled 3-D model, and new engineering hinted at the viability of hybrid gas and electric engines.[7] The Chronos evoked romantic visions of the past, mining a glamorous period of Chrysler's heritage for ideas that would appeal to contemporary eyes. ❖

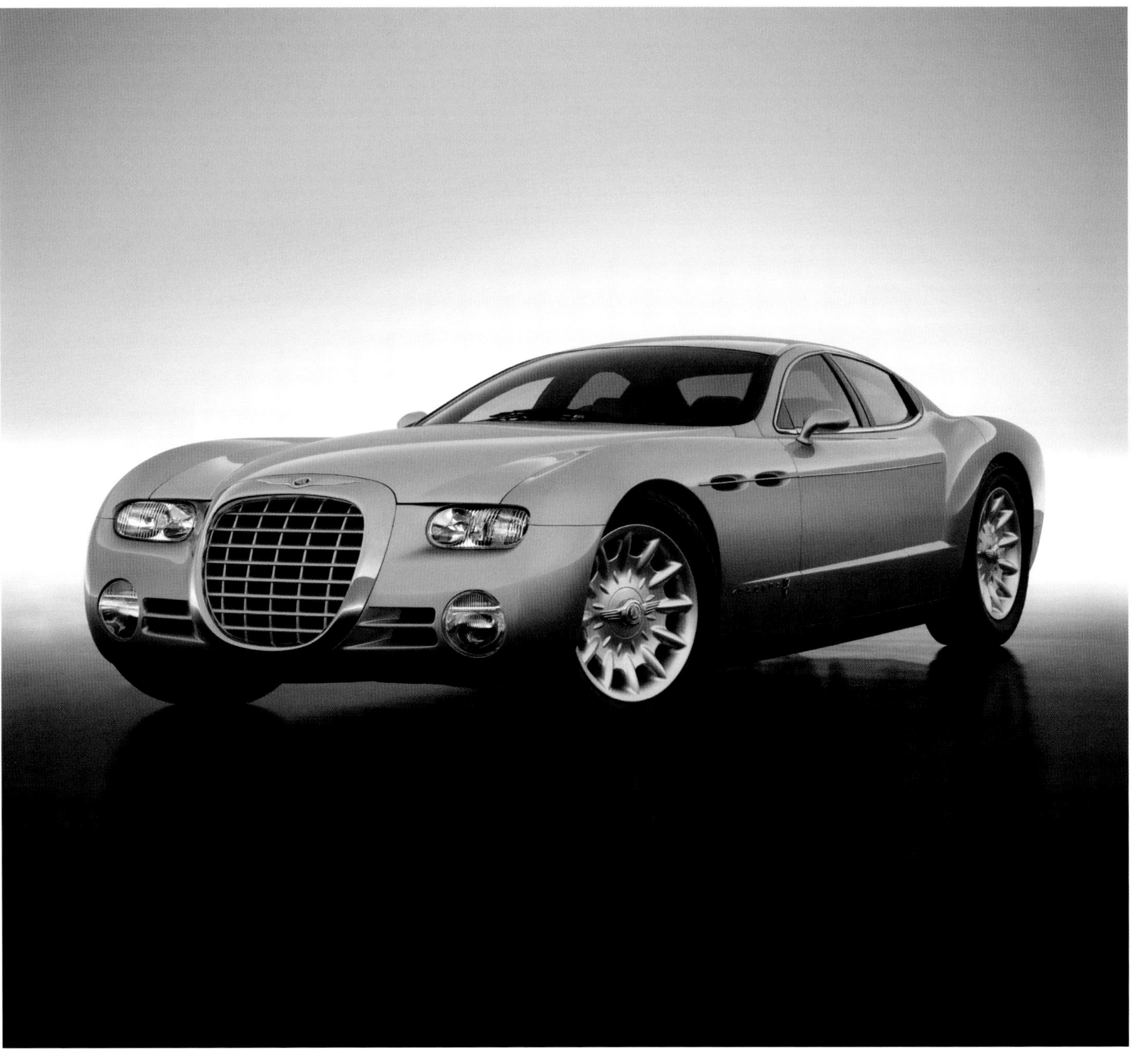

Chrysler Corporation, Chronos, 1998. *p. 110:* Front view (detail); *pp. 112–13:* Left side view; *above:* Front three-quarter view showing side ornament and fender modeling; *opposite:* Front view showing grille referencing 1950s Chrysler designs.

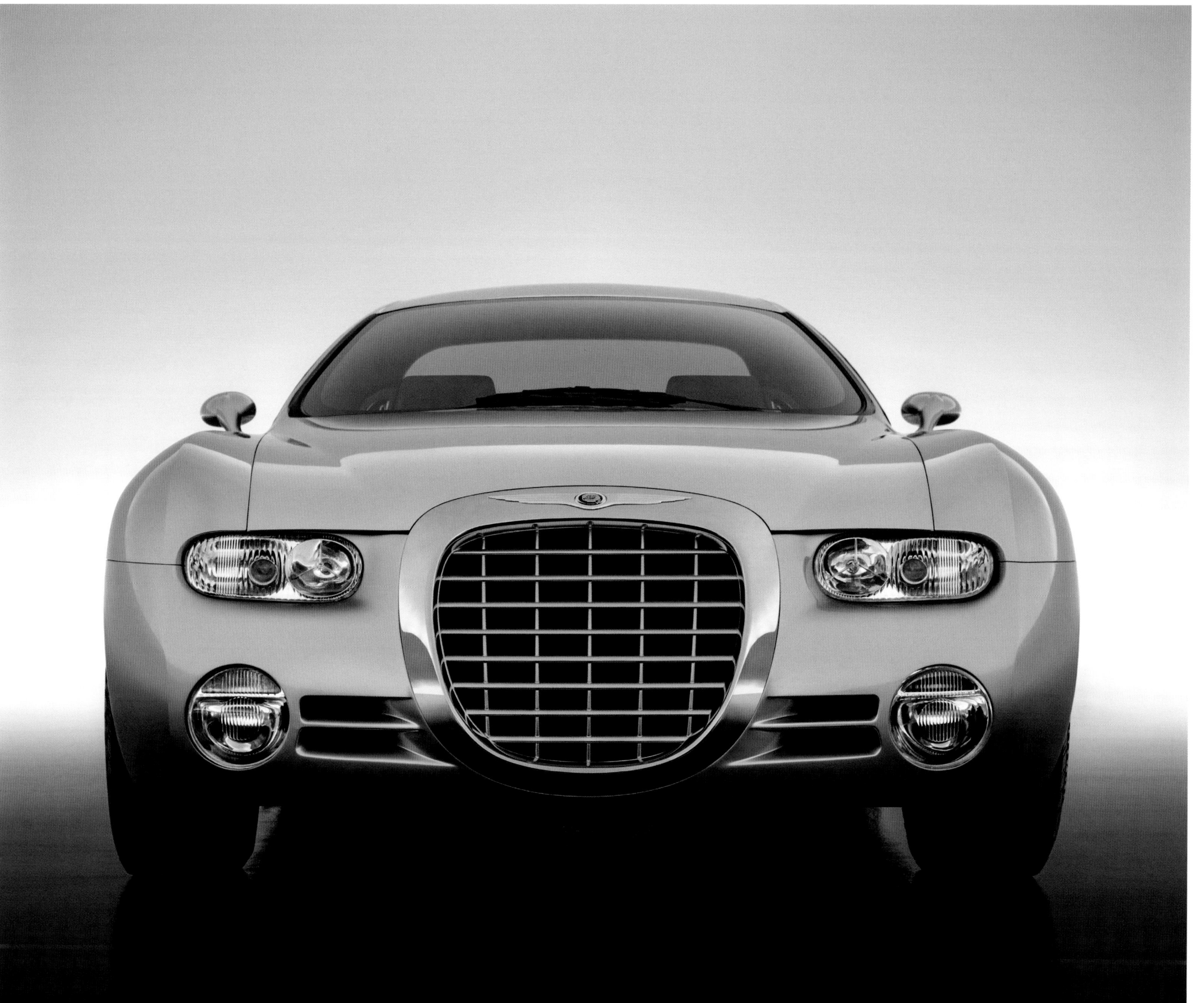

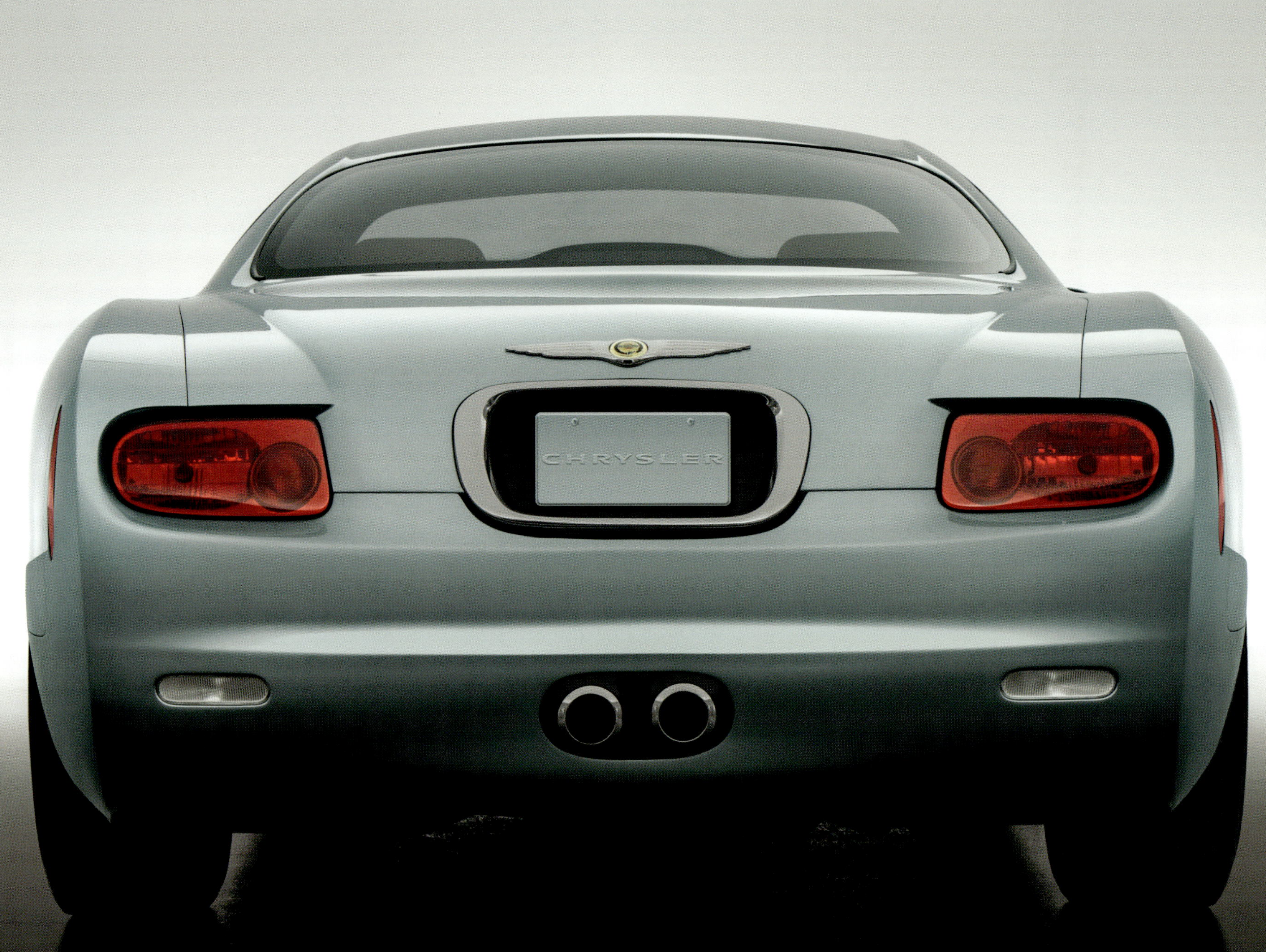
CHRYSLER

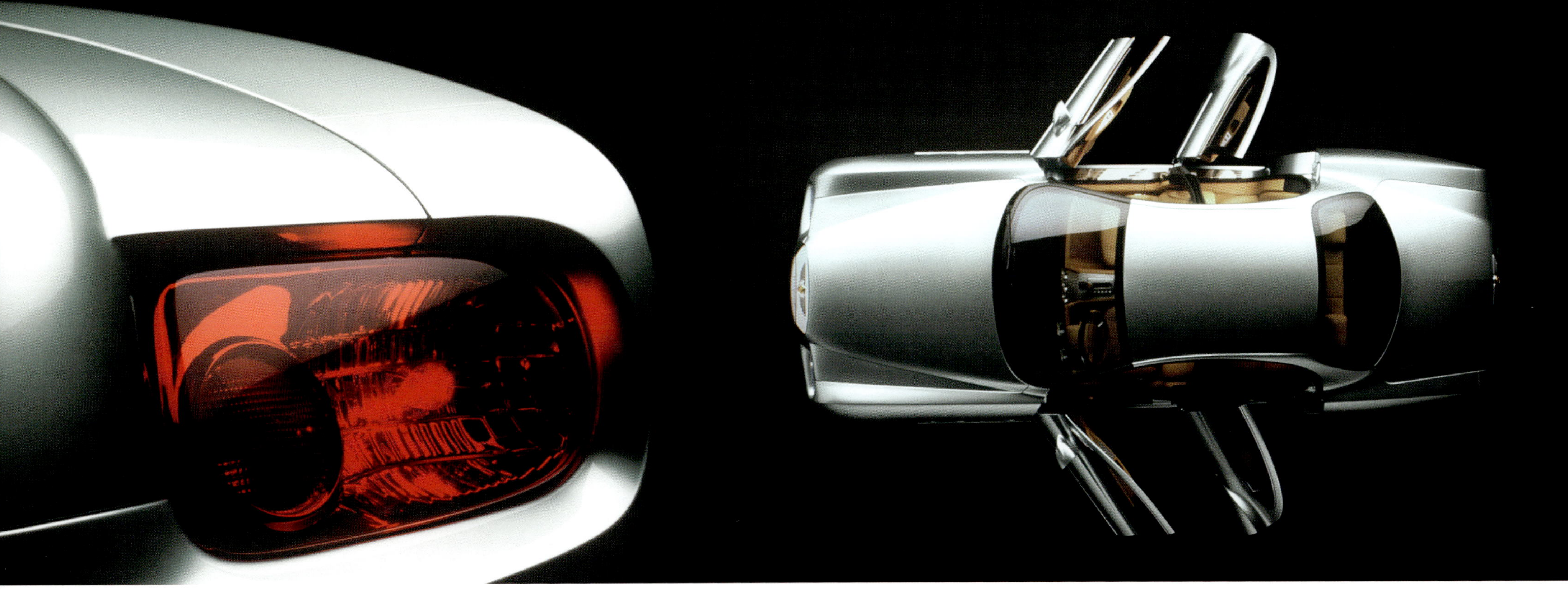

Chrysler Corporation, Chronos, 1998. *opposite:* Rear view; *above left:* Taillight; *above right:* Top view showing tapering body form.

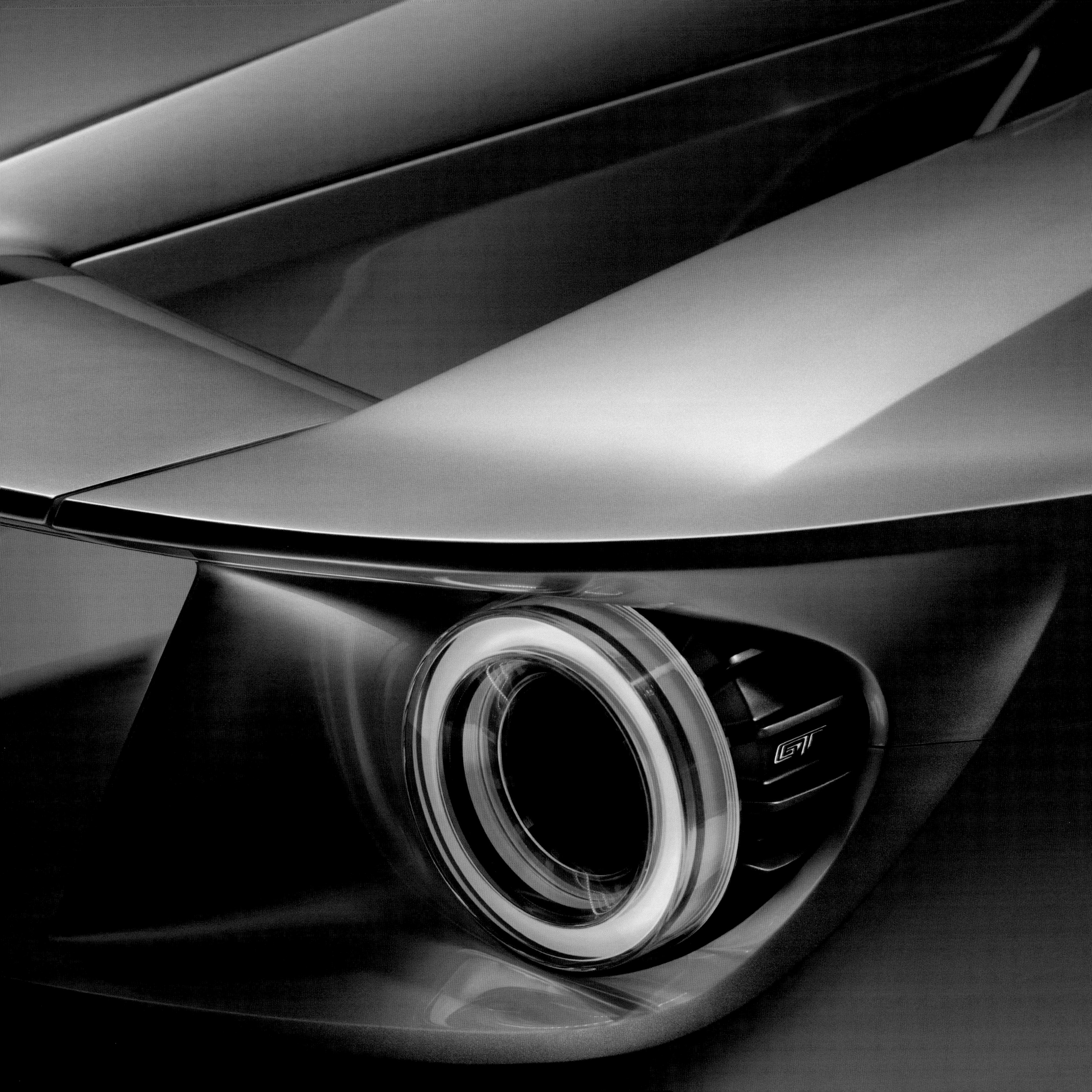
GT

2002
FORD GT CONCEPT

2017
FORD GT

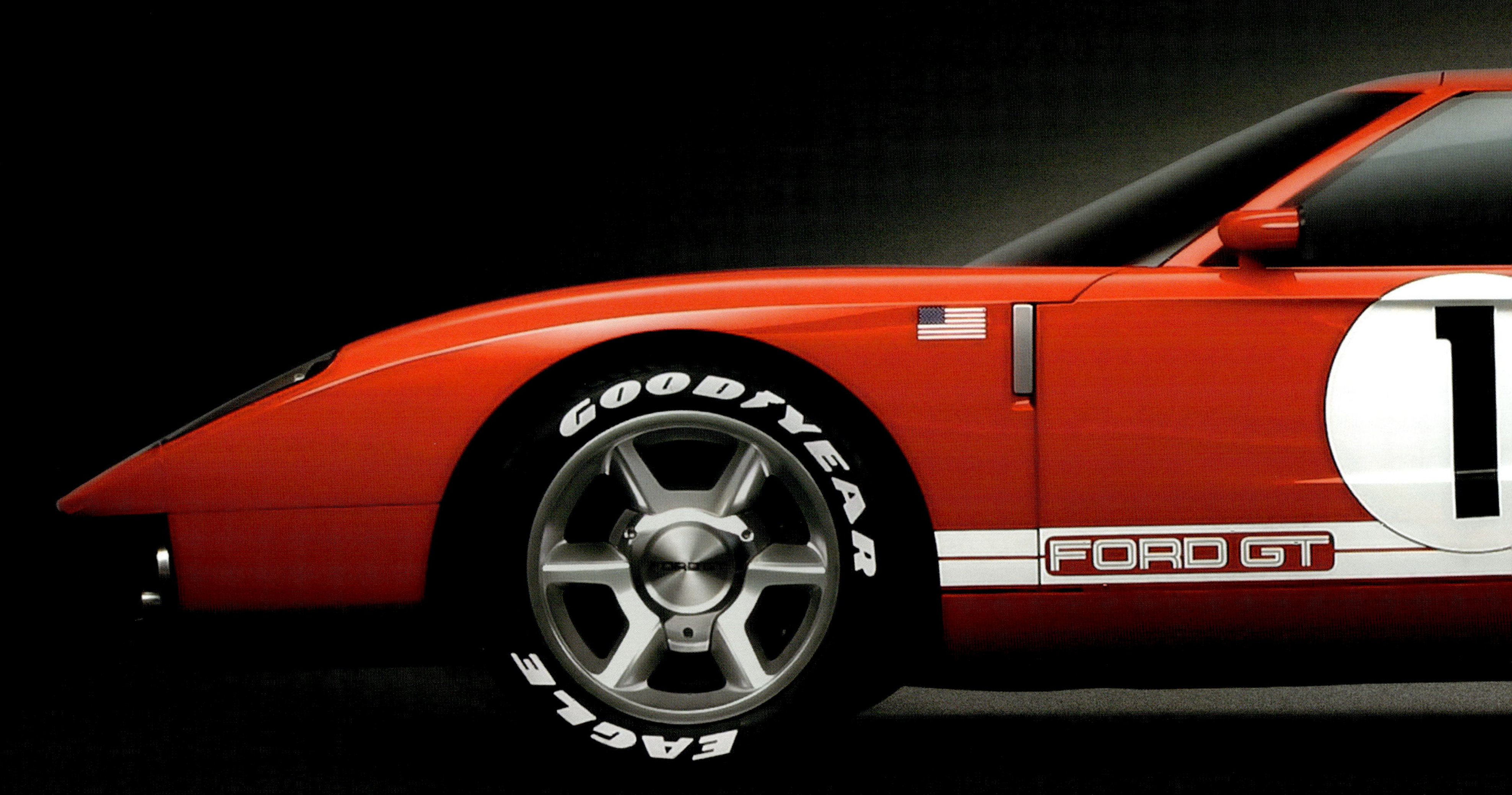
GOODYEAR
EAGLE
FORD GT

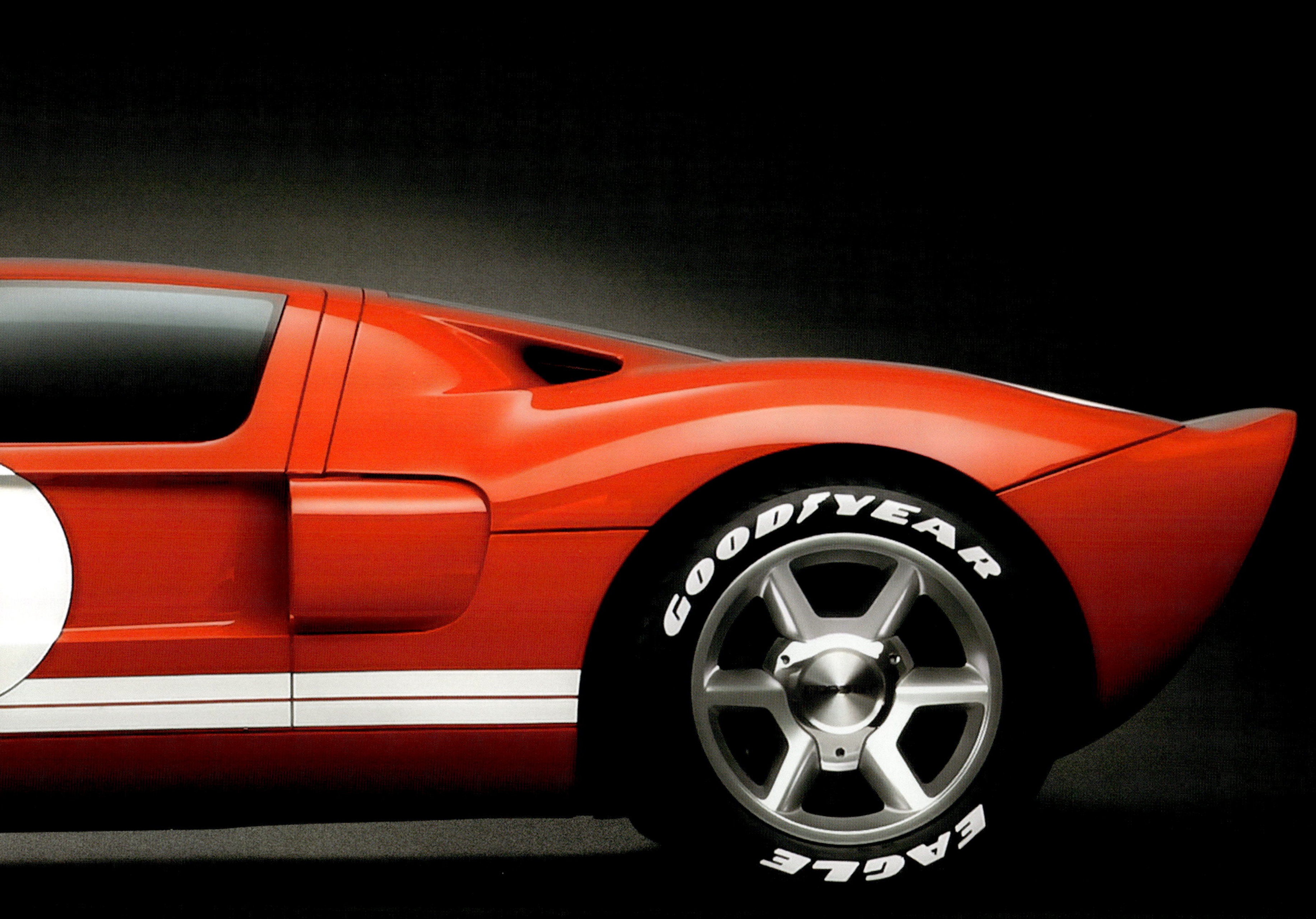
GOODYEAR
EAGLE

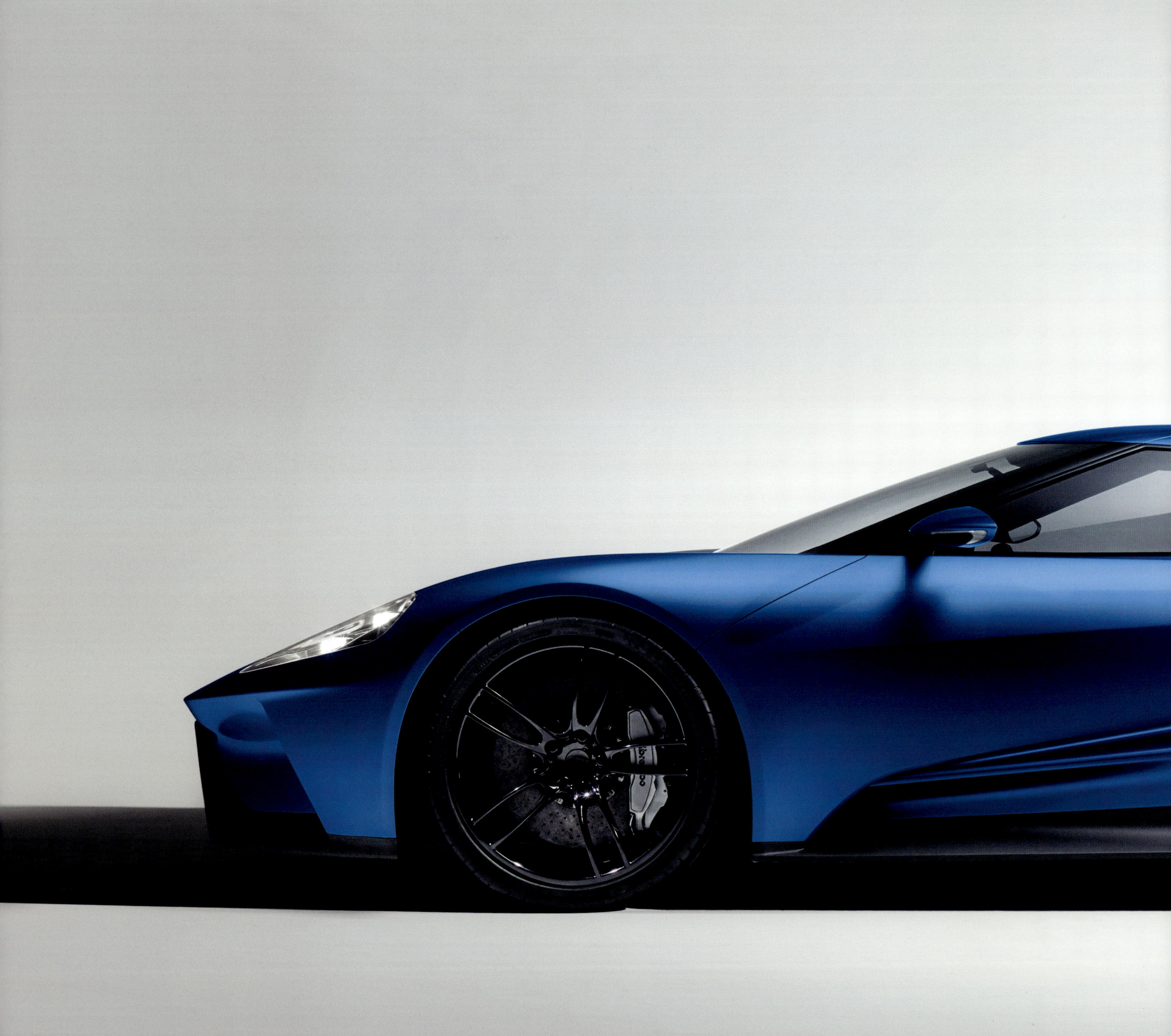

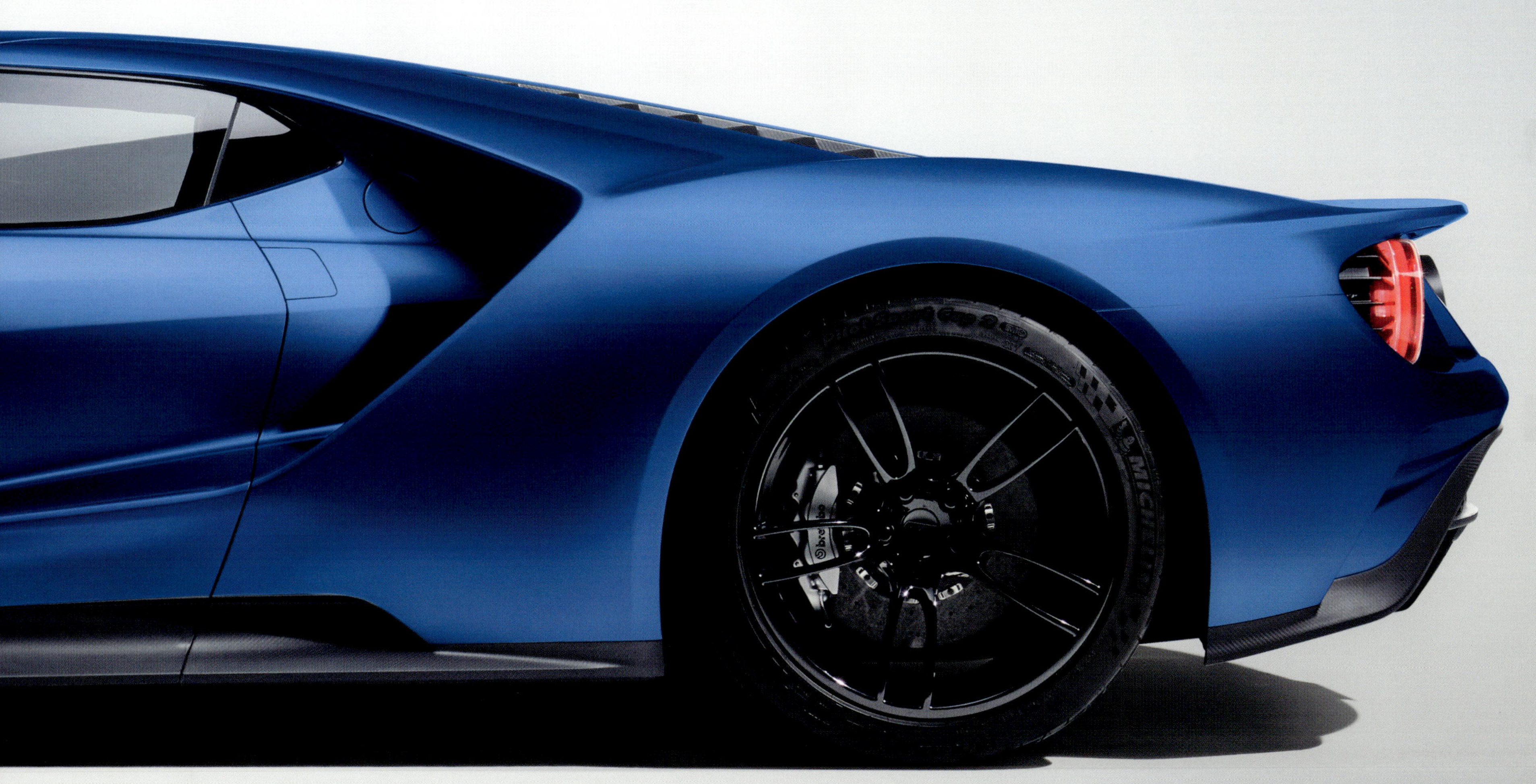
MICHELIN

RICHARD PRINCE

Pro Street, 1992–2002, fiberglass hood in two parts with Bondo, acrylic, flake paint, and enamel mounted on wooden frame

The original Ford GT was born of a 1960s rivalry. The fame of that race car inspired subsequent designers to revive and revisit its sleek and powerful proportions for reintroduced models. Together, these updated GTs offer different visions for how design history can shape contemporary forms.

In 1963 a group of Ford representatives traveled to Maranello, Italy, to negotiate the purchase of Enzo Ferrari's eponymous company. The deal was meant to energize Ford's racing profile and elevate its reputation for styling. When it collapsed late in the process, a feud was sparked between the two companies, and Ford became determined to break Ferrari's string of prominent victories in the most important car races. The result was a rapid program to develop a new race car at Ford Advanced Vehicles in England, led by legendary American designer and racer Carroll Shelby and the English racer John Wyer. Their team created the GT40 that won first, second, and third places in the twenty-four-hour Le Mans race in 1966, keeping Ferrari out of the winner's circle it had dominated in the early 1960s. The GT40 went on to take first at Le Mans from 1967 to 1969.[1] The 1966 GT40—a sleek and sinuous midengine design with a low-slung form and fluid curves that suggested a powerful machine—became an instant racing legend.

When Ford set out to celebrate its corporate centenary in 2003, a proposal was developed for a car that paid homage to the 1966 classic, layered with associations of power, machismo, and speed. As Ford product developer Chris Theodore said, the project appealed to design history to "polish the Ford oval to bring the luster back."[2] Overseen by Ford product developers Theodore and Richard Parry-Jones, and head of design J. Mays, the project was called Petunia to keep prying eyes away from the secretive special vehicles team studio where the car was being developed.

The revived GT needed to succeed on two fronts. It had to function as an innovative car whose speed, performance, and exotic appeal rivaled that of its European competitors, and it had to be legible as a Ford. The design was led by Camillo Pardo, whose first attempt updated the look of the classic GT40 to suit the modern sports car, with a profile that "was simpler, smooth, organized."[3] Initial proposals suggested a car similar to a number of high-end European sports cars of the day, but not enough like a Ford GT40. The design team's ultimate 2002 concept model hewed more closely to the lines of the 1966 car, with subtle updates. Introduced during a period of retrospective assessment of the company's design heritage, this car instantly called to mind the iconic form of its inspiration. By 2003 the initial concept design went into production. Three prototypes were produced in time for the June centennial celebration, in anticipation of a limited production run for the 2005 model year.[4]

The same pull of nostalgia that drew designers to the 1966 GT40 attracted the eyes of artists like Richard Prince (born 1949) to explore the narrative and form of American automotive history. In the 1980s Prince began a series of sculptures from fiberglass reproductions of parts of classic American muscle cars. Blurring the line between ready-made art object, minimalist sculpture, and pop art, works like his 1992–2002 *Pro Street* highlight the formal features, vernacular traditions, and lived beauty of the automobile (opposite). To him, a car hood was a "great thing that actually got painted out there, out there in real life. ... It got 'teen-aged.' Primed. Flaked. Stripped. Bondo-ed. Lacquered. Nine coats. Sprayed. Numbered. Advertised on. Raced."[5]

When Ford set out to reimagine the GT again for a 2015 public debut, it took a different approach. Moray Callum, vice president for design, described the project as a reinterpretation of the original GT with a contemporary vocabulary, saying, "if the GT40 emerged for the first time, today, this is how it would look."[6] Chris Svennsson, then design director for Ford in North America, said the goal was to capture the sensibility of the 1966 GT40, particularly with respect to the relationship between experimental materials and forms. While very different from midcentury molded plywood, the carbon fiber used for the GT's body and the lightweight aluminum of its substructure reflect a parallel meditation on the relationship between novel materials, streamlined function, and beautiful form.[7]

Like its predecessor, the GT supercar was developed in secret, in a basement studio at Ford's product development center in Dearborn. Only a small circle of designers and engineers were granted access to the space. The project began in late 2013, with the goal of exhibiting at the January 2015 North American International Auto Show in Detroit. The rapid progress from drawing to prototype meant that the car was a direct expression of the designer's hand. Callum observed, "There's certain areas of the car that are as sketched—we didn't over-sweat it. There's even a rawness to the car."[8]

The car that made its public debut in 2015 and went into limited production beginning in the 2017 model year is a muscular design that replicates some of the styling features of its 1960s predecessor but updates others in a radical departure from existing Ford cars. The curved front fenders and rounded bubble-like headlamps, for instance, recall the sleek forms of the original GT. The radically buttressed rear fenders extend away from the teardrop-shaped body. The car's swept-back lines and fragmented surfaces suggest an object in motion at extreme speed. Its form was developed in close collaboration with engineers and aerodynamicists, assuring that styling decisions would contribute to the car's racing prowess. Garen Nicoghosian described the form as a "collection of items that collect air, avoid air, or make better use of air."[9]

Considered together, the 2002 and 2015 Ford GTs offer different visions for how design history can shape contemporary forms. Implicit to both is the power and allure of high-speed racing in American culture. Although the everyday vehicles Americans drive are increasingly sport utility vehicles, trucks, or crossovers, the cars of the American imagination continue to recall Detroit's legacy of powerful muscle cars and sleek racers. The speed, energy, and danger of the sport are evoked by American artist Kristin Baker (born 1975) in a series of large-scale paintings inspired by the grand public spectacle and potential for chaotic danger in races staged for popular entertainment (opposite).

The 2002 GT concept takes direct formal inspiration from the past. With modest updates, the car reflects the general motifs and concept of its 1960s predecessors. The 2017 GT interprets the spirit of the 1960s with a radically different form making use of the possibilities of new materials. Its relationship to the past is through a shared sensibility. Each car offers a striking vision for the ways Detroit's history continues to resonate in the minds and eyes of designers, both as a formal vocabulary and as an attitude. ❖

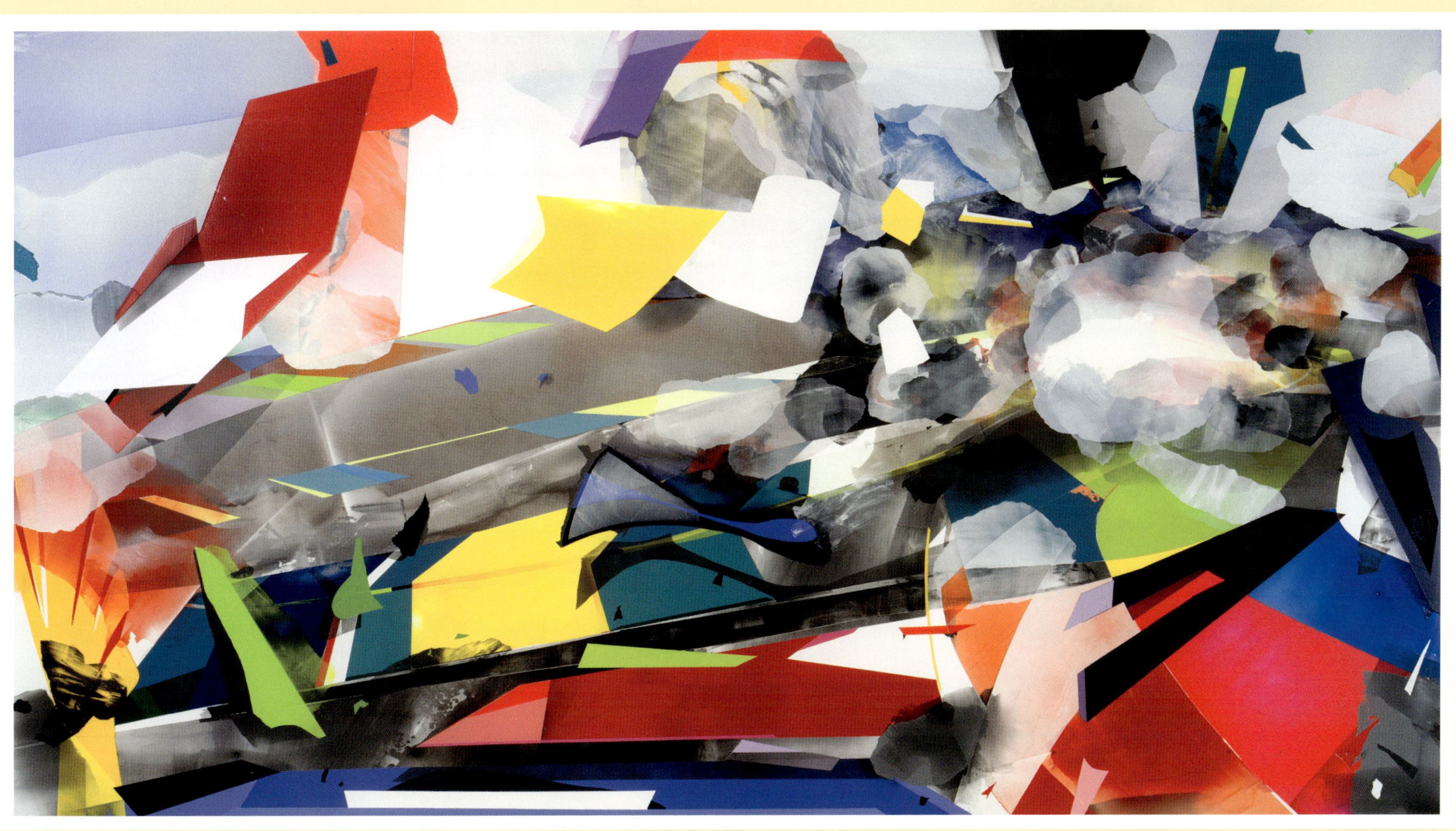

KRISTIN BAKER

The Unfair Advantage, 2003, acrylic on PVC board

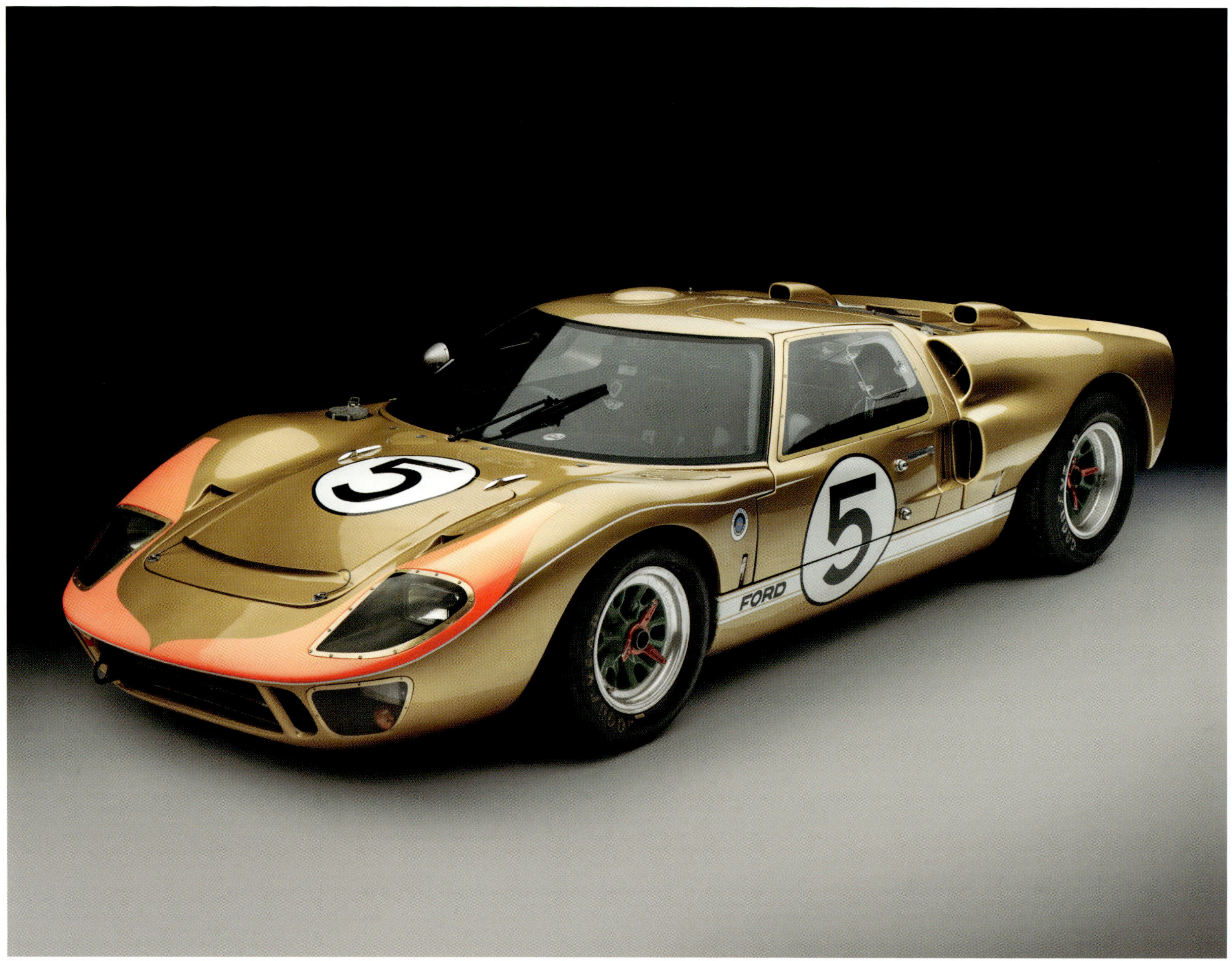

p. 120: Ford Motor Company, GT, 2017, front end (detail); *pp. 122–23:* Ford GT Concept, 2002, left side view; *pp. 124–25:* Ford GT, 2017, left side view; *above:* Ford GT40 Mk II, 1966; *opposite:* Ford GT, 2017, front view from above showing body's tapering teardrop shape.

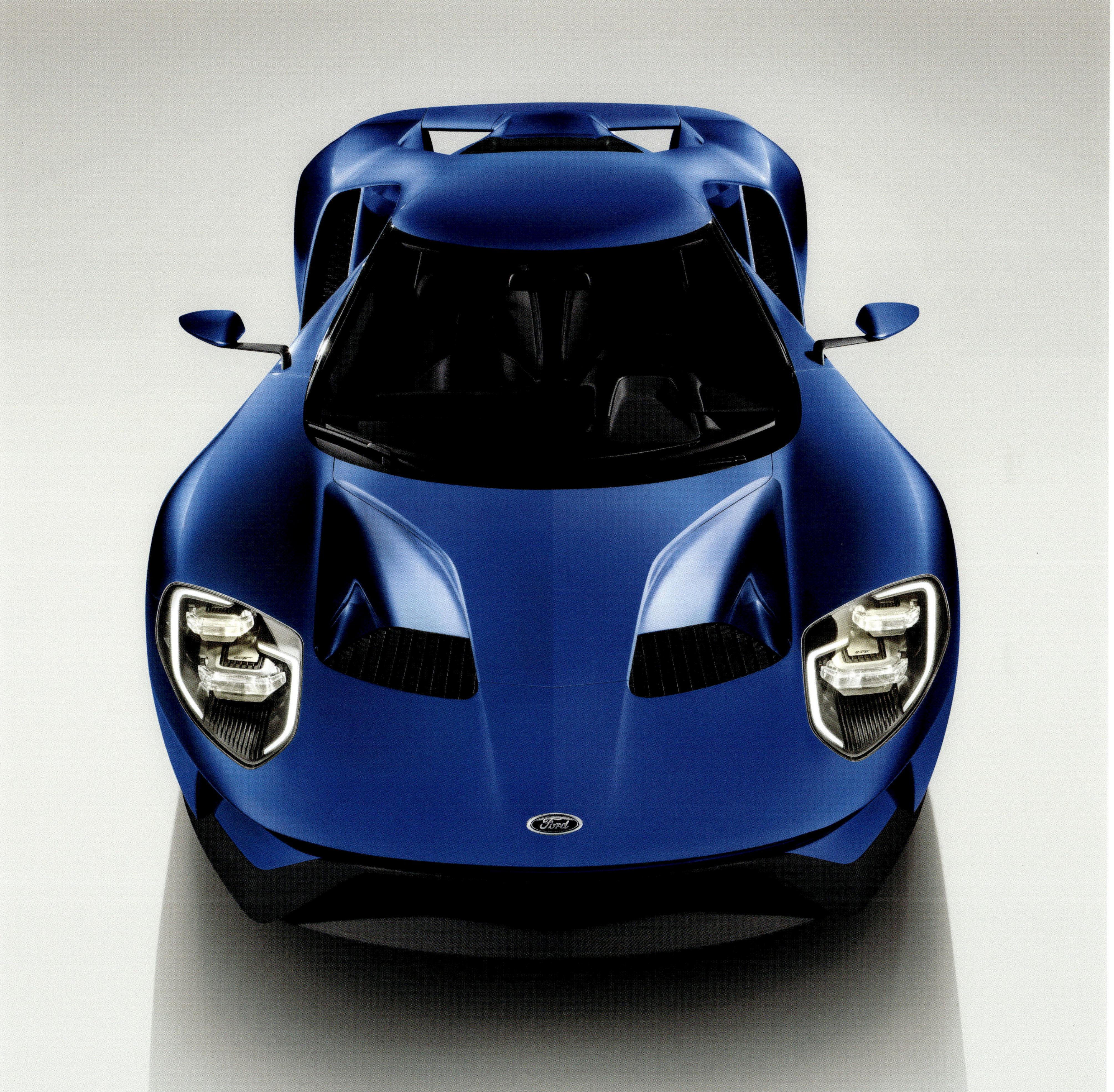
Ford

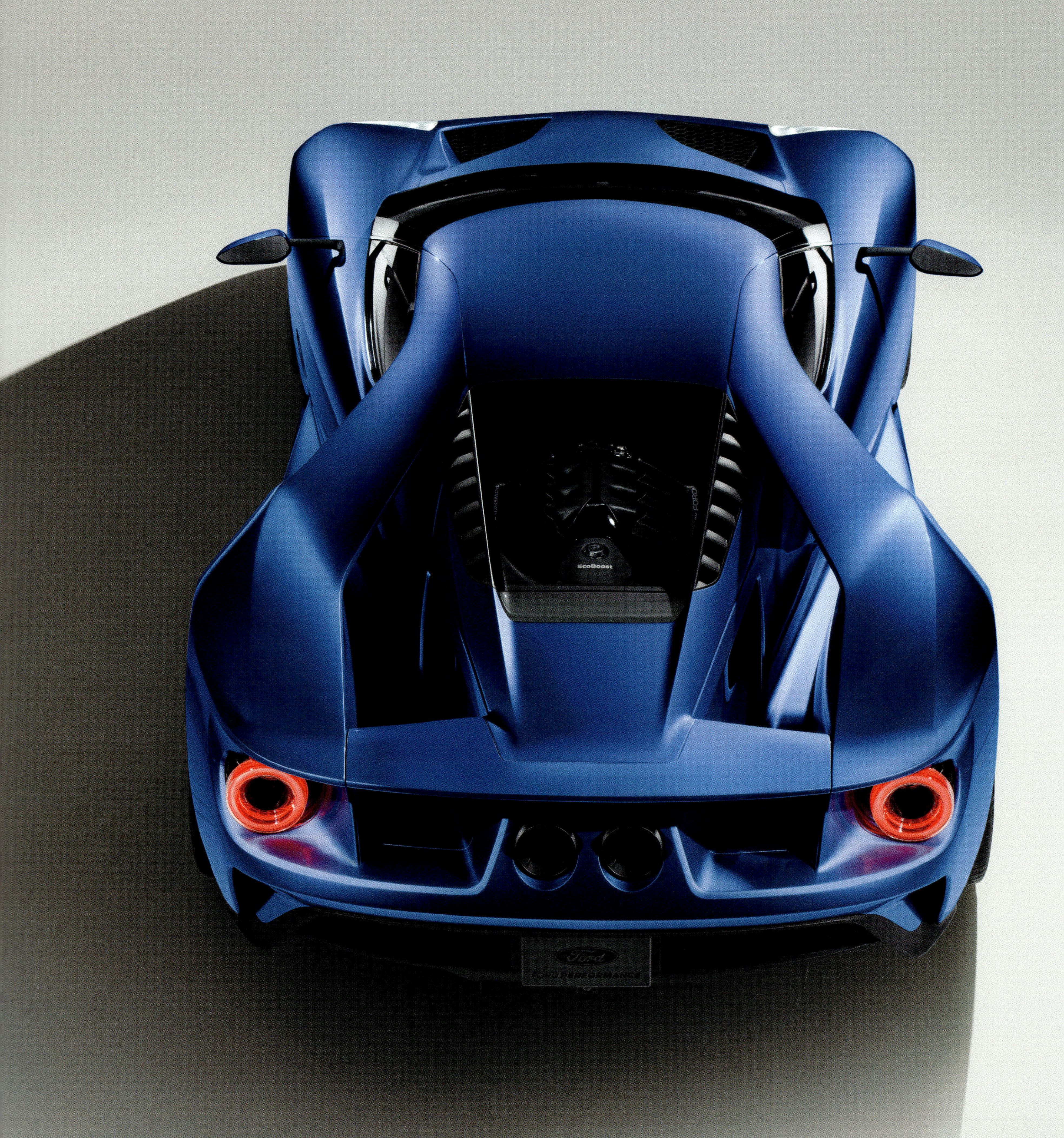
EcoBoost
Ford
FORD PERFORMANCE

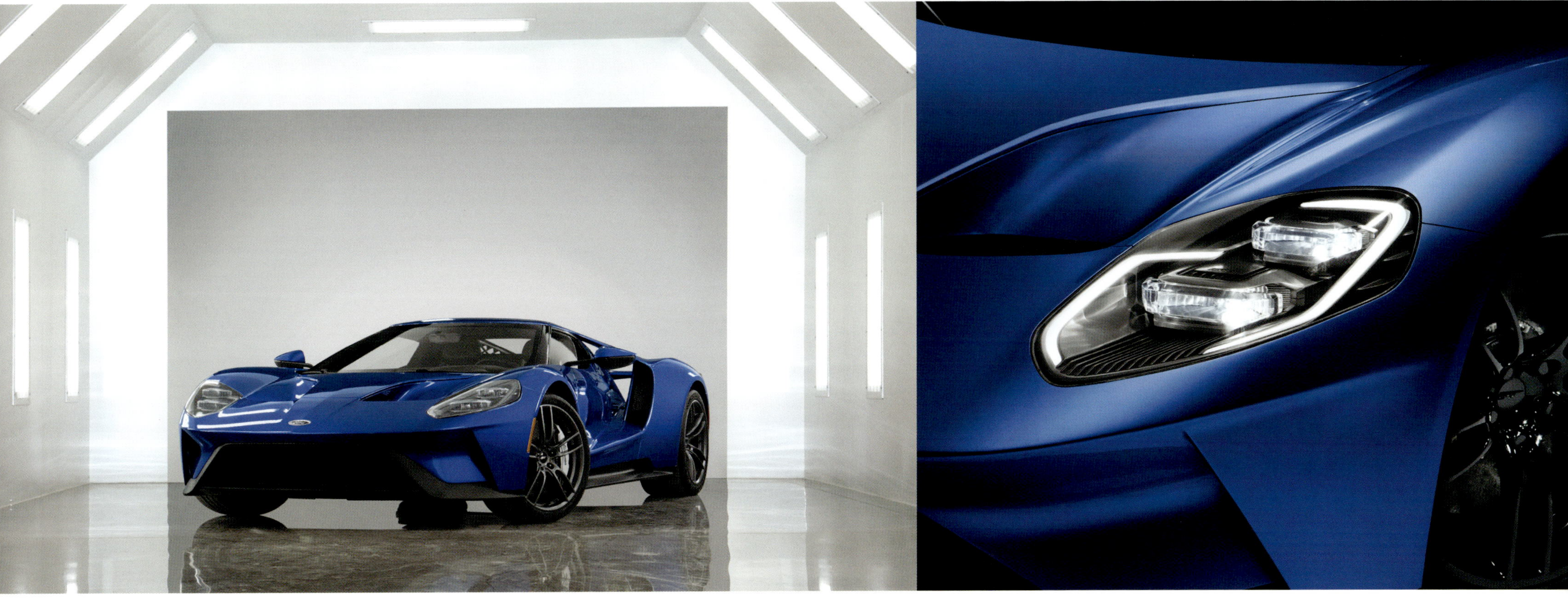

Ford Motor Company, GT, 2017. *opposite:* Rear view from above showing buttress support around rear wheels; *above left:* Front three-quarter view showing rear fender buttress; *above right:* Headlamp.

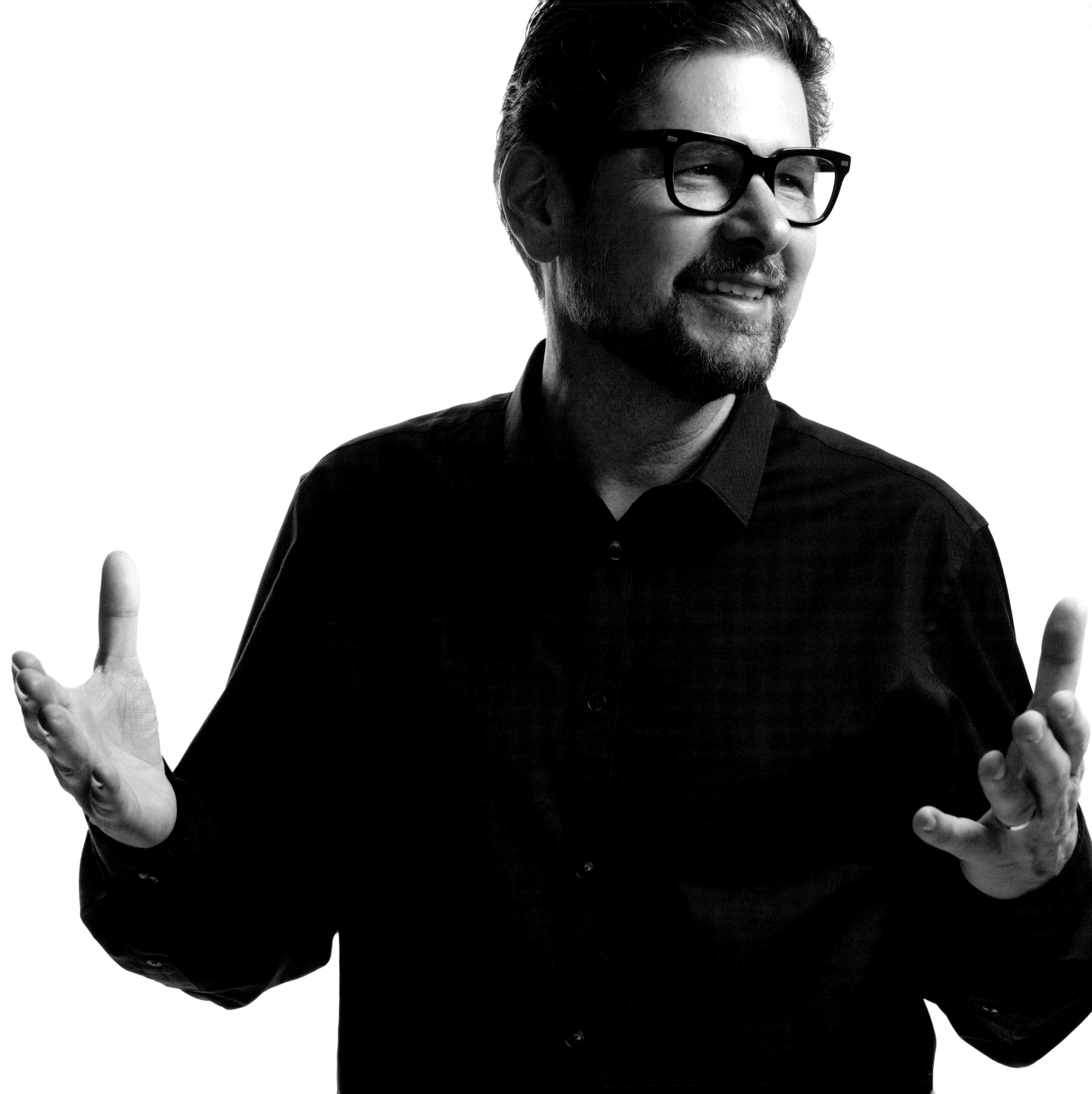

INTERVIEW WITH CRAIG METROS

Craig Metros is the director of exterior design for the Americas at the Ford Motor Company, a position he has held since 2014. A native of Dearborn, he has worked at Ford since 1986.

Benjamin W. Colman: At what age did you know you wanted to be a car designer?

Craig Metros: I knew really early on. My dad was an engineer for General Motors and he was taking me to car shows before I could walk. I've been making art and drawing as long as I can remember, and I was sketching cars as far back as second grade.

BC: Did your family only drive GM cars?

CM: We did. I grew up in Dearborn, and we were the only family in the neighborhood to have GM cars in the driveway. I remember my dad bringing home Camaros, and my mom had a Corvette. We lived about four blocks from the Ford product development center, and I would see all the latest Fords coming out—cars camouflaged, mule cars, prototype cars. I thought that was the coolest thing in the world. Seeing it all at a very early age had a big influence on me.

BC: When it came time to go to college, did you know you wanted to go to design school?

CM: I knew I wanted to design cars. I wasn't sure I would be able to because I thought it would be very engineering heavy, and I was horrible at math. But in about seventh grade I started entering a design-the-car-of the-future contest sponsored by the National Hot Rod Association. My senior year of high school I won first place and got a small scholarship to the Center for Creative Studies in Detroit, now the College for Creative Studies. I started CCS in 1981. We were in a bit of a recession at the time, and auto companies weren't hiring. I was told immediately to be sure I had a diverse portfolio so that if there were no automotive jobs when I graduated, I could work in other areas of design.

BC: What other types of design did you study?

CM: My first studio class was actually furniture design. I remember thinking, "What am I doing?," but by the end I absolutely loved it. That opened my eyes to other aspects of design, especially industrial design. In the automotive industry we are constantly looking at things that are happening in fashion, product design, industrial design. Those are a huge influence on what we do in the car studio.

BC: When you finished your degree in 1986, did you go directly to Ford?

CM: I did. In 1984 I had a summer internship at Chrysler. Then, in 1985, I had an internship at the Ford Ghia studio in Turin. That was huge. I had never been out of the United States before. I came back to finish my senior year, but from that point on I wanted to live and work in Europe. So I completed my senior year, finished my portfolio, and started interviewing. I hired in at Ford in 1986 and in 1987 they sent me back to the Ghia studio in Turin for eight months. I absolutely loved it. I've moved around my entire career—the United Kingdom, Italy, Germany, Japan, and Australia. I spent a total of seventeen years overseas, which is more time than I have spent in Dearborn.

BC: What was your career trajectory within Ford?

CM: I bounced around quite a bit at first. As time went on I became more of an exterior guy, but I never minded being put on an interior. Car design is holistic. I find the exterior to be a bit more on the emotional side and interiors much more challenging. On the exterior you're dealing with the shape, but in the interior there are a thousand more parts and it needs to interface with the human. It needs to look great, feel great, function great. To me it's far more intricate.

BC: When I think of Ford in the 1980s, I think of a very rational and functional design ethos for the aerodynamic cars coming out of the design studio. Was that something that drew you to the company?

CM: Cars like the Ford Topaz, the Ford Taurus, the Ford Thunderbird, and the Mercury Sable had just hit the market when I was hired. They had a big influence on me.

BC: I'd like to hear about your relationship as a designer to design history and to brand and corporate history within Ford. When you're creating a new car, how do you set about engaging with the history of that model?
CM: Car design is becoming much more about strategic thinking, and leveraging our brand is now a big deal. For me heritage is a big thing. I love classic cars and have a few old cars in the garage. I enjoy looking to the past and seeing what we can pull into our current products, making sure there's a lineage, a DNA, that extends through them. That gives the products a bit of soul.

BC: What Fords from the past influenced the cars coming out of the studio today?
CM: If you were to talk to a group of car designers, the 1966 GT40 would probably be in the top five or ten cars. The Ford GT is the holy grail of cars. It's a huge piece of racing history, and having the chance to work on the modern interpretation of that car is every car designer's dream. In 2001 Ford in Dearborn started doing a new generation GT40. I wasn't involved in the project. The concept model came out in 2002, and then it was announced that during our hundred-year anniversary we would be bringing back the GT for production years 2005 and 2006. It was a car that really paid homage to our heritage. It was retro and looked like the original GT40.

When the 2015 Ford GT project began, I had just come back from Australia and assumed the role of the North American design director for exteriors. The challenge with the 2015 car was incorporating the latest technology. This car needed to be innovative. With race cars it's all about air management, down force, how you direct the air over and under the car. It's one thing to hit those numbers functionally, but we also wanted to make sure the car was drop-dead gorgeous. Even if you walked into a room and didn't see the badge on the car, we wanted it to visually resonate as a GT40. The goal was to capture the spirit of that original car in a very modern, state-of-the-art race car. Aesthetically it is very different from the original GT40, but the lamp shapes, air outlet ducts in the front, round taillights, and the way the C-pillar is executed—in my mind it visually resonates as a Ford GT.

BC: How did the orientation and placement of the rear wheels, buttressed out from the body, come to be?
CM: If you look at the GT40 and then the 2005–6 car, there are two air intakes right in front of the rear wheel—a lower intake and an upper intake. In gestural sketches from the studio, those intakes started to get bigger and bigger until they became one.

At the time we were starting to learn about the packaging and the layout of the chassis and motor. The car is all carbon fiber, so it has this carbon fiber tub that's actually part of the chassis, the structure. We were using a V-6 EcoBoost engine that is extremely narrow. Looking at this layout in plan view, we realized we were basically developing a teardrop shape, which is the most aerodynamic shape in the world—it's perfectly clean. We put the car in the wind tunnel and confirmed the shape worked. The buttress is also functional. The outer quarter panels that are now separated house the oil coolers and duct through the buttress back into the engine compartment.

BC: What are the cars or technologies you're most excited about in the near future?
CM: When you start to talk about the car driving itself and no longer having an internal combustion engine, that's a whole different way of thinking for the industry and for designers. There are two schools of thought. You've got people who are skeptical and are going to miss the internal combustion engine, and you've got people who are really excited for the future and the technology. I'm a bit of both. I love the old cars, the race cars, the V-8 engine, the sound, the smell, all of that. But I've also driven electric cars, and they're awesome. The performance is fantastic, superefficient, clean.

Car designers are pretty passionate people, myself included. I'm really excited for some of the technologies and materials we have coming because it's allowing us to do things we weren't able to do fifteen or twenty years ago. The GT is a great example. We couldn't have created that car if it was done in the traditional way, if we were stamping sheet metal. It was the technology of the carbon fiber that allowed us to do the tunnel and the buttress and all these extreme shapes. That's how I look at the future. I see it as exciting, allowing us to do really great things.

This July 3, 2019, interview has been edited and condensed.

Introduction

[1] Arthur Drexler, *8 Automobiles* (New York: Museum of Modern Art, 1951), n.p.

1951 General Motors Le Sabre

[1] William Knoedelseder, *Fins: Harley Earl, the Rise of General Motors, and the Glory Days of Detroit* (New York: Harper Business, 2018), 61–4.
[2] Sally Clarke, "Managing Design: The Art and Colour Section at General Motors, 1927–1941," *Journal of Design History* 12, no. 1 (1999): 65–79; David Gartman, "Harley Earl and the Art and Color Section: The Birth of Styling at General Motors," *Design Issues* 10, no. 2 (Summer 1994): 3–26; Michael Lamm, "The Beginning of Modern Auto Design," *Journal of Decorative and Propaganda Arts* 15 (Winter–Spring 1990): 60–77. [3] David W. Temple, *The Cars of Harley Earl* (Forest Lake, MN: CarTech, 2016), 47–48. [4] Karl Ludvigsen, "Two GM Showsters That Startled the Fabulous Fifties: Le Sabre and XP-300," *Special Interest Autos* (April–May 1973): 22–27; Temple, *The Cars of Harley Earl*, 53.
[5] "'Sabre' Is the Car of the 1960s," *Life*, January 1, 1960, 60–61. [6] Ludvigsen, "Two GM Showsters," 23–24; Michael Lamm, "1951 GM LeSabre: The Future Was Then," *Special Interest Autos* 158 (March–April 1997): 20–27, 66–67.
[7] David Temple, *Motorama: GM's Legendary Show and Concept Cars* (North Branch, MN: CarTech, 2015), 22; Lamm, "1951 GM LeSabre," 22.
[8] *Styling: The Look of Things* (Detroit: General Motors, 1955), from the Collections of The Henry Ford, 90.48.4. [9] Gartman, "Harley Earl," 12.

1957 Chrysler 300C

[1] Richard Langworth, "SIA Profile: Virgil Exner," *Special Interest Autos* 72 (December 1982): 22–27; David Gartman, *Auto-Opium: A Social History of American Automobile Design* (New York: Routledge, 1994), 147–48. William B. Harris, "Chrysler's Private Depression," *Fortune*, 1958, http://fortune.com/2014/01/05/chryslers-private-depression-fortune-1958/; Peter Grist, *Virgil Exner: Visioneer* (Poundbury, UK: Veloce, 2007), 72.
[2] The campaign was named by the New York advertising firm McCann Erickson, which issued a copyright for a string of "Forward Look" slogans in late 1954. [3] Grist, *Virgil Exner*, 78. [4] Richard Rutter, "Chrysler Leaves 1954 Far Behind," *New York Times*, May 8, 1955. [5] Harris, "Chrysler's Private Depression"; Kenneth Rudeen, "The New Models Wheel In," *Sports Illustrated*, October 20, 1958, 66.
[6] Virgil Exner, "Styling and Aerodynamics," Detroit Section, Society of Automotive Engineers, Greenbrier Meeting, White Sulphur Springs, WV, September 14, 1957. [7] Grist, *Virgil Exner*, 71–75.
[8] Gartman, *Auto-Opium*, 150.

1958 General Motors Firebird III

[1] "1953 Firebird I," Collection, General Motors Heritage Center, https://www.gmheritagecenter.com/gm-vehicle-collection/1953_Firebird_I.html, accessed October 12, 2018; Paul J. C. Friedlander, "Two New Engines," *New York Times*, December 9, 1956; "1953 Firebird II," Collection, General Motors Heritage Center, https://www.gmheritagecenter.com/gm-vehicle-collection/1953_Firebird_II.html, accessed October 12, 2018; "Imagination in Motion," General Motors (1958), The Benson Ford Research Center, 90.7.2. [2] Norman J. James, *Of Firebirds and Moonmen* (n.p. 2007), 104. [3] "XP-73 Firebird III (Running Car)" memo, December 2, 1957, General Motors Design Archive and Special Collections.
[4] James, *Firebirds*, 123. [5] James, *Firebirds*, 104.
[6] "First of the 1959 Cars," *Popular Science*, October 1958, 83. [7] "The '59 Caddy: Traditional Luxury in a Flamboyant Package," *Popular Science*, October 1958, 88–9, 244.

1959 Custom Stingray Racer

[1] Damon Stetson, "Personality: He Tapped 'Gas' in His Blood," *New York Times*, February 7, 1960.
[2] "Corvette Shows the Way for Plastic Cars," *Life*, January 4, 1954, 71; Leo Donovan, "Detroit Listening Post," *Popular Mechanics*, April 1955, 100; Ken W. Purdy, "New Corvette Challenges Thunderbird and Hawk," *Popular Science*, February 1956, 136–39.
[3] Peter Brock, *Corvette Stingray: Genesis of an American Icon*, 2nd ed. (Henderson, NV: Brock Racing Enterprises, 2017), 67–113; Ken Gross and Ronald Labaco, *The Allure of the Automobile* (Atlanta: High Museum of Art, 2010), 116. [4] Brock, *Corvette Stingray*, 69. [5] Brock, *Corvette Stingray*, 41–85.
[6] Brock, *Corvette Stingray*, 67–113: Gross and Labaco, *Allure of the Automobile*, 116.

1966 Oldsmobile Toronado

[1] GM Styling Staff Program Planning, "Timing Highlights of the 1966 'E' Body Program at G.M. Styling Staff," July 12, 1965, General Motors Design Archives. [2] "Oldsmobile to Make Car with Front-Wheel Drive," *New York Times*, July 14, 1965; Walter Rugaber, "Detroit Looks to Another Big Year," *New York Times*, October 17, 1965; William L. Mitchell, "The Toronado Takes Shape," *General Motors Engineering Journal* 13, no. 1 (First Quarter 1966): 22.
[3] Jim Dunne and Alex Markovich, "Coast to Coast in a Toronado," *Popular Mechanics*, December 1965, 76. [4] Mitchell, "Toronado Takes Shape," 23.
[5] Mitchell, "Toronado Takes Shape," 22–31; David North, phone conversation with author, November 11, 2018. [6] Mitchell, "Toronado Takes Shape," 22–31; North, November 11, 2018.

1967 Ford Mustang

[1] James Dinsmore and James Halderman, *Mustangs by Design: Gale Halderman and the Creation of Ford's Iconic Pony Car* (Forest Lake, MN: CarTech, 2018), 21–34. [2] *The Ford Book of Styling: A History and Interpretation of Automotive Design* (Dearborn: Ford Motor Company, 1963), 4, From the Collections of The Henry Ford, Dearborn.
[3] Joseph C. Ingraham, "Ford's 'Mustang' on Display Today," *New York Times*, April 17, 1964; "New Ford Mustang," advertisement, *Ebony*, July 1964, 32.
[4] "Specialty Models Pacing Auto Sales," *New York Times*, June 19, 1967. [5] Colin Date, *Original Mustang, 1967–1970: The Restorer's Guide*, 18–22; Ford Motor Company, "Three New Ways to Answer the Call of the Mustang ... Mustang '67," From the Collections of The Henry Ford, Dearborn.

1970 Plymouth Barracuda

[1] Peter Grist, *Dodge Challenger and Plymouth Barracuda: Chrysler's Potent Pony Cars* (Poundbury, UK: Veloce, 2007), 8–36. [2] Grist, *Challenger and Barracuda*, 37–70; Antonick interview with author, April 2, 2018. [3] Antonick, April 2, 2018; Grist, *Challenger and Barracuda*, 71–76. [4] Grist, *Challenger and Barracuda*, 71–75; Milton Antonick interview with author, March 20, 2018.
[5] Ron Eyerman and Orvar Lofgren, "Romancing the Road: Road Movies and Images of Mobility," *Theory, Culture, and Society* 12, no. 53 (1995): 53–79.
[6] Julie Sylvester, "Auto/Bio: Conversations with John Chamberlain," in Sylvester, *John Chamberlain: A Catalogue Raisonné of the Sculpture, 1954–1985* (New York: Hudson Hills in association with the Museum of Contemporary Art, Los Angeles, 1986), 15. [7] E. W. Kenworthy, "Conferees Back Car Fumes Curb," *New York Times*, December 17, 1970.
[8] "Detroit's Sporty Cars Are Due to Be Sportier," *New York Times*, February 15, 1970.

1983 Ford Probe IV

[1] Donald F. Kopka remarks, Ford Probe V press conference, August 20, 1985, Ford Motor Company Technical and Regulatory Affairs, Dearborn.
[2] Herbert Shuldiner, "Probe IV," *Popular Science*, March 1983, 64–66. [3] Phil Patton, "The Shape of Ford's Success," *New York Times Magazine*, May 24, 1987, 24. [4] Patton, "Shape of Ford's Success," 72.
[5] Patton, "Shape of Ford's Success," 72.
[6] Shuldiner, "Probe IV," 66; Patton, "Shape of Ford's Success," 72. [7] John Holusha, "New Lures for a New Type of Buyer," *New York Times*, January 30, 1983; Patton, "Shape of Ford's Success," 19–22.

1987 Lamborghini Portofino

[1]John Holusha, "Lamborghini Goes to Chrysler," *New York Times*, April 24, 1987.
[2] Blake Z. Rong, "On This Day in 1987, Chrysler Bought Lamborghini," *Road and Track*, April 23, 2016, https://www.roadand- track.com/car-culture/news/a28926/on-this-day-in-1987-chrysler-bought-lamborghini; Nick Georgano, ed., *The Beaulieu Encyclopedia of the Automobile: Coachbuilding* (Chicago: Fitzroy Dearborn Publishers, 2001), 118.
[3] "Art of the Impossible Made Probable," *New York Times*, September 8, 1988. [4] Bob Nickas, "Re-Make/Re-Model: The Car Paintings of Peter Cain," in *Peter Cain: More Courage and Less Oil* (New York: Matthew Marks Gallery, 2002), 49–54. [5] Marshall Schuon, "A Pretty Car Is Like a Melody," *New York Times*, June 30, 1991. [6] Jeffrey J. Taras, "Driving Smart; What's the Big Deal about 'Cab Forward' Cars?" *New York Times*, December 11, 1994.

2002 Ford GT Concept | 2017 Ford GT

[1] Rob Sass, "The GT40, Born of Ford's Feud," *New York Times*, June 6, 2014, https://www.nytimes.com/2014/06/08/automobiles/collectibles/the-gt40-born-of-fords-feud.html; Preston Lerner, *Ford GT* (Minneapolis, Quarto, 2015), 6–28.
[2] Jim Mateja, "Divine Secrets of an Exotic Named Petunia," *Chicago Tribune*, June 23, 2003, https://www.chicagotribune.com/news/ct-xpm-2003-06-23-0306230002-story.html.
[3] Larry Edsall, *Ford GT: The Legend Comes to Life* (St. Paul, Motorbooks International, 2004), 50.
[4] Keith Martin, "A Latter-Day Odyssey in Ford's Mythic Machine," *New York Times*, October 17, 2004, https://www.nytimes.com/2004/10/17/automobiles/a-latterday-odyssey-in-fords-mythic-machine.html; Mateja, "Divine Secrets"; Edsall, *Ford GT*, 42–51.
[5] Randy Kennedy, "The Duchamp of the Muscle Car," *New York Times*, September 23, 2007, https://www.nytimes.com/2007/09/23/arts/design/23kenn.html; Nancy Spector, *Richard Prince* (New York: Solomon R. Guggenheim Foundation, 2007), 42–45; Alisa Priddle, "Go Inside Secret Lair Where Ford Developed the GT Super Car," *Detroit Free Press*, May 12, 2015, https://www.freep.com/story/money/cars/ford/2015/05/12/ford-gt-development-secret-design-studio-engineering-moray-callum/27131883/.
[6] Larry Webster, "How Ford Kept the GT Secret,"*Road and Track*, January 13, 2015, https://www.roadandtrack.com/car-shows/detroit-auto-show/news/a24753/how-ford-kept-the-gt-top-secret. [7] Jeff Jablonsky, "Ford's Design Director Explains the Secrets behind the 2017 Ford GT Supercar," *Architectural Digest*, May 22, 2017, https://www.architecturaldigest.com/story/fords-design-director-explains-secrets-behind-2017ford-gt-supercar. [8]Thom Taylor, "Interview with the Designers Behind the 2016 Ford GT," *Hot Rod Network*, April 20, 2015, https://www.hotrod.com/articles/interview-with-the-designers-behind-the-2016-ford-gt.
[9] Taylor, "Interview with the Designers."

EXHIBITION CHECKLIST

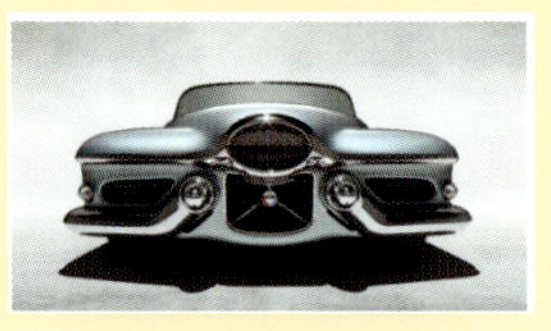

1 GENERAL MOTORS
Le Sabre, 1951
General Motors Heritage Collection

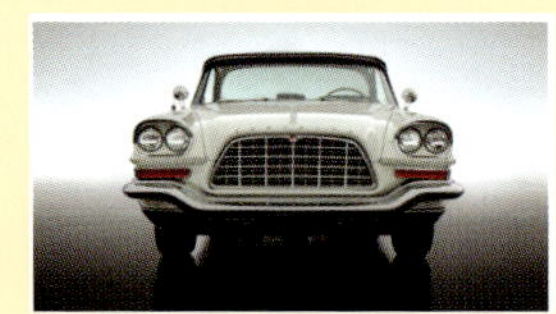

2 CHRYSLER CORPORATION
300C, 1957
Fiat Chrysler Automobiles

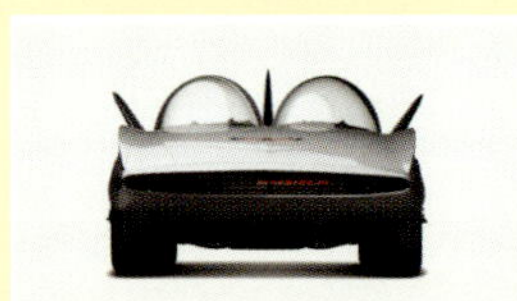

3 GENERAL MOTORS
Firebird III, 1958
General Motors Heritage Collection

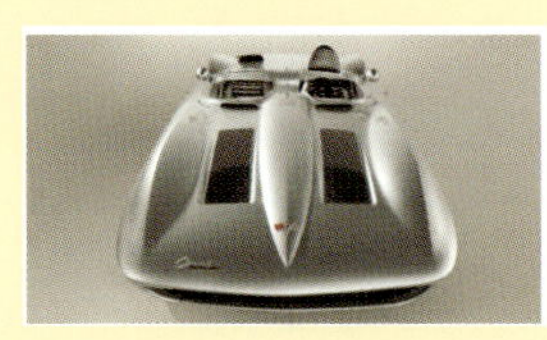

4 GENERAL MOTORS
Corvette Stingray Racer, 1959
General Motors Heritage Collection

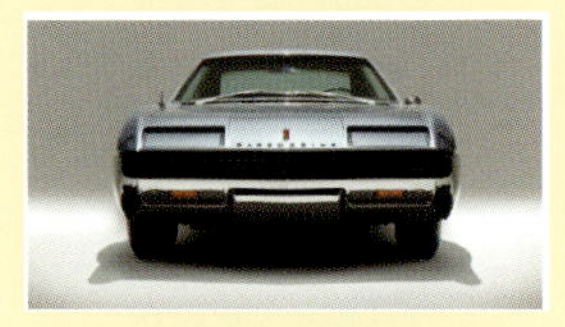

5 GENERAL MOTORS
Oldsmobile Toronado, 1966
General Motors Heritage Collection

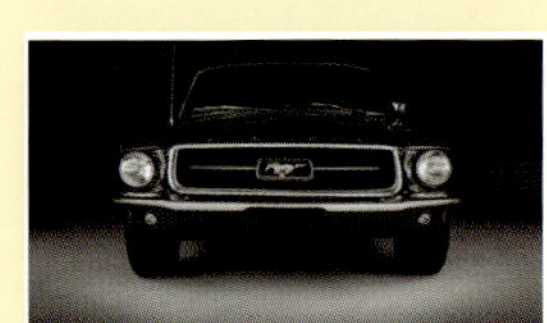

6 FORD MOTOR COMPANY
Mustang, 1967
Lent by Moray Callum

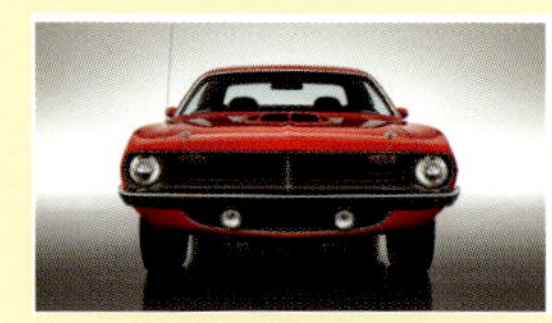

7 CHRYSLER CORPORATION
Plymouth Barracuda, 1970
Fiat Chrysler Automobiles

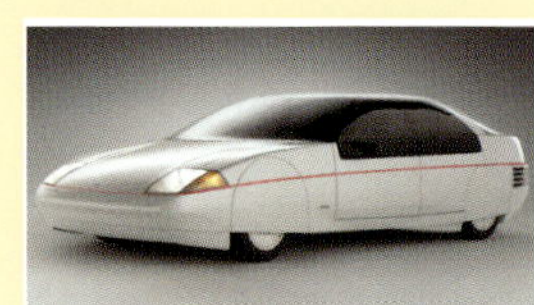

8 FORD MOTOR COMPANY
Probe IV, 1983
Collection of Fred and Dan Kanter

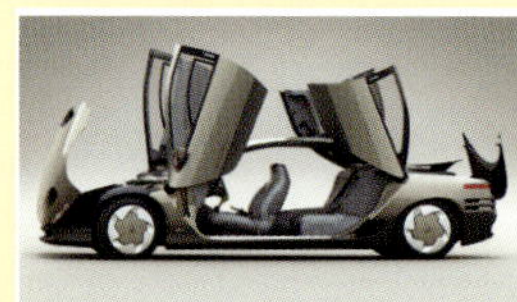

9 CHRYSLER CORPORATION.
Lamborghini Portofino, 1987
Fiat Chrysler Automobiles

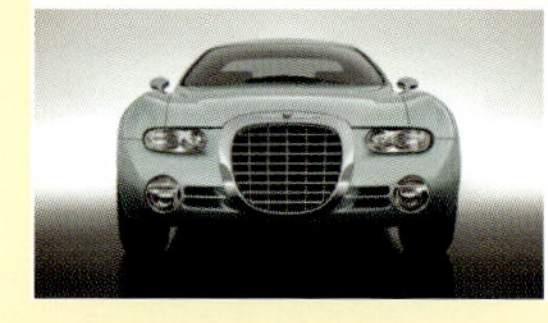

10 CHRYSLER CORPORATION
Chronos, 1998
Fiat Chrysler Automobiles

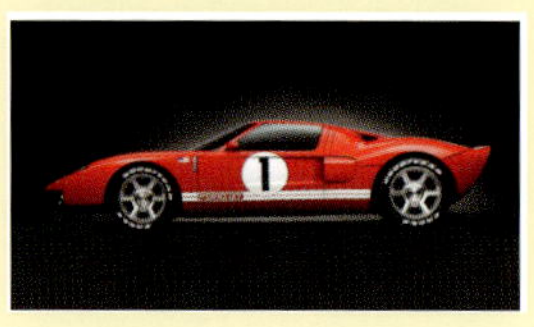

11 FORD MOTOR COMPANY
GT Concept, 2002
On loan from Ford Motor Company Global Design

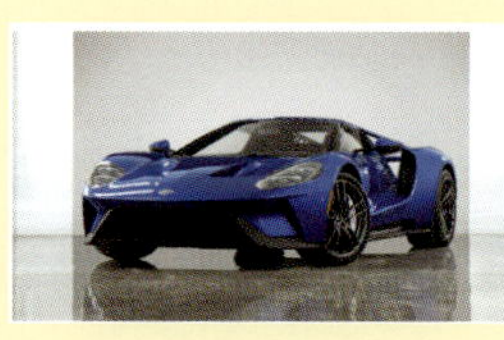

12 FORD MOTOR COMPANY
GT, 2017
Collection of Jody and Tara Ingle

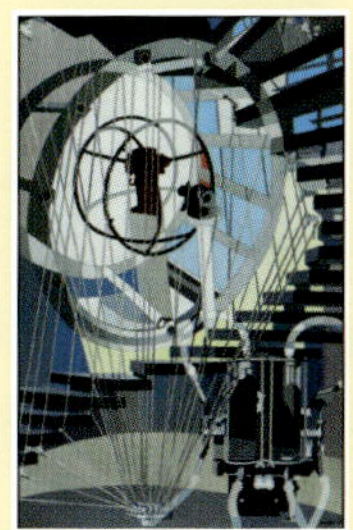

13 CHARLES SHEELER
(American, 1883–1965)
General Motors Research, 1955
Oil on canvas
48 × 30 in. (121.9 × 76.2 cm)
General Motors Research and Development

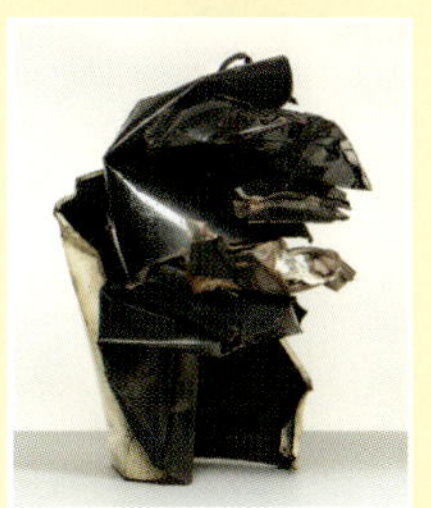

14 JOHN CHAMBERLAIN
(American, 1927–2011)
Coo Wha Zee, 1962
Painted steel
72 × 60 × 50 in. (182.9 × 152.4 × 127 cm)
Detroit Institute of Arts, Gift of Mr. and Mrs. S. Brooks Barron, 65.76

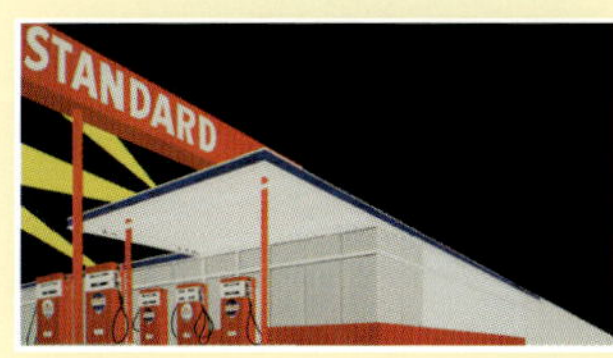

15 EDWARD JOSEPH RUSCHA
(American, born 1937)
Standard Station, Amarillo, Texas, 1963
Oil on canvas
64 15/16 × 121 13/16 in. (164.9 × 309.4 cm)
Hood Museum of Art, Dartmouth College, Hanover, New Hampshire: Gift of James Meeker, Class of 1958, in memory of Lee English, Class of 1958, scholar, poet, athlete and friend to all; P.976.281

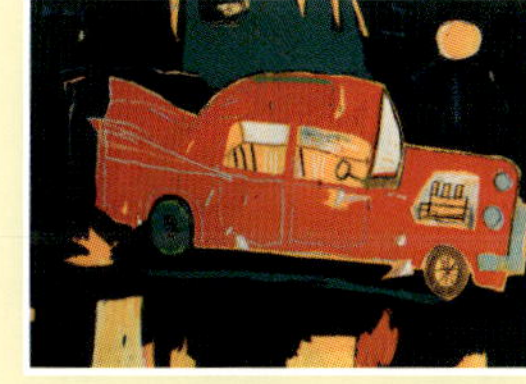

16 JEAN-MICHEL BASQUIAT
(American, 1960–88)
Rusting Red Car in Kuau, 1984
Oil stick and oil on canvas
72 × 96 in. (182.8 × 243.8 cm)
Private collection, Courtesy of Vito Schnabel Gallery

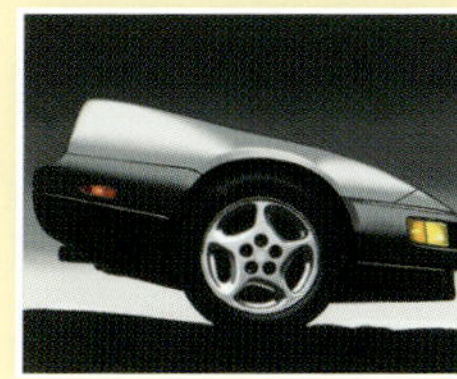

17 PETER CAIN
(American, 1959–97)
Z, 1989
Oil on canvas
58 1/4 × 70 1/8 in. (148 × 178.1 cm)
Whitney Museum of American Art, New York; Purchase with funds from the Painting and Sculpture Committee
Courtesy Matthew Marks Gallery

18 RICHARD PRINCE
(American, born 1949)
Pro Street, 1992–2002
Fiberglass hood in two parts with Bondo, acrylic, flake paint, and enamel mounted on wooden frame
65 5/8 × 56 1/8 × 6 3/8 in.
(169.2 × 142.6 × 15.9 cm)
Collection of Peter Marino

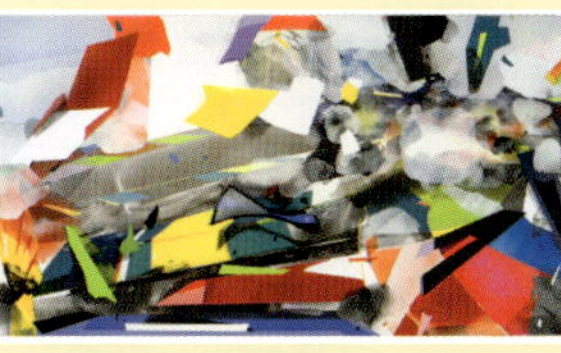

19 KRISTIN BAKER
(American, born 1975)
The Unfair Advantage, 2003
Acrylic on PVC on board
60 1/4 × 108 1/4 in. (153 × 275 cm)
Mattatuck Museum, Waterbury, Connecticut,
Gift of Pam and Jack Baker, 2017

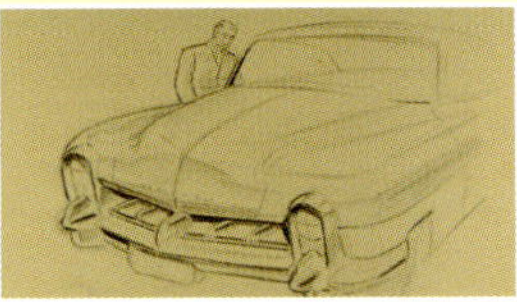

20 JOHN G. ALDRICH
(American, 1895–1977)
Sketch of Lincoln Automobile, Front End Detail, 1947
Graphite pencil on paper
8 1/2 × 10 7/8 in. (21.6 × 27.6 cm)
From the Collections of The Henry Ford, Dearborn, Michigan

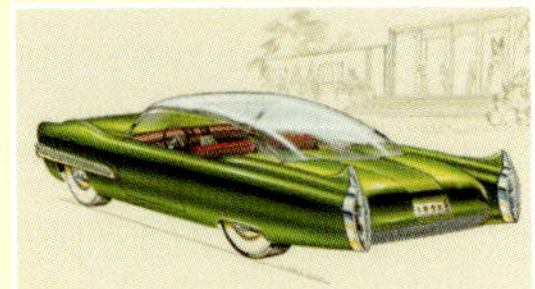

21 CHARLES E. BALOGH
(American, 1924–2013)
Lincoln XL-500 Concept Car, 1952
Watercolor, gouache, airbrush, ink, and graphite on illustration board
17 1/8 × 23 1/2 in. (43.5 × 59.7 cm)
Collection of Robert L. Edwards and Julie Hyde-Edwards

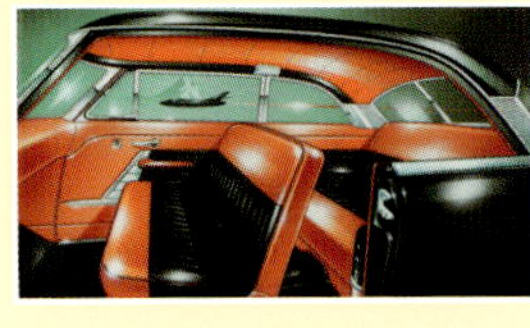

22 ART MILLER
(American)
Rendering of Automobile Interior, 1952
Airbrush and pastel on paper
19 5/8 × 25 5/8 in. (49.9 × 65.1 cm)
From the Collections of The Henry Ford, Dearborn, Michigan

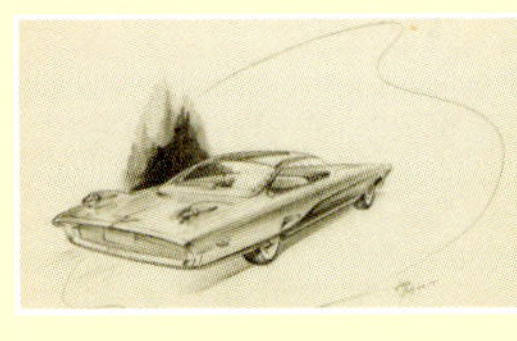

23 CLIFF VOSS
(American, 1926–94)
Chrysler Proposal, 1955
Crayon and Prismacolor on vellum
11 13/16 × 17 13/16 in. (30 × 45.2 cm)
Collection of Robert L. Edwards and Julie Hyde-Edwards

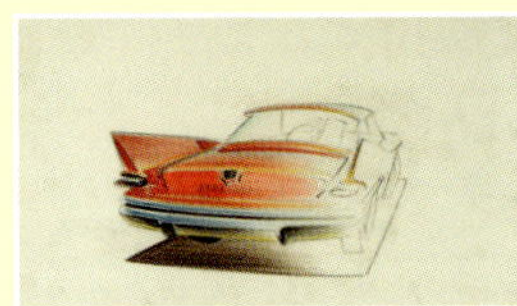

24 DAVE CUMMINS
(American, born 1934)
1960 Chrysler, 1956
Prismacolor on vellum
14 1/16 × 17 1/16 in. (35.7 × 43.3 cm)
Collection of Brett Snyder

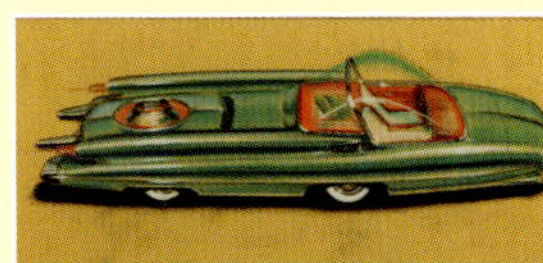

25 ALBERT L. MUELLER
(American, 1927–2009)
"Ford Nucleon" Atomic Powered Vehicle, Rear Side View, 1956
Gouache, pastel, Prismacolor, and brown-line print on vellum
12 1/2 × 28 1/2 in. (31.8 × 72.4 cm)
Collection of Robert L. Edwards and Julie Hyde-Edwards

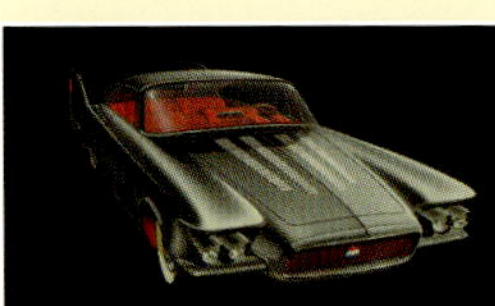

26 WILLIAM BROWNLIE
(American, 1926–96)
Chrysler 300 Front End, ca. 1957
Gouache and Prismacolor on black charcoal paper
19 11/16 × 25 1/2 in. (50 × 64.8 cm)
Collection of Brett Snyder

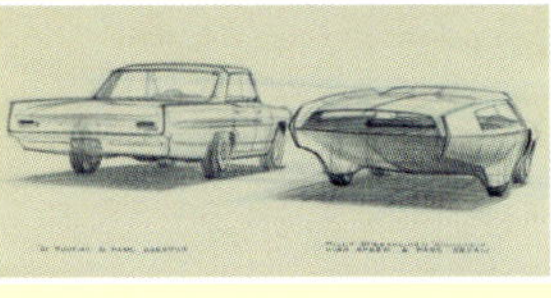

27 WILLIAM PORTER
(American, born 1931)
'61 Pontiac Catalina vs. Aerodynamic Streamlined Sedan, 1959
Prismacolor on vellum
14 × 16 15/16 in. (35.6 × 43 cm)
Collection of William L. and Patsy H. Porter

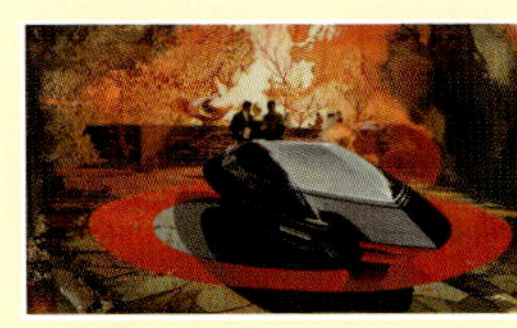

28 SYDNEY JAY MEAD
(American, 1933–2019)
Elwood Engel Design for a Gyroscopically Stabilized Two Wheel Car, ca. 1960
Gouache, liquid resist, and graphite on illustration board
17 15/16 × 29 15/16 in. (45.6 × 76 cm)
Collection of Brett Snyder

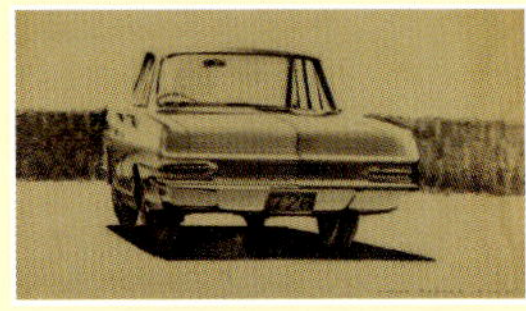

29 WILLIAM PORTER
(American, born 1931)
Rear End Proposal for 1962 Model Pontiac Tempest, 1960
Ink and felt marker on newsprint
20 13/16 × 26 3/4 in. (52.9 × 67.9 cm)
Collection of William L. and Patsy H. Porter

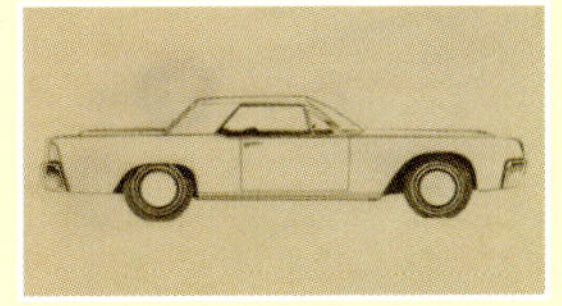

30 JOHN GILSON GUMP
(American, 1922–2011)
Lincoln Continental, ca. 1961
Graphite on vellum
9 × 11 7/8 in. (22.9 × 30.2 cm)
Collection of Robert L. Edwards and Julie Hyde-Edwards

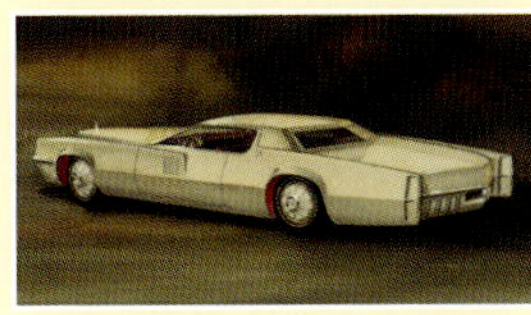

31 WAYNE KADY
(American, born 1937)
Rendering of Proposed 1967 Cadillac Eldorado Design, 1964
Watercolor, gouache, and ink on paper
22 × 34 3/4 in. (55.9 × 88.3 cm)
From the Collections of The Henry Ford, Dearborn, Michigan

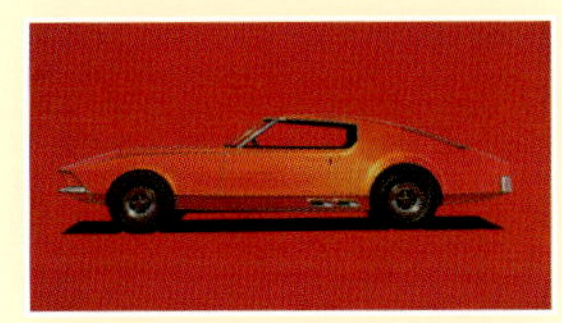

32 HOWARD PAYNE
(American, 1934)
Ford Mustang, 1965
Prismacolor and gouache on red charcoal paper
13 15/16 × 21 7/16 in. (35.4 × 54.5 cm)
Collection of Brett Snyder

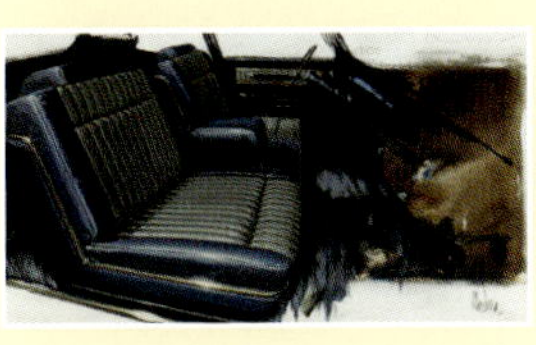

33 JAMES SHERBURNE
(American)
Ford Interior Proposal, ca. 1965
Gouache and acrylic on paper
17 15/16 × 30 3/4 in. (45.6 × 78.1 cm)
Collection of Robert L. Edwards and Julie Hyde-Edwards

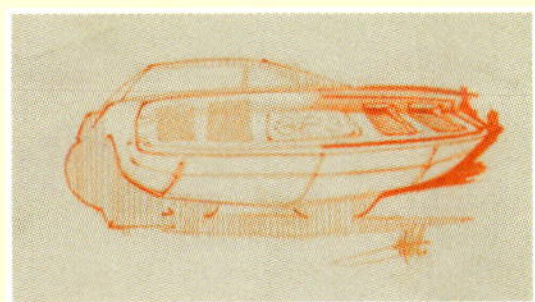

34 MILTON ANTONICK
(American, born 1936)
Barracuda Rear Form Sketch for Clay Development, 1967
Orange Prismacolor on vellum
7 3/8 × 11 15/16 in. (18.7 × 30.3 cm)
Milton Antonick Collection

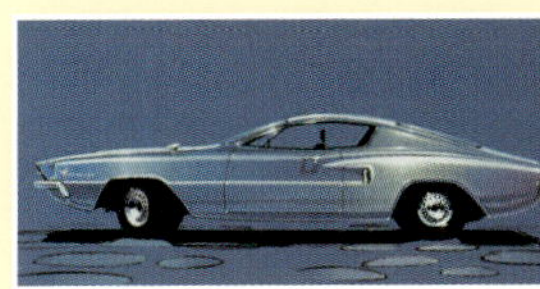

35 WILLIAM SHENK
(American, born 1933)
Rendering of Mustang Design Proposal, 1967–68
Pastel on paper
10 3/4 × 25 5/8 in. (27.3 × 65.1 cm)
From the Collections of The Henry Ford, Dearborn, Michigan

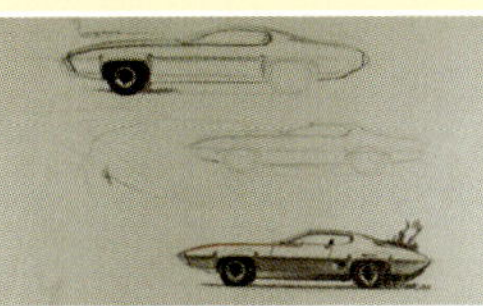

36 JOHN HERLITZ
(American, 1942–2008)
Original Design Sketch of 1971 Plymouth Roadrunner GTX, 1968
Graphite and color pencil on tracing paper
11 13/16 × 17 3/4 in. (30 × 45.1 cm)
From the Collections of The Henry Ford, Dearborn, Michigan

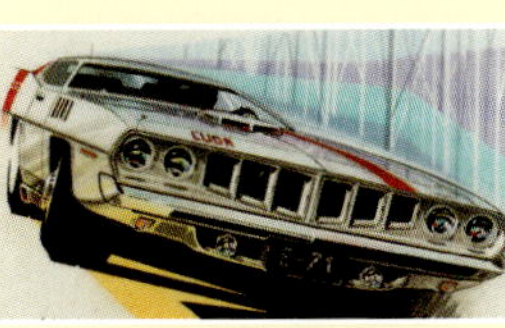

37 DONALD HOOD
(American, 1934–2018)
'71 Barracuda Front End Facelift Concept, 1968
Crayon, gouache, ink, felt marker, Prismacolor, and pastel on vellum
20 1/4 × 26 7/8 in. (51.4 × 68.3 cm)
Collection of Robert L. Edwards and Julie Hyde-Edwards

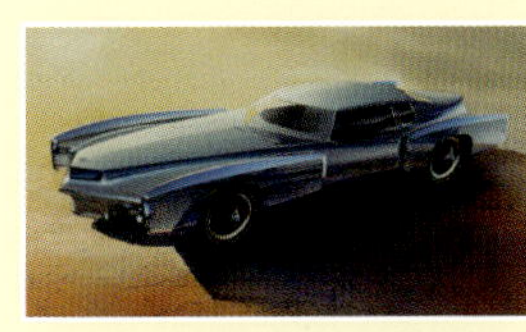

38 ROGER HUGHET
(American, born 1937)
Toronado Proposal, 1968
Gouache and Prismacolor on illustration board
22 × 31 7/16 in. (55.9 × 79.9 cm)
Collection of Roger Hughet

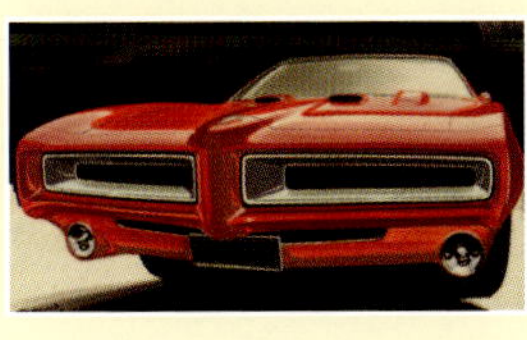

39 JOHN PERKINS
(American, born 1940)
Rendering of Proposed 1970 Pontiac GTO Design, 1968
Ink on tracing paper
22 × 28 in. (55.9 × 71.1 cm)
From the Collections of The Henry Ford, Dearborn, Michigan

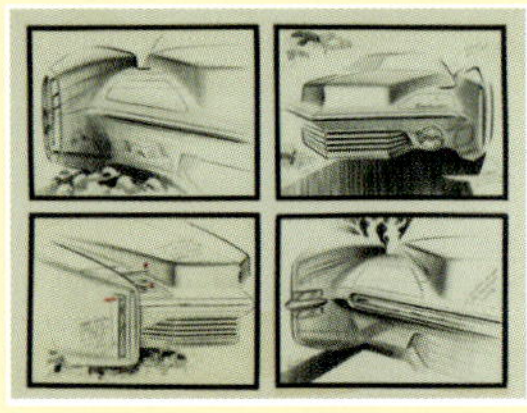

40 RALPH AMPRIM
(American, 1939–87)
Toronado Fender Detail Studies, ca. 1970
Crayon and Prismacolor on vellum attached to board
22 × 28 in. (55.9 × 71.1 cm)
Collection of William L. and Patsy H. Porter

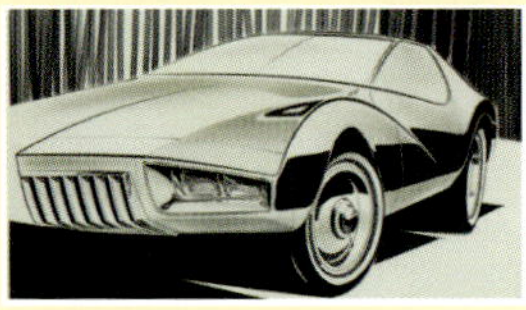

41 WILLIAM MICHALAK
(American, born 1944)
1975 Monte Carlo Proposal, ca. 1972
Crayon, graphite, felt marker, and Prismacolor on vellum
14 × 16 15/16 in. (35.6 × 43 cm)
Collection of William Michalak, Rochester, MI

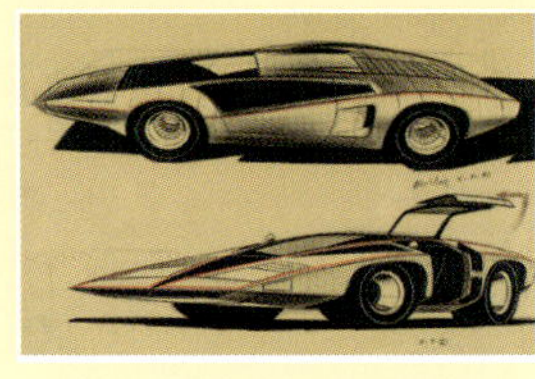

42 ALLEN YOUNG
(American, born 1938)
Sports Car, 1973
Ink, crayon, and Prismacolor on paper
18 3/4 × 22 1/2 in. (47.6 × 57.2 cm)
Collection of Brett Snyder

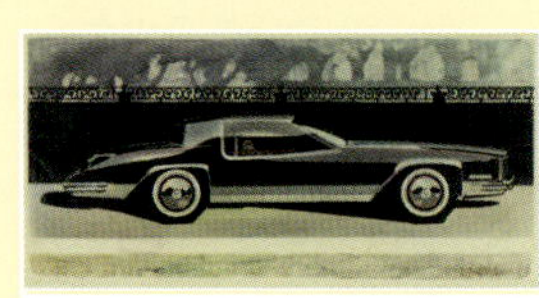

43 JACK GABLE
(American, born 1944)
Cadillac Proposal, ca. 1975
Ink, Prismacolor, and red tape on vellum; verso: watercolor
14 1/2 × 26 5/8 in. (36.8 × 67.6 cm)
Collection of Brett Snyder

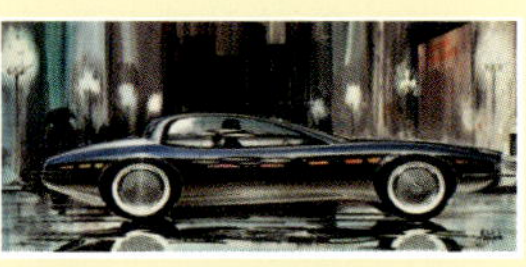

44 DAVID MCINTOSH
(American, born 1941)
Grand Prix Sketch, 1975
Felt marker, ink, gouache, Prismacolor, and pastel on vellum
23 15/16 × 54 in. (60.8 × 137.2 cm)
David McIntosh Collection

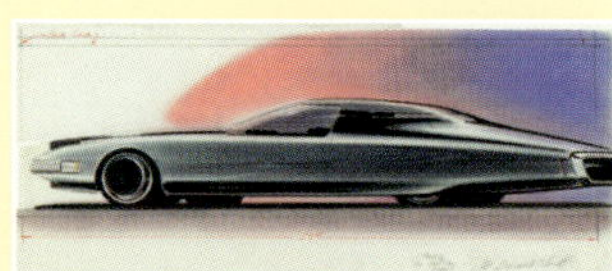

45 JOE PEREZ
(American, born 1942)
Cadillac Proposal, ca. 1975
Pastel, ink, Prismacolor, gouache, crayon, and felt marker on vellum; verso: ink and pressure-sensitive tape
11 × 26 15/16 in. (27.9 × 68.4 cm)
Dennis Burke Collection

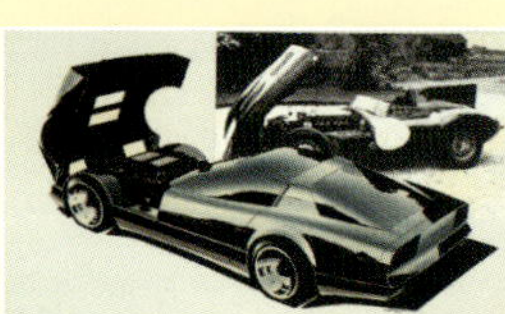

46 JOHN CAFARO
(American, born 1955)
Rendering of Proposed Chevrolet Corvette Design, ca. 1979
Photographic print, airbrush, marker, and collage on paper board
17.5 × 27 in. (44.5 × 68.6 cm)
From the Collections of The Henry Ford, Dearborn, Michigan

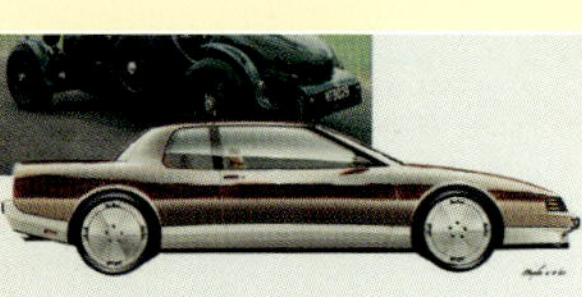

47 DENNIS BURKE
(American, born 1951)
Coupe Proposal, ca. 1980
Crayon, gouache, ink, colored tape, watercolor, collage, and graphite attached to board; photographic reproduction attached to board
14 11/16 × 25 5/8 in. (37.3 × 65.1 cm)
Dennis Burke Collection

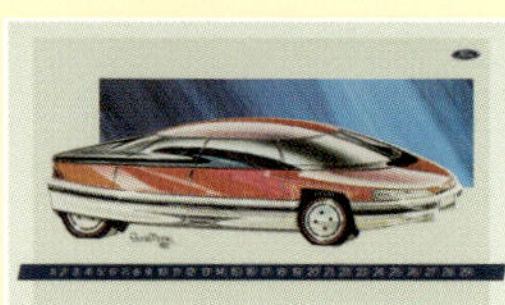

48 HOWARD "BUCK" MOOK
(American, born 1942)
Granada Mid-Engine Proposal, 1982
Offset lithograph on paper
14 13/16 × 20 3/16 in. (37.6 × 51.3 cm)
Collection of Buck Mook

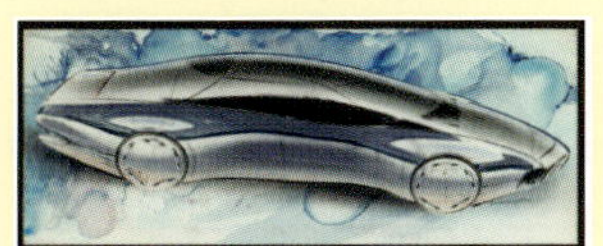

49 MAURICE CHANDLER
(American, 1941–95)
Aerodynamic Car Proposal, ca. 1985
Pastel, ink, Prismacolor, gouache, graphite, felt marker, and pressure-sensitive tape on vellum; collage over drawing: watercolor on vellum
10 15/16 × 26 15/16 in. (27.8 × 68.4 cm)
Dennis Burke Collection

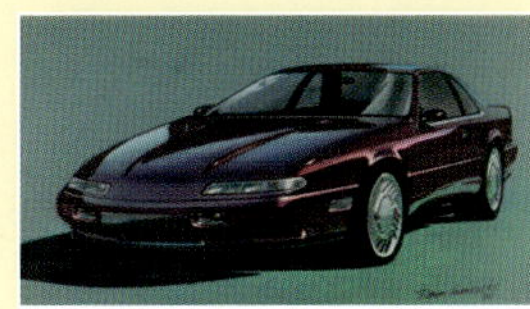

50 ROBERT HUBBACH
(American, born 1938)
Coupe Proposal, 1985
Gouache, ink, felt marker, pastel, and Prismacolor (scribing) on blue paper
16 × 27 9/16 in. (40.6 × 70 cm)
Lent by Robert Hubbach

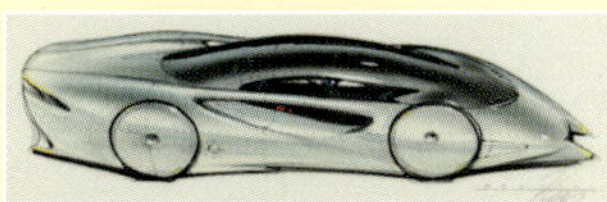

51 KEN OKUYAMA
(American, born 1959)
Race Car Proposal, ca. 1990
Gouache and Prismacolor attached to board; verso: pastel, graphite, and pressure-sensitive tape
10 15/16 × 28 1/16 in. (27.8 × 71.3 cm)
Collection of Robert L. Edwards and Julie Hyde-Edwards

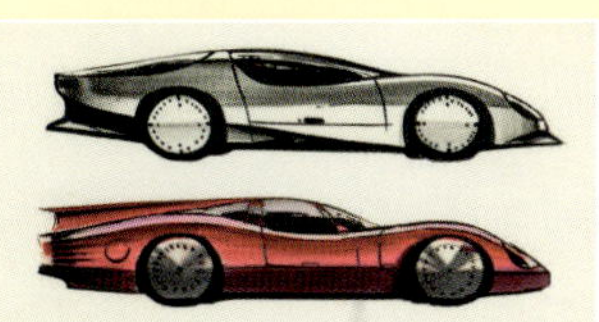

52 ELIA RUSSINOFF
(American, born 1930)
Two Sketches, ca. 1990
Crayon and felt marker on vellum attached to paper
11 × 17 in. (27.9 × 43.2 cm)
Collection of Robert L. Edwards and Julie Hyde-Edwards

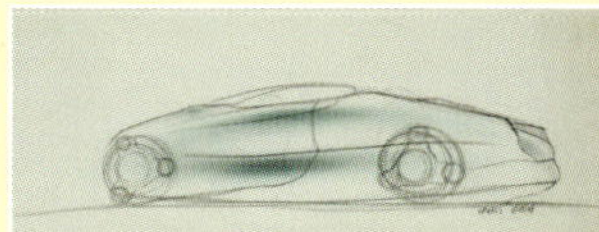

53 TARU LAHTI
(American, born 1966)
Cutline Concept, 1991
Prismacolor and pastel on vellum
11 7/8 × 36 1/8 in. (30.2 × 91.8 cm)
Collection of the artist

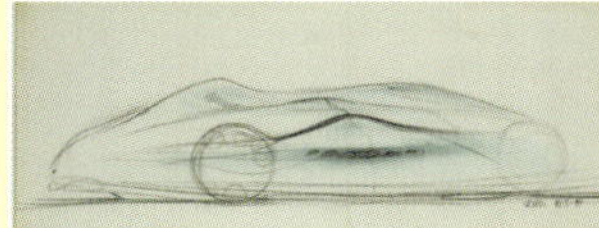

54 TARU LAHTI
(American, born 1966)
Two Seat Concept, 1991
Prismacolor and pastel on vellum
12 × 36 1/16 in. (30.5 × 91.6 cm)
Collection of the artist

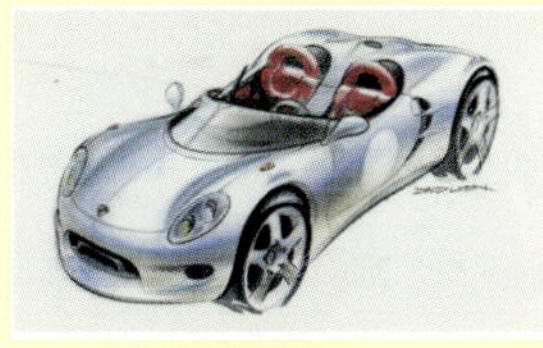

55 DAVID LYON
(American, born 1968)
Sports Car Proposal, ca. 2000
Inkjet print on paper
11 × 16 15/16 in. (27.9 × 43 cm)
Dennis Burke Collection

Detroit Style: Car Design in the Motor City, 1950–2020, celebrates the often overlooked artistry of the designers and stylists who shaped American cars. Appropriately, this exhibition and catalog would not have been possible without the support and wisdom of people throughout the city and region who generously contributed their expertise, made accessible their collections, and refined the ideas in the exhibition and catalog.

The project began with the encouragement of two people. The late Robert Edwards, an artist, historian, and consummate collector of automotive designer drawings, planted the initial idea at the museum. William L. Porter, retired car designer, instructor, and historian, acted as a consulting curator and font of design history throughout the exhibition. Bill and his wife, Patsy, graciously opened their home to me, and together we spent many hours discussing automotive history and examining drawings.

At the development stage, an advisory committee was formed that helped refine and focus the ideas in this volume. Its members included Teckla Rhoads and Susan Skarsgard from General Motors; Brandt Rosenbusch from Fiat Chrysler; Craig Metros from the Ford Motor Company; Matt Anderson from The Henry Ford; Tom Roney from the College for Creative Studies; David McIntosh from the League of Retired Automobile Designers; Edward Welburn, former vice president of global design at General Motors; and collectors Julie Hyde-Edwards and Robert L. Edwards.

Colleagues throughout the DIA contributed immeasurably to the exhibition's physical and intellectual form. Salvador Salort-Pons, director, president, and CEO, provided important support and advice at every stage. Interpretive planner Megan DiRienzo played a foundational role in giving shape to its abstract ideas. I am grateful for the help in realizing the project provided by director of exhibitions Jennifer Paoletti, executive director of strategic initiatives Felicia Eisenberg Molnar, exhibition project manager Elena Berry, exhibition coordinator Sabrina Hiedemann, director of registration Terry Segal, registrar for exhibitions Kimberly Dziurman, director of collections management Terry Birkett, collections management senior technician James Johnson, paper care specialist Douglas Bulka, conservator of paper and photographs Christopher Foster, manager of photography Eric Wheeler, research library director Maria Ketcham, curator of American art Kenneth Myers, chief development officer Nina Holden, director of development Rosemarie Gleeson, and senior major gifts officer Edward Maki-Schramm.

The exhibition would not be possible without generous loans of cars, designer drawings, and paintings provided by public institutions and private individuals. Those lenders include the General Motors Heritage Collection, with special thanks to Michael Simcoe, Susan Skarsgard, Christo Datini, Natalie Morath, and Shelly Joseph; Fiat Chrysler Automobiles, with special thanks to Ralph Gilles and Brandt Rosenbusch; Ford Motor Company; Moray Callum; Jody and Tara Ingle; Fred Kanter; Hood Museum of Art; Whitney Museum of American Art; Mattatuck Museum; The Henry Ford; Peter Marino; Bill and Patsy Porter; Brett Snyder; Robert Edwards and Julie Hyde-Edwards; Dennis Burke; Taru Lahti; Milton Antonick; Robert Hubbach; Roger Hughet; David McIntosh; William Michalak; Buck Mook, and others. Alexandra May and Jane Holzer deserve special thanks for their tireless work in helping to arrange important loans. This catalog took shape under the generous guidance of Curt Catallo as well as his team at Union AdWorks, with design by Katherine Lorenzetti and Scott Markel, and stewardship of the effort by Suzanne Coleman, Maureen Meyers, Sandra Curtis, and Maureen Silvi. Thanks also to Mark DeDona and Bernie Potochnik at LaDriere Digital Art Studio, and the editing efforts of Lisa Bessette and Catherine Comeau.

Although it would be impossible to list every individual who contributed behind the scenes to this exhibition, I am immensely thankful to all who shared ideas, fielded phone calls, made collections accessible, and answered questions as it took shape.

Benjamin W. Colman
Associate Curator, American Art
Detroit Institute of Arts

Ford dust jacket (front and back), www.alexhowe.com. FCA dust jacket (front and back), Chrysler is a registered trademark of FCA US LLC. General Motors dust jacket (front and back), Photograph © Michael Furman. End pages: Photo by John Roe. P. 4, General Motors. Pp. 6, 141 no. 15, Hood Museum of Art, Dartmouth: Gift of James Meeker, Class of 1958, in memory of Lee English, Class of 1958, scholar, poet, athlete and friend to all, © Ed Ruscha. Pp. 8, 141 no. 14, Detroit Institute of Arts, © 2019 Fairweather & Fairweather LTD / Artists Rights Society (ARS), New York. Pp. 12–13, Photograph © Michael Furman. P. 14, Detroit Institute of Arts, Eric Perry Photography. P. 18, James Haefner. Pp. 20–21, James Haefner. Pp. 22, 142 no. 22, The Henry Ford. Pp. 24–25, General Motors. Pp. 26–27, 140 no. 1, James Haefner. P. 28, Chrysler is a registered trademark of FCA US LLC. Pp. 30–31, Chrysler is a registered trademark of FCA US LLC. Pp. 32, 142 no. 24, Detroit Institute of Arts, Chrysler is a registered trademark of FCA US LLC. Pp. 34–35, Chrysler is a registered trademark of FCA US LLC. Pp. 36–37, 140 no. 2, Chrysler is a registered trademark of FCA US LLC. P. 38, Photograph © Michael Furman. Pp. 40–41, General Motors. Pp. 42, 141 no. 13, GM Research & Development. Pp. 44–45, General Motors. Pp. 46–47, 140 no. 3, Photograph © Michael Furman. Pp. 48, 50–52, 54–55, 140 no. 4, General Motors. P. 56, Detroit Institute of Arts, Eric Perry Photography. Pp. 60, 62–63, Mark Bramley. Pp. 64, 66–67, General Motors. Pp. 68–69, 140 no. 5, Mark Bramley. Pp. 70, 72–73, betweenthewhitelines. Pp. 74, 143 no. 32, Detroit Institute of Arts. Pp. 76–77, 140 no. 6, betweenthewhitelines. P. 78, Ford Motor Company Archives. P. 79, All content copyright © 2019, County of Santa Clara. Pp. 80, 82–83, Chrysler is a registered trademark of FCA US LLC. Pp. 84, 143 no. 34, Detroit Institute of Arts, Chrysler is a registered trademark of FCA US LLC. Pp. 86–87, 140 no. 7, Chrysler is a registered trademark of FCA US LLC. Pp. 88, 90–91, 140 no. 8, Ford Motor Company Archives. P. 92, 144 no. 49, Detroit Institute of Arts. Pp. 94–97, Ford Motor Company Archives. Pp. 98, 100–101, 140 no. 9, Chrysler is a registered trademark of FCA US LLC. Pp. 102, 141 no. 17, © Whitney Museum of American Art / Licensed by Scala / Art Resource, NY, Courtesy Matthew Marks Gallery. Pp. 104–5, Chrysler is a registered trademark of FCA US LLC. P. 106, Detroit Institute of Arts, Eric Perry Photography. P. 110, Chrysler is a registered trademark of FCA US LLC. Pp. 112–13, Chrysler is a registered trademark of FCA US LLC. Pp. 114, 141 no. 16, Detroit Institute of Arts, Courtesy of Vito Schnabel Gallery, © Estate of Jean-Michel Basquiat. All rights reserved. Licensed by Artestar, New York. Pp. 116–19, 140 no. 10, Chrysler is a registered trademark of FCA US LLC. P. 120, www.alexhowe.com. Pp. 122–23, 140 no. 11, Ford Motor Company Archives. Pp. 124–25, www.alexhowe.com. P. 126, 141 no. 18, ç 2011 Christie's Images Limited. Pp. 129, 141 no. 19, Kristin Baker, P. 130, Kidston, SA. Pp. 131–32, www.alexhowe.com. Pp. 133 (L), 140 no. 12, Collection of Jody and Tara Ingle. P. 133 (R), www.alexhowe.com. P. 134, Detroit Institute of Arts, Eric Perry Photography. P. 142 no. 20, The Henry Ford. P. 142 no. 21, Elliot Thayer. P. 142 no. 23, Elliot Thayer, Chrysler is a registered trademark of FCA US LLC. P. 142 no. 25, Elliot Thayer. P. 142 no. 26, Detroit Institute of Arts, Chrysler is a registered trademark of FCA US LLC. P. 142 no. 27, Detroit Institute of Arts. P. 142 no. 28, Detroit Institute of Arts. P. 142 no. 29, Detroit Institute of Arts. P. 143 no. 30, Elliot Thayer. P. 143 no. 31, The Henry Ford. P. 143 no. 33, Elliot Thayer. P. 143 no. 35, The Henry Ford. P. 143 no. 36, The Henry Ford, Chrysler is a registered trademark of FCA US LLC. P. 143 no. 37, Elliot Thayer, Chrysler is a registered trademark of FCA US LLC. P. 143 no. 38, Detroit Institute of Arts. P. 143 no. 39, The Henry Ford. P. 144 nos. 40–43, Detroit Institute of Arts. P. 144 no. 44, David McIntosh Collection. P. 144 no. 45, Detroit Institute of Arts. P. 144 no. 46, The Henry Ford. P. 144 nos. 47–48, Detroit Institute of Arts. P. 145 no. 50, Detroit Institute of Arts, Chrysler is a registered trademark of FCA US LLC. P. 145 no. 51–52, Elliot Thayer. P. 145 nos. 53–55, Detroit Institute of Arts.

This catalog was published in conjunction with the exhibition *Detroit Style: Car Design in the Motor City, 1950–2020,* Detroit Institute of Arts, June 13, 2020–January 10, 2021.

Detroit Style: Car Design in the Motor City, 1950–2020 is organized by the Detroit Institute of Arts.

Major funding is generously provided by the Ford Motor Company Fund and General Motors.

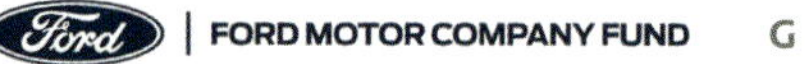

GENERAL MOTORS

Additional funding is provided by the Marvin and Betty Danto Family Foundation, FCA US LLC, and The Suburban Collection, Jennifer & David Fischer and Darcy & David Fischer, Jr.

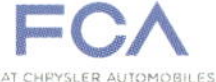

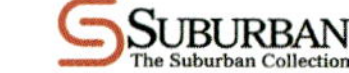

Additional support is provided by Barbara and William U. Parfet and TCF National Bank.

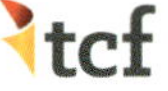

Major funding for the exhibition catalog is generously provided by the Margaret Dunning Foundation.

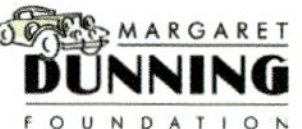

Detroit Style: Car Design in the Motor City, 1950–2020, Detroit Institute of Arts, Benjamin W. Colman

Includes bibliographical references.
Library of Congress Control Number: 2019949249
ISBN 978-0-89558-183-7 (Detroit Institute of Arts)
ISBN 978-0-300-24708-4 (Trade edition, Yale University Press)

Director, Detroit Institute of Arts, Salvador Salort-Pons; Managing Editor, Felicia Eisenberg Molnar; edited by Lisa Bessette and designed by Union Adworks
Printed and bound in South Korea
Published by the Detroit Institute of Arts, www.dia.org

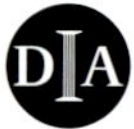

Distributed by Yale University Press, 302 Temple Street, PO Box 209040, New Haven, CT 06520-9040, www.yalebooks.com/art

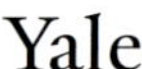

Endpapers: Sunrise over Detroit, 900 feet above Jefferson Avenue, 2018.
Opposite table of contents: Oldsmobile Toronado (E-Body) development at styling, 1965.